The Minard System

The Complete Statistical Graphics
of Charles-Joseph Minard

FROM THE COLLECTION OF THE ÉCOLE NATIONALE
DES PONTS ET CHAUSSÉES

Sandra Rendgen

PRINCETON ARCHITECTURAL PRESS   NEW YORK

The Story Behind
the Masterpiece

*As for my maps, I have heard people say that illustrative maps have
been made for a long time. My maps do not just show, they also count,
they calculate for the eye; that is the crucial point, the amendment
I have introduced through the width of the zones in my figurative maps
and through the rectangles in my graphic tableaus.*

—CHARLES-JOSEPH MINARD, 1861

The French civil engineer Charles-Joseph Minard, whose long life spanned the final
years before the French Revolution through the latter half of the nineteenth century,
left behind an impressive body of statistical graphics and maps. Motivated by the
intellectual problems he encountered during his professional practice, Minard embarked on a quest to create compelling visualizations to support the analysis of
statistical results. He conducted in-depth studies over many decades, and his efforts
finally led him to create one of the most famous information graphics ever made:
a statistical map of Napoléon's Russian campaign of 1812.

Published in 1869, one year before Minard's death, this graphic eloquently
summarizes Napoléon's disastrous military endeavor. On a basemap of what are now
Lithuanian, Belarusian, and Russian territories, it visualizes one particularly telling
statistical variable: the sharp and steady loss of soldiers that Napoléon's army suffered
during the roughly six months covered in the graphic. Though 420,000 men trium-
phantly invaded Russia in June 1812, the army was already significantly reduced by
the time it arrived in Moscow three months later. When Napoléon ordered the troops
to retreat from Moscow in the fall, he sent his men to certain death, as they faced
an extremely harsh winter in the wide plains of western Russia without any support
or infrastructure. The map shows that only some ten thousand soldiers survived [60].

This work has stood out from Minard's extensive oeuvre for a long time and
continues to do so today. Its fame has even produced some curious mementos, such
as a T-shirt featuring the Napoléon flow (currently available, along with other
Minard-related merchandise, in several online shops).[1] With its singular rhetorical
power, the graphic is often treated as an isolated effort, which ignores the fact that
Minard had originally published it alongside a second campaign map recounting
an event from antiquity. Much of this selective fame can be traced back to the enthu-
siastic praise that the American statistician and political scientist Edward Tufte
bestowed on this graphic. He reasoned that "it may well be the best statistical graphic
ever drawn," and published a facsimile of it.[2] Tufte, through his groundbreaking
books on the principles of designing statistical graphics, can be credited with having
brought the work of Minard to the attention of a wider contemporary audience.

The Royal engineer Lieutenant Henry Drury Harness drew this map in 1837 as part of an atlas to accompany a report by the Irish Railway Commissioners. It is considered to be the first flow map and preceded Minard's work by a few years. However, there is no sign that the latter had any knowledge of this atlas.

Tufte was by no means the first author to ardently praise Minard's work. As early as 1878, the French scientist Étienne-Jules Marey reproduced the Napoléon map in his comprehensive compendium, *La méthode graphique dans les sciences expérimentales et particulièrement en physiologie et en médecine* (The graphic method in the experimental sciences and particularly physiology and medicine). He also recognized the immediate visual power of this work, celebrating it with the much quoted remark about "its brutal eloquence, which seems to defy the pen of the historian."[3] Marey also referred to Minard's larger body of work, labeling his method "the Minard system" and stating that it had inspired numerous imitations and applications.[4] Over the course of the twentieth century, cartography and statistical visualization historians —namely Howard Gray Funkhouser, Arthur Howard Robinson, François de Dainville, Josef W. Konvitz, Gilles Palsky, and Michael Friendly—provided more extensive accounts of Minard's oeuvre of statistical maps.[5] Unfortunately, despite these historians' groundbreaking work, many of Minard's maps have remained unknown to the broader public; all the while, general interest in the history of thematic mapping and statistical graphics has grown exponentially following the surge in information visualization since the 1990s.

It is no coincidence that we should take a renewed interest in Minard's impressive body of work. There are several powerful forces shaping his oeuvre that resonate in our contemporary culture. One of these is an unprecedented abundance of data. The early nineteenth century saw the rise and establishment of the new science of statistics, and Minard, as well as many of his contemporaries, viewed it as a fertile source of information and began to work with this data. Though statistics is now a well-established scientific field, we too are experiencing an unprecedented abundance of structured data, brought about by the rise of digital technology—and it is no coincidence that visualization research has seen a massive rise over the past decades.

Another factor that shaped Minard's oeuvre was the profound change that new communication and transit technologies—such as steam locomotion, the railroad, and the telegraph—brought to the nineteenth century. We also find ourselves in the middle of a technological revolution, which has led to an urgent need to discuss, reflect, and understand the machines that pervade ever more aspects of our lives and create an atmosphere of unprecedented complexity. Minard worked within a sphere of well-educated people who embraced the challenge of grappling with the new developments. He was a pioneer in a movement that aspired to make statistical data useful in the face of monumental cultural changes, and he contributed more works to the emerging field of information visualization than any other single person in the nineteenth century.

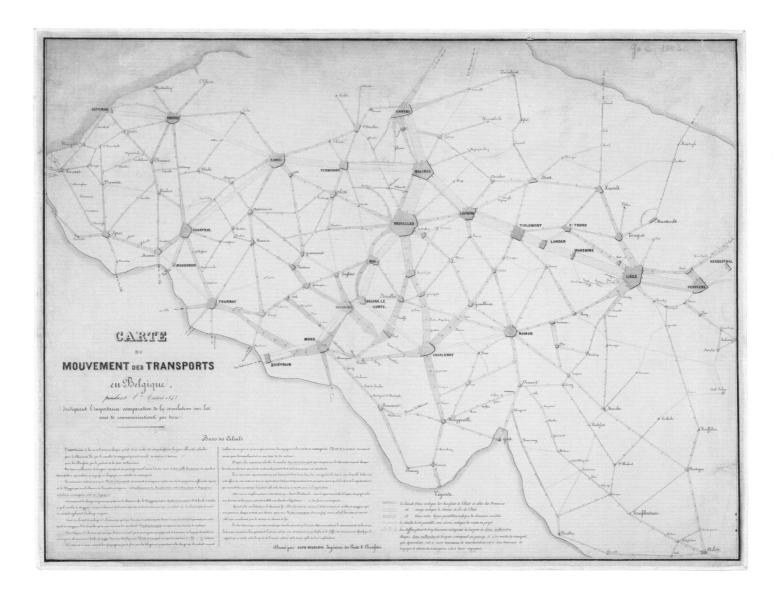

Although he worked with various methods, Minard is particularly associated with the development of the flow map.[6] However, he was neither the first nor the only one to attempt an integration of cartography and the "graphical method" in the form of the flux.[7] We know today that at least one man preceded Minard in creating a flow map: the engineer Henry Drury Harness, who created an atlas of six thematic maps relating to railroad traffic in Ireland in 1837.[8] A few years later, and seemingly parallel to Minard's, the Belgian railway engineer Alphonse Belpaire produced a flow map of his own.[9] Regardless of these instances, the flow method can be considered Minard's major theme in and contribution to information visualization, with forty-one such maps in large-format by his hand alone.

This book will explore the following questions: What is the "Minard system"? What prompted Minard to develop this method? What lucky coincidences were involved in creating such a large body of work? What obstacles did he encounter in visualizing data in this manner? And when and why did he resort to other visualization methods? The introductory essay highlights the major influences that shaped Minard's intellectual life and set the stage for his oeuvre of statistical graphics. The catalog presents a complete collection of Minard's statistical graphics as well as detailed documentation of his technical drawings. This book thus creates an integrated view that will allow for a thorough account of Minard's studies in statistical visualization, and that aims to make the conditions and results of his efforts known to a larger public.

Independently and parallel to Minard, the engineer Alphonse Belpaire created a flow map on traffic in Belgium over the year 1843. The map does not bear a date, but it is likely to have been published in 1845. Blue bands refer to roads, rose bands to railroad lines. The flow width shows quantities of transport, such that a half millimeter represents either 10,000 tonnes of goods, 5,000 tonnes of baggage, or 30,000 travelers.

Introduction

The Minard System: A Geography of Flux

Life and Career

Charles-Joseph Minard was born in 1781 to a middle-class family in Dijon, France, where he was educated at the local college. He showed a preference for mathematics and physical sciences early, and, at the age of fifteen, he entered the recently founded École polytechnique in Paris, where he studied from 1796 to 1800. He was subsequently admitted to the prestigious École des ponts et chaussées in Paris to pursue a degree in civil engineering (ca. 1800–03). To this day, this school is the training center for the renowned state-run Corps des ponts et chaussées (now a part of the Corps des ponts des eaux et des forêts), a national body of expert engineers tasked with overseeing the French traffic infrastructure. All through his professional career, Minard remained closely associated with both the École and the Corps; the École archive continues to maintain the complete collection of Minard's works. After graduating from the École des ponts et chaussées, Minard pursued a long and successful career that took him from civil engineer, to inspector, to member of the Corps. In 1822, at the age of forty-one, he married the daughter of a college friend from Dijon. The couple had two daughters who grew to adulthood; one son was lost in early infancy.

In 1831, at the age of fifty, Minard joined the faculty of the École des ponts et chaussées as professor and inspector while continuing his duty as an engineer of the Corps. The *Almanach royal* lists 29 Rue de l'université, in Paris, as Minard's address from 1839 to 1844, though he may have lived there longer.[1] In 1846, in his mid-sixties, he was given the honor of becoming a permanent member of the Conseil général des ponts et chaussées, a council that directed the work of both the École and the Corps. Minard retired in 1851 at the age of seventy. He then enjoyed almost twenty years of retirement in sufficient health to follow his personal research interests—to read, write, and publish and, most significantly, to create a comprehensive body of statistical maps. In September 1870, at the age of eighty-nine, amid the accelerating events of the collapsing Second Empire and the approach of the Prussian troops, Minard rashly fled to Bordeaux with a part of his family, leaving behind everything except for light baggage and some papers he was working on. He died in Bordeaux from a fever a few weeks later.[2] Curiously, no portrait of him seems to have survived.

Minard's early career was dedicated to engineering services such as inspecting, securing, and building waterways, port installations, and bridges. He was regularly sent on assignment all over France, and in 1839 he was named district inspector to oversee the maintenance and construction of local infrastructure, first in the ninth inspection district, which comprised six departments (administrative districts of France) in the south, and later in the fifteenth inspection district, encompassing several regions in central France.[3]

Traveling and field study were an important part of his work, as was recording his findings and projects in notes, technical drawings, and plans. In 1830, in addition to his duties as a member of the public engineering corps, he was named inspector

OVERLEAF One of Minard's first engineering assignments was the terrain study and construction planning for the extension of the Canal du Charleroi in Belgium (then French territory) between 1802 and 1804. The legend of this 1839 map mentions Minard as one of the engineers sent by the French government to advance the project, even though their designs were not ultimately considered in the execution.

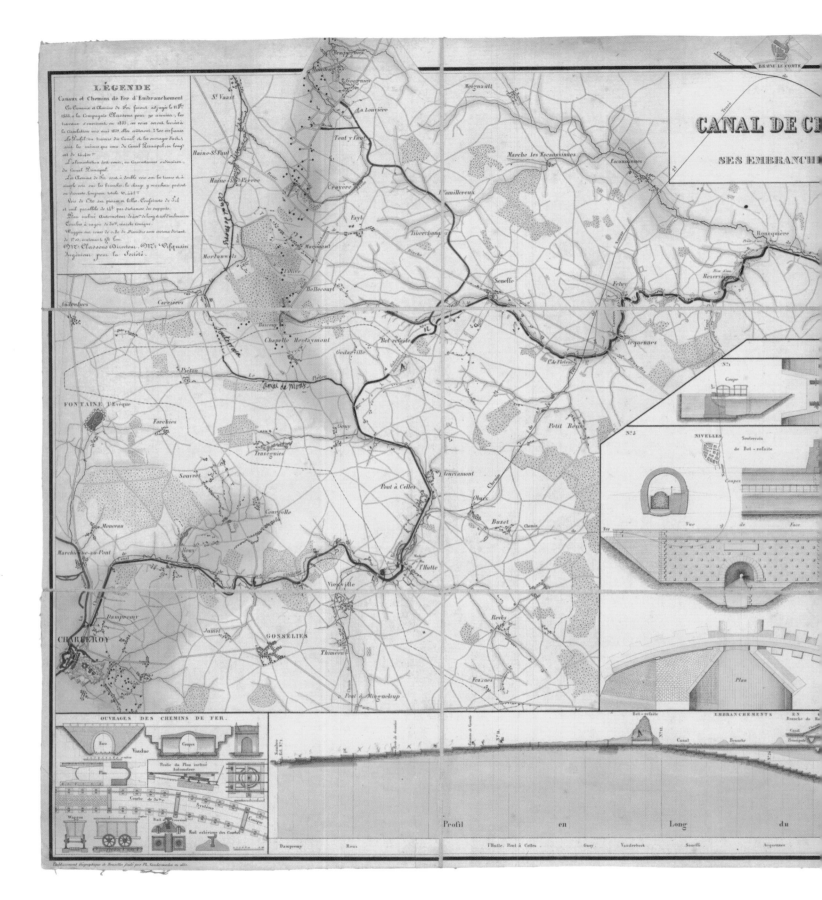

of the École des ponts et chaussées. He taught one course on construction works for canals and riverbeds, and another on fortification works for maritime harbors.[4] As the innovative technology of the railroad steadily gained a foothold in England and was tested throughout the 1820s in early applications in France, Minard found himself tasked with teaching a course about the new technology, though he had little theoretical or practical knowledge about it. However, he devoted himself to the new

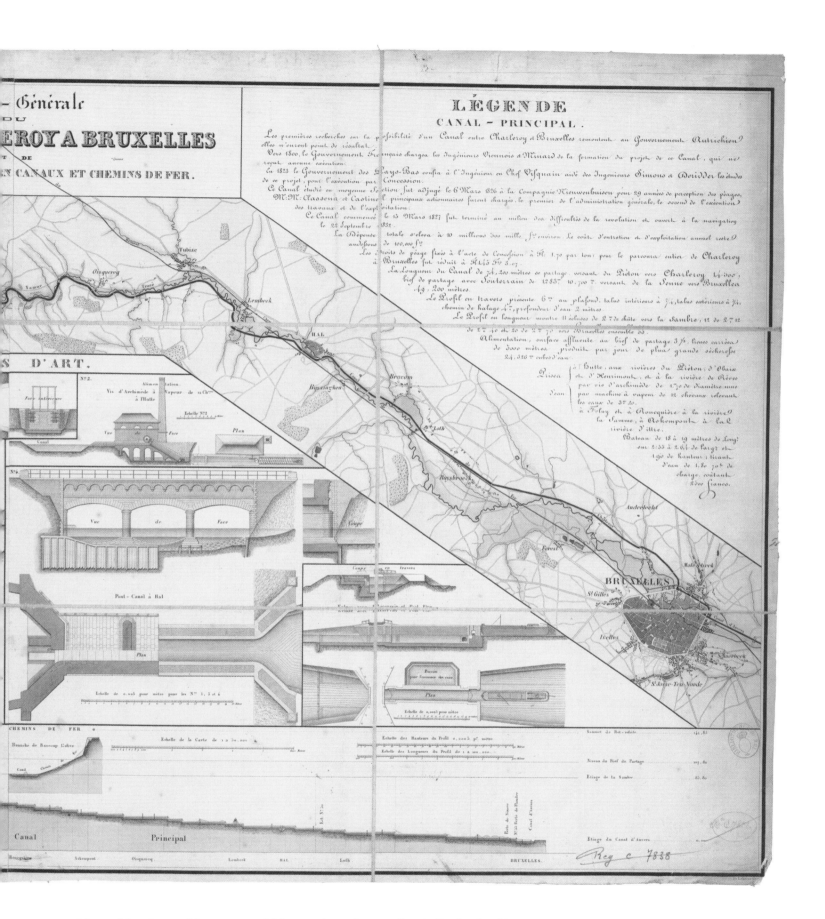

subject with ardor, seeking to expand his experience by traveling to England at his own expense to learn about the latest developments. He published his findings in a 1834 transcript of his course.[5] In addition to these various endeavors, in 1831 he joined the editorial board of the newly founded *Annales des ponts et chaussées*—the oldest modern professional civil engineering journal—to which he regularly contributed articles on a variety of technical issues.[6]

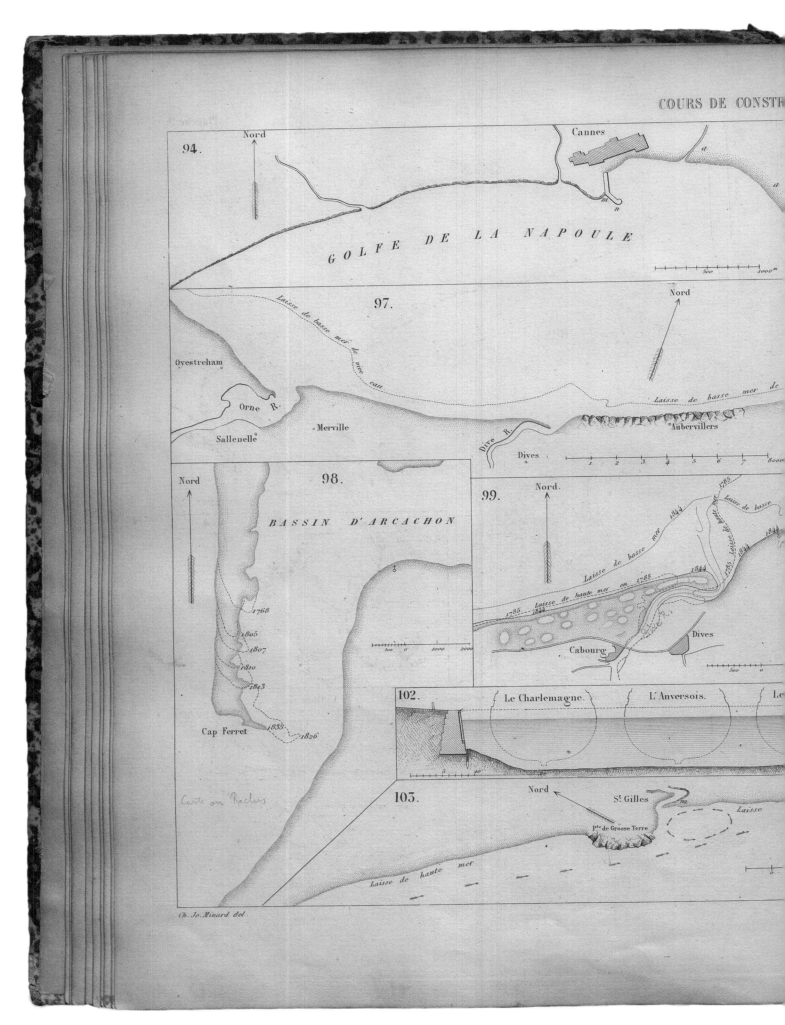

94.

Nord

Cannes

GOLFE DE LA NAPOULE

500   1000ᵐ

97.

Nord

Laisse de basse mer de vive eau

Oyestreham

Orne R.

Merville

Sallenelle

Laisse de basse mer de

Dive R.

Dives

Aubervillers

1   2   3   4   5   6   7   8000ᵐ

98.

Nord

BASSIN D'ARCACHON

1768
1805
1807
1810
1843

Cap Ferret   1835   1826

500   0   1000   2000

Carte ou Rochers

99.

Nord.

1785

Laisse de basse

1844

Laisse de basse mer

1844

Laisse de basse mer en 1785

1844   1844

1785   *Laisse de haute mer en 1785*

1785   1844

Dives

Cabourg

500

102.

Le Charlemagne.   L'Anversois.   Le

103.

Nord   St. Gilles   m

Pte de Grosse Terre   *Laisse*

Laisse de haute mer

Ch. Jo. Minard del.

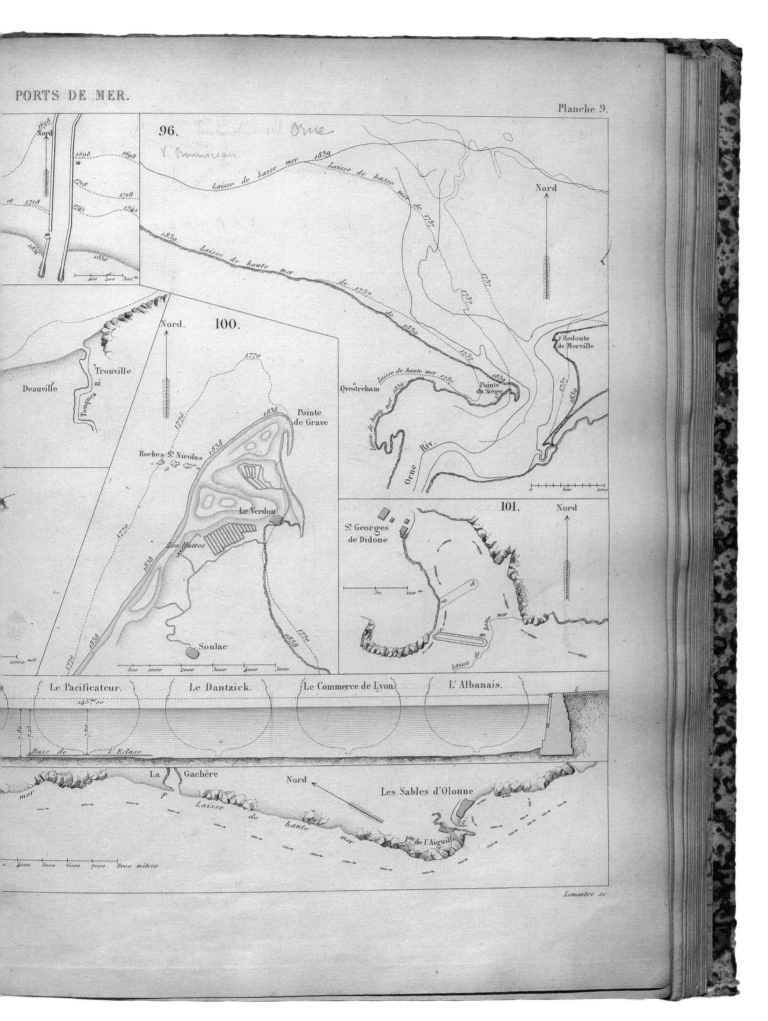

96.

100.

101.

Nord

Nord.

Nord

Deauville

Trouville

Touques R.

Pointe de Grave

1770

1838

Roches St Nicolas   1838

Le Verdou

Les Huttes

1838

1770

Soulac

2000 mèt

500   1000   2000   3000   4000   5000

Qvestreham

Pointe du Siège

Redoute de Merville

Orne Riv.

Laisse de haute mer 1737

St Georges de Didone

Le Pacificateur.   Le Dantzick.   Le Commerce de Lyon.   L'Albanais.

Buse de l'Ecluse

La Gachère

Nord

Les Sables d'Olonne

Laisse   de   haute   mer

Pte de l'Aiguille

4000   5000   6000   7000   8000 mètres.

Lemaitre sc.

Out of the various currents shaping Minard's professional career, there are three particularly interesting aspects that set the stage for him to develop a keen interest in charting economic data in diagrams and maps. First, the daily practice of drawing and mapping had always been an integral part of his engineering work; he used visual aids as a tool for both the analysis and the communication of technical and related engineering issues. Second, midway through his career Minard developed an understanding that complex infrastructural projects such as the ones he was working on must be considered not only in terms of technical feasibility but also in regard to their financing, usage, and public utility. Minard was interested in introducing a political economy framework into the more technically oriented discipline of civil engineering. And third, his work in statistical mapping is marked by a general appreciation of a fact-based scientific practice, which tends to value empirical evidence over abstract reasoning and intuition—a tendency that Minard shared with many of his contemporaries and that accompanied the rise of statistics as a science over the course of the nineteenth century. It is along these lines that we will observe the evolution of Minard's oeuvre of statistical maps.

Drawing and Mapping for Engineering

In the rich body of Minard's work, we encounter an engineering practice that utilizes drawing and mapping on a regular basis to record and communicate technical issues as well as to design and project technical constructions. This is not an achievement that can be attributed solely to Minard. Rather, we should see him as having been trained within a European engineering tradition that for centuries had valued drawing and mapping as an indispensable tool to communicate issues of technical construction.[7]

This deeply rooted appreciation for the practice of drawing and mapping was engrained in the training of aspiring engineers from the early days of the École des ponts et chaussées in the Ancien Régime. The institution started in 1747 as the *Bureau des dessinateurs*, which coordinated the work of the Corps des ponts et chaussées. Not only engineering and technical drawing, but also measurement techniques, linear and aerial perspective, and mapping all formed a regular part of the curriculum at the school, which Minard joined in 1800.[8]

We may presume that he acquired sufficient proficiency in technical drawing and mapmaking through his education, a fact that is confirmed by drawings and plans in his early writings. One of his first brochures, published around 1825, contains two plates: one regional project plan and one diagram. The brochure was written and drawn while Minard was engaged in municipal service in Paris and devoting himself to the subject of the city's pavement.[9] The pamphlet first analyzed the history of the ways in which the municipal pavements in Paris had been maintained throughout the previous 188 years, before proposing a new canal—supported by several short, horse-drawn railway lines—to provide Paris with large amounts of high-quality yet affordable cobblestones from the banks of the river Yvette.[10]

The preceding historical analysis is accompanied by Minard's earliest known diagram [1]. Notably, this piece utilizes the abstract representation space of the timeline to follow various key figures throughout a period of 188 years. In Minard's era, the concept of a timeline was less prevalent than it is today. The plotted graphs are hand colored for better legibility and differentiation. For each graph, the legend provides a scale, so that the reader—using a ruler—would be able to measure the precise values on the vertical axis. While this way of deriving exact numbers from the charted graphs is certainly tedious, the diagram also reveals more general temporal patterns.[11]

This early venture in abstract statistical representation was not, however, promptly followed by similar attempts. We don't know exactly what inspired Minard to create this sort of timeline, although it does seem fair to assume he was influenced in part by the work of William Playfair. Playfair's *Commercial and Political Atlas* had appeared in French translation as early as 1789, and Playfair himself experienced a somewhat more favorable reception in Paris than in his native Great Britain. Minard could very well have drawn on this in the early 1820s; however, there is no proof of his familiarity with Playfair until 1861.[12]

Minard does not proceed on the path of statistical representation until the mid-1840s. However, several of his publications in the intervening years testify to his continuing practice of recording and communicating information in technical drawings and plans. In particular, all three of the comprehensive transcripts of his courses (published between 1834 and 1846) contain extensive visual documentation.[13] For instance, the latest of these publications, the *Cours de construction des ouvrages hydrauliques des ports de mer*, contains twenty-five plates of delicately engraved drawings, bound in a separate atlas to accompany the volume of text. These visuals cover natural phenomena, such as wind patterns, recorded in diagrams; sea currents and shifting coastlines in large-scale inset maps; plans of local harbors and the layouts of several existing ones; and construction drawings. All plates are signed "Ch. Jo. Minard del.," clearly demonstrating Minard's authorship.

Even if we attribute some credit for the exquisite execution of these prints to the engraver ("Lemaitre sc."), the plates still testify to the fact that Minard had perfected his draftsmanship and paid attention to the smallest visual detail. For instance, he used an intricate dotting or a delicate hachure to separate the shore from the sea in large-scale maps of estuaries and islands, and he employed several different types of lines to plot the ever-shifting course of a coastline.[14] Also notable are the clean and minimalist aesthetics that these drawings convey. Not only are they refined in every detail of their rendering, including the lines, the dotting, the hachure, and the concise labeling, they also have a very "modern" appeal to them, narrowly focusing on the technical issues at hand and refraining from any graphic decoration. This is a characteristic that we will continue to observe in Minard's later statistical representations.[15]

Given this habitual practice of drawing on visual aids—whether to clarify pre-existing conditions or to draft a new technical structure—it is unsurprising that Minard would employ these skills when facing a very new sort of problem.

Infrastructural Projects and Economic Thinking

Cost estimates and, more generally, the economic evaluation of an infrastructural project had long formed an important part of engineering work. However, as the construction works of both the Corps des ponts et chaussées and the engineers themselves were all paid for by the royal and, later, the national budget, it is plausible that they were not as concerned with economic considerations as private businesses would have been. Furthermore, the evaluation of investments in infrastructure often proved to be intrinsically difficult during the eighteenth century. For instance, the Crown did not impose any nationwide road charges, meaning that the return on investing in good streets did not come back to the state but stayed with streets' users, thus eluding deeper analysis. This changed with the arrival of the railroads in the 1820s and 1830s, which combined investment (in the infrastructure) and operation (of the trains) into one system, which would yield returns by requiring users to pay for their tickets. This enabled the engineers to assess in detail the investments made in a particular railroad line versus the returns that its operation would yield.[16]

In Minard's obituary, Victorin Chevallier, Minard's son-in-law and fellow engineer, wrote that when Minard entered the faculty of the École des ponts et chaussées in 1831, he wanted to establish a new position to teach applied economics to the engineering students.[17] Chevallier further recounts that Minard had pondered economic questions for a long time and had read the works of the most eminent economists. The new teaching position did not come into fruition until 1847; however, the debate about its creation inspired Minard to write a paper in 1831 that outlined his ideas of what an applied economic science for engineers could look like.[18] This extensive treatise, *Notions élémentaires d'économie politique appliquées aux travaux publics* (Basic notions of political economy applied to public works), is a detailed effort to assess the utility of public works. While there was sufficient experience among engineers to figure out the necessary investments for a given construction, it was difficult to assess the expected returns. Minard wrote, "In the current state of our society, public constructions…almost always have as their goal to improve existing conditions; it is this improvement that we should try to express economically, and it is the economies which represent the utility created."[19] In the paper, he tried to develop methods for how exactly the economies of a structure—whether a bridge, canal, or railroad line—could be expressed in a common unit such as money.

It is no coincidence that such considerations would resurface with renewed relevance in the late 1820s, when the railroad gained traction in England and saw its first small-scale applications in France. The new technology confronted the state engineers of the Corps with a whole complex of intricate questions: How can we predict the future usage of the railroads? How can we assess their utility against the investments that will have to be made? Is the relation of investments and utility such that we should envision a national railroad system? As previously mentioned, Minard investigated the new technology and laid out his knowledge on the subject in a publication in 1834. At the time, his economic assessment of the railroad was rather ambiguous: Minard considered its utility to consist mostly in saving time. He acknowledged that faster travel might be helpful for passengers such as businessmen; he felt, however, that saving time was not really necessary in freight traffic. Therefore, he was not certain if steam-powered locomotives were preferable to horse-drawn railroad carriages for the transport of merchandise, given the high investments necessary for the former. It is ironic that Minard—a celebrated innovator in the field of statistical representation—is remembered by some historians of technology as a witness to the inherent inertia of the state-run engineering corps, whose members were not visionary enough to see the full potential of the railroad.[20] His reserve, however, can be understood in the context of his efforts to assess the balance of investments and predicted future usage for traffic infrastructure projects.

When turning to the first group of statistical works that Minard created, beginning in 1844, we can see this rationale at work: he systematically investigated the demand for particular traffic infrastructures. He had formed the belief that new railroad lines would pay off only if they were conceived to serve not just their end points but also the smaller towns along the route, since most passenger and freight traffic was to be gained on short distances between intermediate stations.[21] In order to support his argument, Minard embarked on a quest to assess as precisely as possible the current usage of existing traffic routes, both as an analytic tool and to help predict future demands on specific lines. The first elaborate example to have survived is a sheet of six diagrams dating from May 1844 [3]. The diagrams each represent one particular railroad line in a bar chart, over a horizontal axis subdivided proportionally by the distance between intermediate stations. The vertical axis represents the number of passengers who traveled each section during a given period of time. As the product of distance and passenger trips, the surface area of each rectangle represents the transportation performance for the given part of that railroad line. Minard distinguished between two different types of voyage: the dark hachure refers to passengers traveling the distance from one end point to the other, while the brighter areas represent passengers who traveled only along one or several sections of the route.[22]

In analyzing the traffic flow for existing railroads, Minard sought ways to help predict demand on existing or projected routes. And indeed, these diagrams were very helpful in comparing passenger flux along particular lines. They support Minard's argument that most travel happens between intermediate sections (except for the line between Orléans and Paris in the lower right, where passengers traveling the full distance account for a substantial share of all traffic). Also, general usage patterns of specific routes become easily discernible, like in the three Belgian lines (the top three diagrams); the most passengers travel between Brussels and Mechlin.

Over the next two years, Minard created three more variations of this format, which he termed "graphic tableau" or "figurative tableau." In a brochure published in 1846, he described his rationale for these diagrams: "However, the numbers—of an undisputable statistical utility—are not as easily apprehended by the eye as figures proportional to them. I have thus drawn a figurative tableau of passenger traffic.... This tableau speaks to the eye and renders accessible the results as a whole at one glance." [23] Among these tableaus, one colored piece from December 1845 is particularly worth examining [5]. It introduces no fewer than nine different categories of merchandise that are observed in their travels along the Canal du Centre. Minard did not confine himself to showing the quantities of each type of merchandise in the height of the stacked sections; he also tried to describe the direction of movement by introducing arrows. However, as he executed this rather erratically, it is difficult to read the orientation for select amounts of goods. In the first brochure about his statistical graphics, *Des tableaux graphiques et des cartes figuratives* (1861), he explored the problems of this distinct diagram: "This mode of representation has a little drawback regarding commercial use: sometimes, the journey of a commodity cannot easily be followed with the eye, because the rectangles of the same color representing it are separated by those of another color. If one would like to track the journey of this commodity, it takes a tableau graphique for this one alone." [24] This way of reflecting on his work continually pervades Minard's oeuvre. For instance, when following Minard's statistical maps over the years, we can see that he gradually developed an understanding of the intricacies of integrating many different flows into one coherent representation, and that he continually worked on avoiding clutter in his multiflow representations. This is particularly evident in the Napoléon campaign map, which combines the countless diverse movements of many different parts of the army into one continuous flow.

The First Flow Maps

In considering how he could refine his graphical method, Minard soon made a crucial decision: he switched from diagram to map. When he placed his proportional section bars on a map, he went from working with one spatial dimension in his graphic tableaus (i.e., the horizontal axis of the route) to the two spatial dimensions of longitude and latitude. His first flow map from 1845 shows road traffic in the area between Dijon and Mulhouse and can be understood as another effort to predict demands for a future railroad line in the region, which was projected and debated at the time [4]. As simplistic as this map is from a cartographic point of view, it successfully served its objective. Minard reported to have distributed two hundred copies to members of the Conseil général des ponts et chaussées, deputies of the concerned districts, and fellow engineers. Apparently, the map shaped the debate to the extent that a fake copy was soon made in an attempt to prove another route to be more promising.[25]

Minard's first productive period in statistical mapping stretched from May 1844 to March 1847. During this time, he created variations of the graphic tableaus as well as the first flow maps. The period was capped by a very intricate and lesser known map, in which Minard introduced several novel features that deepened his approach to statistical mapping [9].[26] For the first time, he colored a flow map to distinguish between the various flows. Furthermore, Minard introduced a historical aspect by comparing data from ten years apart. Lastly, Minard added exact numbers along his flows, making it possible to derive precise data from reading the map. Through the experience of seeing his maps used in public discourse, and by

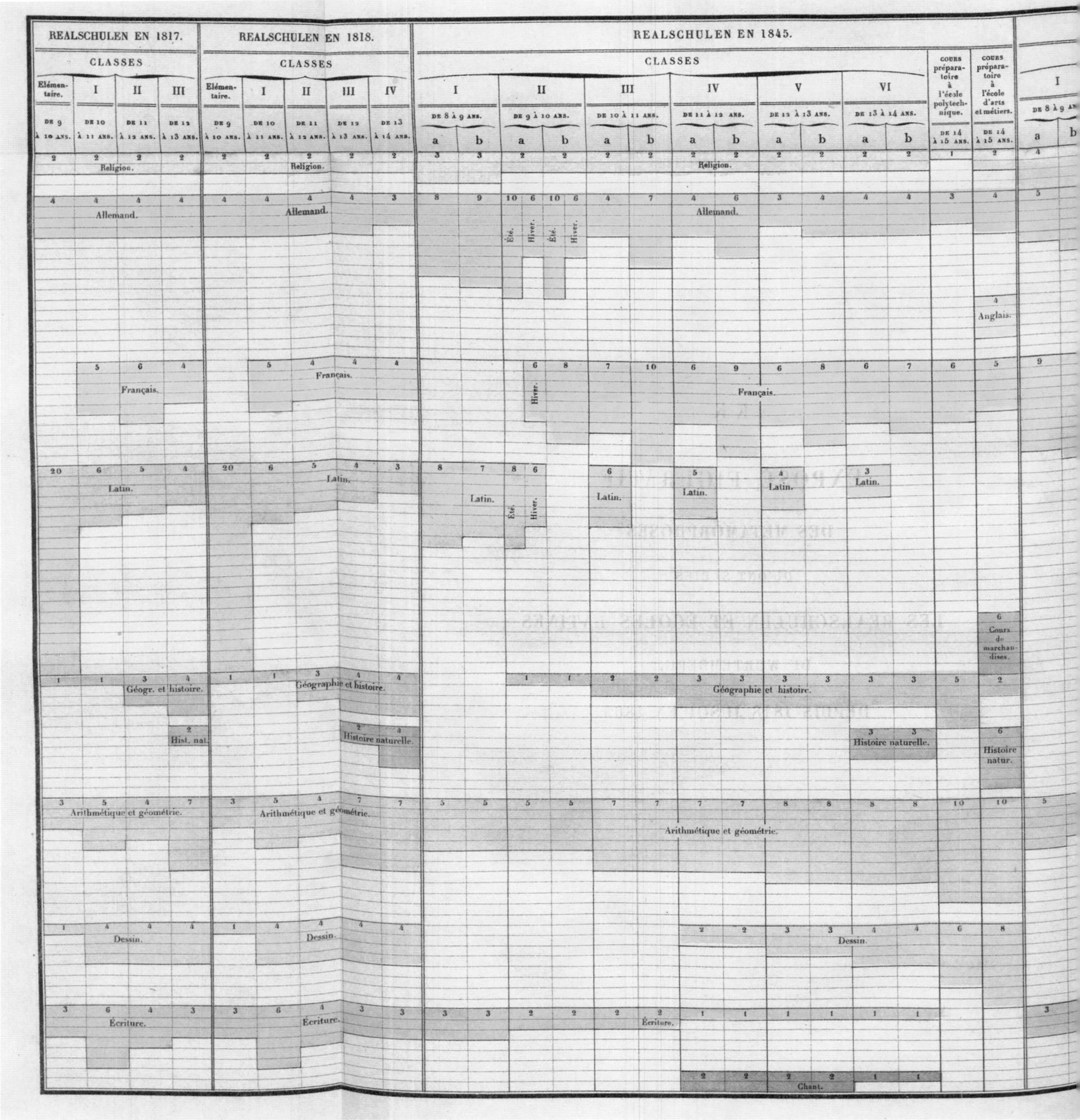
REALSCHULEN EN 1817.
REALSCHULEN EN 1818.
REALSCHULEN EN 1845.
CLASSES
Elémentaire.
COURS préparatoire à l'école polytechnique.
COURS préparatoire à l'école d'arts et métiers.
Religion.
Allemand.
Été.
Hiver.
Anglais.
Français.
Latin.
Cours de marchandises.
Géogr. et histoire.
Géographie et histoire.
Hist. nat.
Histoire naturelle.
Histoire natur.
Arithmétique et géométrie.
Dessin.
Écriture.
Chant.

In his pamphlet *La Statistique* (1869), Minard refers to an administrative report on secondary education in Belgium, Germany, and Switzerland. The French inspector general for education, Jean Magloire Baudoin, had visited these countries and published the report in 1865. Minard mentioned the thirty-plus colored graphics featured in the report, referring to this tableau as one of the most impressive ones. It shows the subjects taught in secondary schools in the Kingdom of Wurttemberg, and inspired him to draw one of his last large-format diagrams [59].

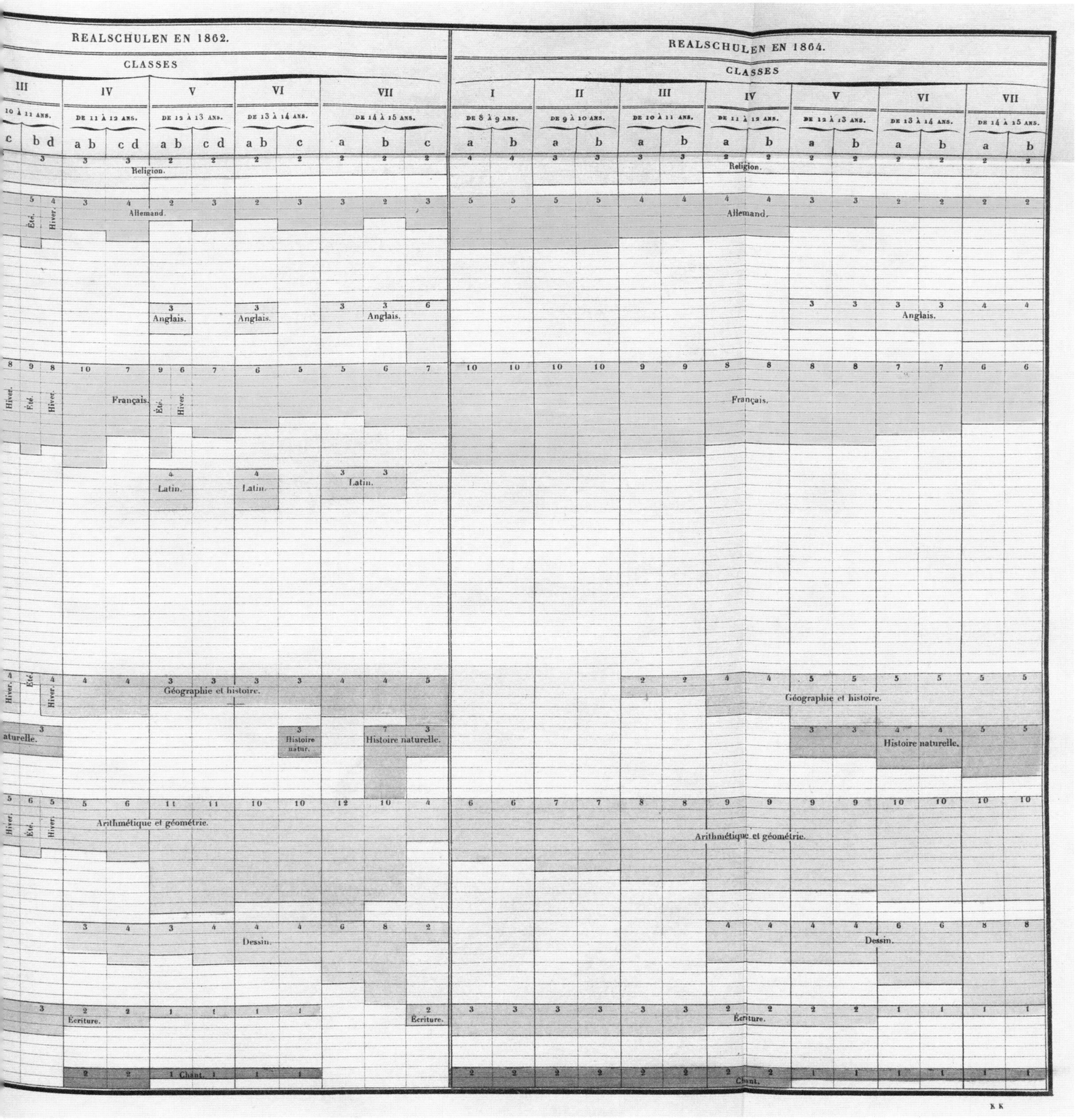

CLASSES

REALSCHULEN EN 1862 — CLASSES

III	IV	V	VI	VII
10 à 11 ans.	DE 11 à 12 ans.	DE 12 à 13 ans.	DE 13 à 14 ans.	DE 14 à 15 ans.
c / b d	a b / c d	a b / c d	a b / c	a / b / c

REALSCHULEN EN 1864 — CLASSES

I	II	III	IV	V	VI	VII
DE 8 à 9 ans.	DE 9 à 10 ans.	DE 10 à 11 ans.	DE 11 à 12 ans.	DE 12 à 13 ans.	DE 13 à 14 ans.	DE 14 à 15 ans.
a / b	a / b	a / b	a / b	a / b	a / b	a / b

Subjects (rows): Religion. — Allemand. — Anglais. — Français. — Latin. — Géographie et histoire. — Histoire naturelle. — Arithmétique et géométrie. — Dessin. — Écriture. — Chant.

1862 side — selected values:

Religion: 3 3 3 2 2 2 2 2 2 2

Allemand: 5 4 3 4 2 3 2 3 3 2 3

Anglais: 3 — 3 — 3 3 6

Français: 8 9 8 10 7 9 6 7 6 5 5 6 7

Latin: 4 4 3 3

Géographie et histoire: 4 4 4 3 3 3 3 4 4 5

Histoire naturelle: 3 3 3 7 3

Arithmétique et géométrie: 5 6 5 5 6 11 11 10 10 12 10 4

Dessin: 3 4 3 4 4 4 6 8 2

Écriture: 3 2 2 1 1 1 2

Chant: 2 2 1 1 1

1864 side — selected values:

Religion: 4 4 3 3 3 3 2 2 2 2 2 2 2 2

Allemand: 5 5 5 5 4 4 4 4 3 3 2 2 2 2

Anglais: 3 3 3 3 4 4

Français: 10 10 10 10 9 9 8 8 8 8 7 7 6 6

Géographie et histoire: 2 2 4 4 5 5 5 5 5 5

Histoire naturelle: 3 3 4 4 5 5

Arithmétique et géométrie: 6 6 7 7 8 8 9 9 9 9 10 10 10 10

Dessin: 4 4 4 4 6 6 8 8

Écriture: 3 3 3 3 3 3 2 2 2 2 1 1 1 1

Chant: 2 2 2 2 2 2 2 1 1 1 1 1

K K

21

elaborating his graphical methods, Minard developed an ever-stronger impulse to draw from the fertile sources of statistics in order to create meaningful visual analyses for engineers and administration officials. Evidently, this also entailed a strong motivation to adhere to the guidelines and "ethics" of statistics.

After a four-year break between 1847 and 1851, and following his retirement in March 1851, Minard entered into his study of graphic visualization with new fervor. He produced a constant output of statistical maps in large format over the next nearly two decades.[27] The majority of these works were flow maps, and while he occasionally tested other methods of statistical mapping (such as proportional and sectioned pie charts placed on maps), he never really returned to using diagrams until very late in his career. We do not know what shaped his specific preference for the flow map method; however, we should not regard it a mere coincidence but rather acknowledge it as a clear decision on Minard's part. Apparently, he appreciated the flow map for its integration of statistical representation and spatial reasoning, and considered this the most promising path to follow in his visualization studies.[28]

Statistical Thinking and Empirical Evidence

One key factor in understanding Minard's work is the rise of statistics through the early nineteenth century.[29] In a pamphlet titled *La Statistique*, published one year before his death, Minard explored the potential of this new field of study and defended it against contemporary criticism, which dismissed it as not being a proper science:

> *Statistics is the registration of homogenous facts in a systematic, numerical or chronological manner. Memory is the intuitive registration in our brain of ideas or sensations which have left more or less of an impression on us....*
> *In indicating at first the analogy between Statistics and one of the elements most necessary to our understanding, I wanted to relieve it from the state of inferiority in which it has been placed by the scholars, as since memory is indispensable for acquiring our intellectual knowledge, Statistics is the foundation of several sciences at which we wouldn't have arrived without it.*[30]

The treatise also proclaimed a new genre of figurative statistics, which according to Minard was developing rapidly at the time. Minard went on to present successful examples of statistics and statistical graphics across a variety of academic disciplines, including lawmaking, botany, paleontology, and history. While the argument seems a little odd at times, as he mentioned several scientific procedures which are not—in our understanding—actually related to statistics (such as the systematic description of human organs and their functions in physiology), there is one common denominator to be found. In all the examples given, Minard celebrated a singular approach to acquiring knowledge: *the systematic gathering and evaluation of facts.*

Minard showed an appreciation for empirical evidence that was shared by many of his contemporaries throughout the nineteenth century. The role of such evidence in statistics and in the emerging social sciences was expressed by the British statistician William Newmarch in 1861:

> *We have, for example, in Statistics no such body of general laws as are to be found in dynamics, as are to be found in chemistry, or in physiology. But then we claim for Statistics—and it is no small claim to put forward for any branch of knowledge—that it is the application of the Experimental or Baconian method to the several divisions of inquiry which relate to man in society. We say, that where there is no careful application of the Statistical method—in other words, where there is an absence of observation and experiment, so far as observation and experiment can be applied to men in societies—there can be but faint hope of arriving at the truth in any line of research connected with social problems.*[31]

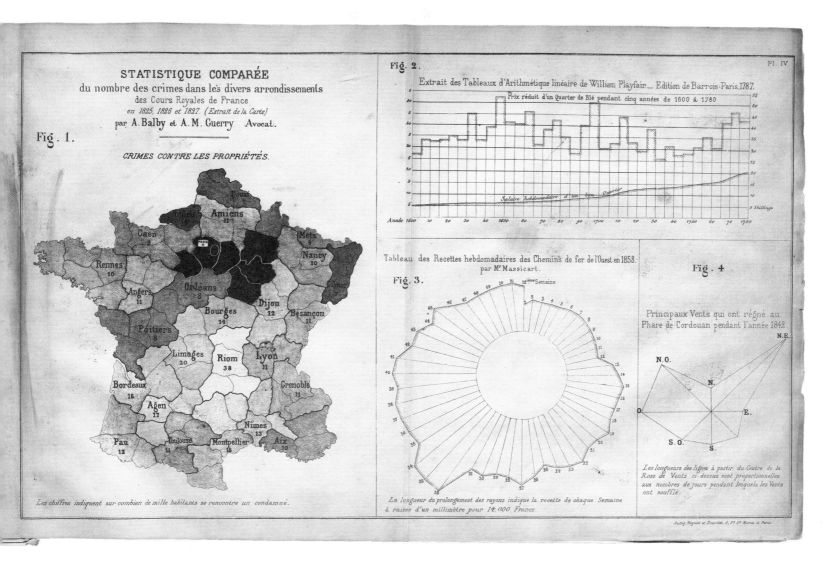

Pl. IV

STATISTIQUE COMPARÉE
du nombre des crimes dans les divers arrondissements
des Cours Royales de France
en 1825, 1826 et 1827. (Extrait de la Carte)
par A. Balby et A. M. Guerry Avocat.

Fig. 1.

CRIMES CONTRE LES PROPRIÉTÉS.

Les chiffres indiquent sur combien de mille habitants se rencontre un condamné.

Fig. 2.

Extrait des Tableaux d'Arithmétique linéaire de William Playfair — Edition de Barrois-Paris, 1787.

Prix réduit d'un Quarter de Blé pendant cinq années de 1600 à 1780

Salaire hebdomadaire d'un bon Ouvrier

Année 1600 10 20 30 40 1650 60 70 80 90 1700 10 20 30 40 1750 60 70 1780

Tableau des Recettes hebdomadaires des Chemins de fer de l'Ouest en 1858.
par M.r Massicart.

Fig. 3.

La longueur du prolongement des rayons indique la recette de chaque Semaine
à raison d'un millimètre pour 14,000 Francs.

Fig. 4.

Principaux Vents qui ont régné au
Phare de Cordouan pendant l'année 1842.

Les longueurs des lignes à partir du Centre de la
Rose de Vents ci-dessus sont proportionnelles
aux nombres de jours pendant lesquels les Vents
ont soufflé

This valuation of experience, empirical research, and exact measurements of social or economic phenomena underlies the intellectual framework of Minard's visualization research. Many details in his maps (particularly in the labeling and text descriptions) testify to Minard's continuing bid for what we might call "data hygiene" —a responsible and transparent handling of the statistical data he processed in his graphics. He continually strove to disclose not just the sources of his numbers but also his methods for aligning and aggregating data or estimating missing figures.[32] Even in his early works, Minard consistently used subheadings or legends to give some explanation of how to read the visualization. In 1847, he began to expand these elements into proper description texts for each map. With very few exceptions, every one of his large-format statistical maps contains one or two texts, which provide information about its topic, sources, and execution, as well as the date of publication and Minard's signature. The maps are designed to be individual works rather than illustrations integrated into a book. From the sources mentioned in the descriptions, as well as from the data portrayed and several brochures accompanying some of the more complex works, we get the sense that each of his maps must have been the result of a personal research project. At the time, statistical information on matters such as population, administration, or transport was not as readily available as it is today. Repeatedly, Minard indicated that he gleaned his data from not only a rich

In his 1861 treatise *Des Tableaux Graphiques et des Cartes Figuratives,* Minard advocated the use of the graphical method to communicate statistical data. He recapped the work of several of his predecessors and reproduced some models of statistical visualization. The table above shows an early choropleth map by Adriano Balbi and André-Michel Guerry (left, with data from 1825–1827), a diagram by William Playfair (ca. 1787, top right), a circular diagram of the weekly receipts of the French Western railroad company by a Mr. Massicart (bottom center, with data from 1858), as well as an unsigned wind diagram from the Cordouan lighthouse (bottom right, with data from 1842).

variety of printed sources but from correspondence with administration officials, fellow engineers, and authorities of commerce or transportation in order to obtain unpublished data for an integrated view of the matter in question.[33]

Two terms Minard frequently used to describe his maps are "figurative" and "approximate." The former appears first in 1851 [10] and the latter in 1852 [12], after which time they consistently are used together in the majority of Minard's maps.[34] From his 1861 treatise *Des tableaux graphiques et des cartes figuratives*, we can discern what Minard meant when speaking of a figurative map—namely, the transformation of statistical numbers into a visual representation:

> *The great extension which our time has given to statistical research gener-*
> *ated the need to record its results in ways which are less dry, more beneficial*
> *and more accessible to rapid exploration than the numbers.... In giving*
> *statistics a figurative direction, I followed a general impulse toward graphi-*
> *cal representations.... In creating a figurative statistics, I satisfied the*
> *current need, but have I not just bowed to the taste of our epoch and have*
> *I not contributed to enhancing the utility and to shortening the time*
> *required for statistical studies?*[35]

This transformation was by no means trivial, and it was also not unanimously supported among statisticians in Minard's time. Even though many statisticians would acknowledge the inherent potential of graphics to render accessible the results of their research, the utility of the graphical method was often considered to be limited. The German-French statistician Maurice Block expressed the reserve of many of his colleagues when he wrote in 1886, "Notwithstanding all the truly remarkable things that have been done, the graphical representations might never achieve the precision of a table of numbers."[36] It is therefore unsurprising that many groundbreaking inventions in the field of information visualization in the nineteenth century were contributed not by statisticians but rather by scientists and professionals such as Minard who had a thorough knowledge of mathematics (thus they were able to process statistical results) and sought to understand phenomena of current interest in their respective fields. For all his passion for creating statistical representations, Minard seems to have been aware of the statisticians' reservations and advocated for his use of figurative maps:

> *The aim of my figurative maps is less to exhibit statistical results, which*
> *could be better established by numbers, than to make relationships quickly*
> *apparent to the eye, relationships that are instantly grasped where numbers*
> *would require the mediation of a mental calculation. The figurative maps*
> *are thoroughly in the spirit of the century in which one seeks to save time in*
> *all ways possible.*[37]

As for the term "approximate," we may assume that Minard started including it as a way to acknowledge that his graphical representations would always have to compromise some scientific standards of precision. On the one hand, he would try to adhere as much as possible to the notion of statistical precision and gradually adopted several measures to achieve the highest possible standard. Those measures included the disclosure of his sources, his estimates, and the facts on which these estimates were based; the inclusion of raw numbers along his flows or next to his pies; and a clear labeling and description of the graphical elements in the legend. The consistent use of graphic scales for the statistical elements, and the precision expended on the exact transformation of raw data into proportional forms, suggests that Minard designed his maps for both an overview and a "close reading," where the reader would use a ruler to actually measure flow widths or intervals in a diagram.[38]

On the other hand, Minard quite deliberately and continually transgressed every idea of cartographic precision. He ruthlessly revised coastlines and omitted even big islands [32], widened the strait of Gibraltar [41] and the Bosphorus [58], and dispensed with Ireland and Scotland in a map of Europe [49]. These are just a few examples, with many more to be discovered throughout his extensive oeuvre. As this rather crude treatment of cartographic principles is such a remarkable and pervasive trait in Minard's maps, it has been much discussed by previous authors. Arthur Howard Robinson, for instance, has written archly of the "tyranny of precise geographical position" from which Minard deliberately escaped.[39] And in his discussion of the distinction between topographic and thematic maps in the nineteenth century, Gilles Palsky explained that this rather liberal approach to mapmaking was considered more than strange by cartographers and was one of the reasons why thematic cartography—such as practiced by Minard—was received rather critically within the circles of geographers and cartographers of the time.[40]

In addition to this "non-Euclidian cartography" (as put by Palsky), it is also interesting to note that Minard's statistical maps are extremely bare.[41] Topographic references are scarce, and landscapes are usually characterized simply by a combination of coastlines and land borders with a few place names positioned loosely on the map. Except for a number of examples where areas are shaded, both land and ocean remain uncolored and are sometimes difficult to distinguish at all. For instance, in the early flow maps of France (prior to 1858), the silhouette of the country is not easily discernable against the dominant flows. Similarly, not all readers immediately understand that the Napoléon campaign graphic [60] is in fact a map. The territory on which this drama unfolds is not visually described, except with a few labels for places and rivers.

Minard was clearly quite skilled in drawing and mapmaking. Had it been a priority to him, he would have been very capable of drawing "proper" maps, or at least of creating ones that do not so boldly defy the principles of cartographic representation. It is evident that his "non-Euclidean cartography" is not the result of coincidence, incompetence, or mere negligence. On the contrary, we must consider it a clear decision on Minard's part to treat cartography as an "auxiliary canvas" on which his main story (i.e., the drama of the statistical numbers) unfolds. An indication of this is given in his own description on the map where he first used the term "approximate" in 1852 [12]:

> The aim of this map was to make apprehensible to the eye the relative importance of several movements of traffic. To this consideration I have sacrificed the topographic exactness. Several distances are altered in order to place the zones and in order not to exceed the measures of the largest stones available for the lithographic printing.[42]

This remark is echoed by many similar comments in the map descriptions, and it points to the fact that his priority was the representation of the statistical data, which was given detailed attention and scrutiny. In his maps, Minard chose a spatial setup for plotting this data. The space, however, is not described in much detail; it is enough that the map references the mental map the reader harbors in her memory. Moreover, the space is not only denied closer attention but must "recede" when it threatens to interfere with the statistical depiction.

Minard—whether consciously or not—systematically worked to carve out a coherent "story" from a given research question. Throughout his oeuvre, we can observe an ever more consequential habit of editing his maps with the aim of shaping a narrative focus. He did so, for instance, by focusing on just one aspect of a given data set, by collecting data from various sources in order to answer a predefined research question, or by juxtaposing maps to compare data sets over time. He thus gradually developed an expertise in composing rich and detailed dataviews while avoiding the clutter and inconsistencies found in some of his earlier maps.

The Reception of Minard's Work

Minard published his maps himself; he was not part of any major scientific society or academy, nor did he publish in any scientific journal other than the *Annales des ponts et chaussées*.[43] The American cartographer Arthur Howard Robinson wondered how exactly Minard circulated his maps, reached a wide audience, and made the impact that he did. Robinson concluded: "He seems to have been a lone worker."[44]

This is congruent with Minard's obituary, where he is described as a rather modest person who didn't have much talent for self-display and whose career, considering his merits, advanced rather slowly.[45]

Other than his technical drawings, which were printed as engravings and bound in books or pamphlets, his broadsheet maps were lithographic prints—most of them hand colored, although some maps were printed with color. According to Minard's writings, two of his early maps were printed and distributed in editions of one hundred and two hundred copies, respectively.[46] Lithographic printing generally allowed for print runs of up to ten thousand copies. However, we have no information about Minard's usual print run, and not many copies of his maps seem to have survived.[47] This may be due to a restrained budget on Minard's part; lithographic prints were an expensive investment for a private budget. Also, with the maps targeted to a specific-interest readership, he may have opted for a limited print run of only a few hundred. As for their conservation, broadsheet maps in general (and even more so statistical maps, whose information grew outdated) were considered tools for daily use (as opposed to precious works of art or decoration) and would usually not have been kept for posterity.

This portrait shows the French statesman Eugène Rouher with a map by Minard draped over the chair. The original painting by Alexandre Cabanel, a famous salon painter in France, was exhibited in Paris at the Salon des Beaux Arts in 1861, and was in possession of Rouher's family until into the twentieth century. This version is a painted copy by Charles Brun. Eugène Rouher gave it to the Musée Mandet in Riom, his home town, where it is kept to this day.

While Robinson's characterization of Minard as a "lone worker" seems exaggerated, the questions remain: If Minard had each of his works printed in only a few hundred copies, where did all these maps go? Who were the readers he addressed? And how did word of Minard's work spread? Some of Minard's notes indicate that he would make the effort to send maps to people whom he thought would be interested, such as fellow engineers, deputies, and local politicians. Apart from that, it may be assumed that his printers would have sold a number of copies in their shops.

Apart from these modes of distribution, there seems to have been one fruitful channel for his oeuvre inside the administration of public works. We know Minard to have been a much respected member of the Corps des ponts et chaussées and its influential Conseil général, which coordinated the work of the Corps and thus all national infrastructure projects. The obituary mentions that he received strong encouragement for his statistical maps from several secretaries of public works.[48] While in office, the secretary would also head the Conseil général des ponts et chaussées. Minard was first a temporary and then, from 1846, a permanent member of the Conseil until his retirement in 1851. We can assume that he continued to engage with his peers after his retirement, and would therefore have managed to circulate his maps among high ranks of the administration of public works.

In his 1861 brochure *Des tableaux graphiques et des cartes figuratives*, Minard mentioned that the general director of the Corps des ponts et chaussées, Alfred de Franqueville, had presented his maps to the French statesman Eugène Rouher, who was secretary of agriculture, commerce, and public works at the time. According to Minard, Rouher readily subscribed "to the majority" of his maps, which enabled Minard to publish some ten thousand copies of maps on a variety of subjects.[49] This suggests that the subscription made by the secretary encompassed not only single copies for himself but larger numbers of copies that Rouher may have circulated

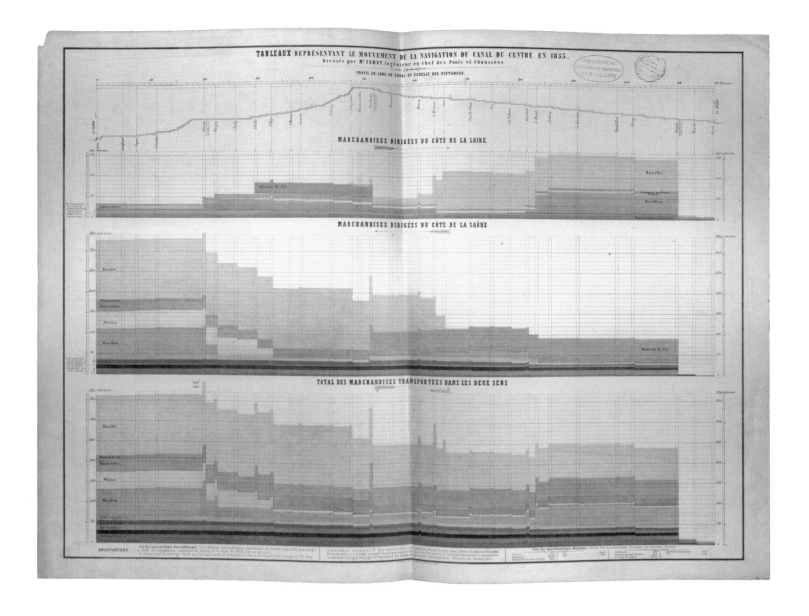

TABLEAUX REPRÉSENTANT LE MOUVEMENT DE LA NAVIGATION DU CANAL DU CENTRE EN 1853.
Dressés par Mr COMOY Ingénieur en chef des Ponts et Chaussées

PROFIL EN LONG DU CANAL ET ÉCHELLE DES DISTANCES

MARCHANDISES DIRIGÉES DU CÔTÉ DE LA LOIRE.

MARCHANDISES DIRIGÉES DU CÔTÉ DE LA SAÔNE

TOTAL DES MARCHANDISES TRANSPORTÉES DANS LES DEUX SENS

among his clerks and officers—an assumption which could explain how Minard financed the printing of large editions of his maps and how large numbers of his maps found their way into the administration's offices.

Rouher went on to be one of the most influential politicians in France over the next decade. (He led the government from 1863 to 1869 and served as a close advisor to emperor Napoléon III and his wife.) Minard reported that his maps had been presented to the emperor Napoléon III, who received them favorably.[50] Minard's obituary states that he had the honor of having one of his maps depicted in a life-size, full-figure portrait of Eugène Rouher, painted and presented to the public at the Salon des Beaux-Arts in 1861.[51] It is clearly an indication of a great appreciation that this high-level politician should have included Minard's map in his official portrait and introduced Minard's work to the emperor. It suggests that Rouher valued applied statistics as a means to comprehend some effects of the accelerating industrialization, and that he considered statistical maps such as Minard's highly expedient tools for administration, suitable to mark Rouher as an icon of modern leadership.

The Impact of Minard's Work

Minard observed in *Des tableaux graphiques et des cartes figuratives* that his innovations were almost instantly imitated. He reported, for instance, that he had sent his 1845 colored tableau graphic on the Canal du Centre [5] to Guillaume-Emmanuel Comoy. At the time, Comoy was the inspector in charge of the canal and had provided

Guillaume-Emmanuel Comoy was the engineer in charge of the Canal du Centre, and provided the data for Minard's graphic tableau showing freight traffic on the canal in 1844 [5]. He found this graphic so useful that he subsequently created his own diagrams visualizing traffic on the canal, including this one showing data from 1853. In representing the two directions of traffic in separate diagrams and in using an elaborate grid as a background, he reconciled some of the difficulties of Minard's 1845 original. As an additional feature, he visualized the cargo for each harbor along the canal.

the data for Minard's diagram. Apparently, Comoy found the graphic so useful that he started publishing his own detailed diagrams following Minard's example, visualizing the traffic on the canal every year from 1851 onward.[52] By 1854 Comoy's works had made such an impact that the administration of public works recommended the application of such graphic tableaus to all main waterways (apparently without referencing Minard). Furthermore, Minard recounts that when two of Comoy's diagrams had been exhibited at the Exposition Universelle in 1855, he felt compelled to claim his anteriority, which was given proper credit when the jury mentioned in their printed report that Comoy's works were based on Minard's system.[53]

Minard also mentioned several other direct followers and applications derived from his examples, including a complex mapping project that the administration of Ponts et chaussées published in twelve sheets to document circulation on national roads.[54] Furthermore, through the described channels of circulation, Minard's maps seem to have gained a large audience among administration officials, social and economic researchers, and employees in private businesses concerned with infrastructure projects, such as the railway companies. It was apparently through a combination of a subscription system, commercial sales in the print shops, many informal contacts, the immediate imitation of his methods by colleagues, and word of mouth that his maps and methods became widely known among technical and scientific circles in France during the second part of the nineteenth century. All told, however, we have no indication that Minard exerted any significant influence in administrative matters, such as in the debates regarding the establishment of the French railroad network. His long-lasting influence lies more in his having inspired many fellow engineers and scientists to pursue the visualization research he so impressively established. Gilles Palsky, in his comprehensive overview of statistical mapping in France through the nineteenth century, summarized the impact of Minard's oeuvre by saying: "If his works exerted an immediate influence, it was primarily by initiating a period of enthusiasm for statistical graphics between 1860 and 1900."[55]

Minard's Legacy

Minard's contribution to the growing movement of data visualization using the "graphical method" is outstanding in its range and extent. It was a lucky concurrence of circumstances that allowed him to create his statistical maps. Apart from the influences described above, we also seem to owe this oeuvre to some simpler, external factors. As most of this work was created after Minard's retirement, it seems noteworthy that he (though his health seems to have been unstable for long periods of his life) was well and motivated enough up until a very old age to pursue his personal research interests, and that he had the time to research the data and draw the maps, as well as the money and the connections to have them printed.

Tarbé de Saint-Hardouin, who published a collection of biographies on the engineers of the Corps des ponts et chaussées in 1884, described Minard as a person of independent spirits: "The slowness of his advancement, compared to his contemporaries, was without doubt the result of the independence of his mind, and of the occupations he chose, with the single goal of satisfying his affinity for research and without considering the progress of his administrative career too much."[56] Whether this is a true description of Minard's character we cannot judge. However, his achievements did require a certain independence of spirit. He developed the impulses of several predecessors to establish a new form of scientific communication. He created a very significant aesthetic in his maps; among hundreds of nineteenth-century maps, it will always be easy to identify works by Minard, with their minimalist design, well-defined color schemes, and fine execution. Most of his many works were self-initiated and well researched. It appears that until his death at the age of eighty-nine, he was a spirited man, ready to engage with new topics and experiment with new methods. Among the later works of his oeuvre, several maps

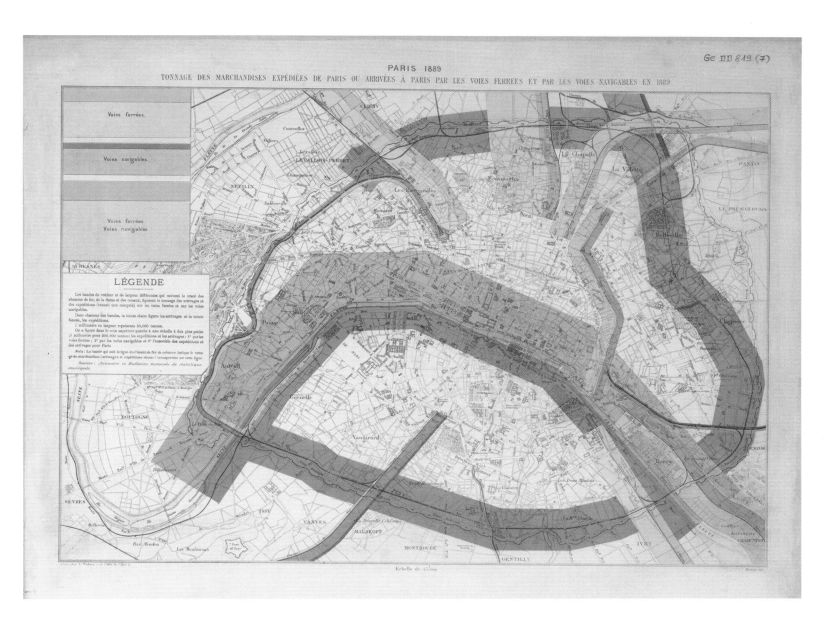

PARIS 1889
TONNAGE DES MARCHANDISES EXPÉDIÉES DE PARIS OU ARRIVÉES À PARIS PAR LES VOIES FERRÉES ET PAR LES VOIES NAVIGABLES EN 1889

deviate from the usual traffic- and trade-dominated topics, such as a map about global migration [38], the development of ancient languages [56], two double pieces (including the Napoléon map) that cover historical military campaigns [46] [60], and two diagrams on higher education [59] [61]. In addition, one year before his death, Minard published a brochure on ancient construction techniques, featuring several technical drawings. All of these works testify to his wide-ranging interest and curiosity, which kept him at work until his very last days.

The archive of the École nationale des ponts et chaussées in Paris, where Minard had close, lifelong associations, keeps a comprehensive portfolio of his works, bound in a volume, that must have been assembled just months or even weeks before his death. In it, Minard had collected and bequeathed to the archive all maps and diagrams he considered relevant in his oeuvre of statistical visualization, certainly with an aim to preserve it for posterity. It would certainly be fulfilling for him to see new generations of engineers, statisticians, and visualization researchers learning from his example. It is unfortunate that at this point no portrait of him is known to exist in the archive of the École des ponts et chaussées or elsewhere. But then it may be most reverent that we should remember him not by his own likeness, but by the power of his celebrated works.

This flow map originates from the *Album de statistique graphique*, by Jacques Bertillon, and shows freight traffic in Paris in 1889. The brighter part of the flow relates to incoming traffic; darker flows show expedient transports. Different modes of communication (waterways, railroads etc.) are distinguished by color. The base map and flows are treated differently than in Minard's works: instead of reducing the base map to the absolute minimum to make room for the flows (as Minard did), the cartographers opted for a transparent flow, which forms a transparent layer over the detailed map.

Catalog of Statistical Graphics

EDITOR'S NOTE: This is a complete catalog of the known statistical maps and diagrams by Charles-Joseph Minard. Not included are technical drawings and plans (a list of those is provided in the appendix). All works in the catalog are kept in the archive of the École nationale des ponts et chaussées in Paris, except for [34], of which there is known to be only one copy, held at the Bibliothèque nationale de France.

The graphics in this catalog are numbered according to the chronology of their creation date, with several undated works listed according to the probable date of their creation. The catalog follows this chronology, except for three distinct series of works. These maps were updated several times over the course of years and are presented here in three associated groups.

The measures given in the catalog pertain to the specific sheet reproduced here. It is important to keep in mind that the measures for Minard's surviving maps vary from copy to copy, sometimes substantially. This is due to the fact that the maps were printed on sheets larger than the actual graphic, and very often were cropped or cut in pieces and subsequently glued on paper, mounted on linen, or bound in a brochure. Therefore, the measures here only serve to give a general size indication for each map.

The explanatory notes and observations included in most of Minard's statistical graphics provide substantial insight to his visualization studies. Although his original language is at times vague or ambiguous, we have included translations of the original map text for a selection of the most interesting works. Digitized versions of his works can be found online at patrimoine.enpc.fr/collections/show/12.

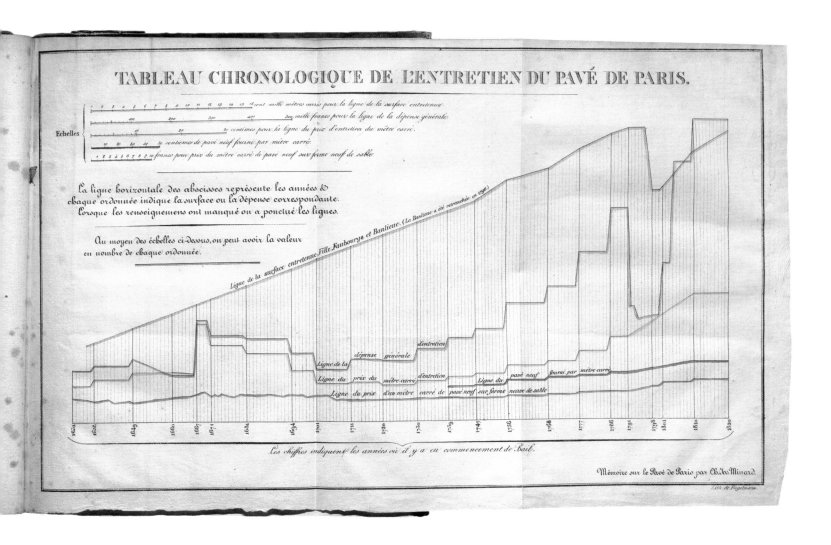

TABLEAU CHRONOLOGIQUE DE L'ENTRETIEN DU PAVÉ DE PARIS.

1

Paris Pavement Maintenance

▲ **"Tableau chronologique de l'entretien du pavé de Paris"**
No date. Lithographic print, hand-colored. 41.5 × 26.0 cm.
Published in: *Tableau des progrès de la dépense du pavé de Paris pendant les deux derniers siècles* (Paris, 1825)

This diagram accompanies a pamphlet about the maintenance of the Paris pavement from 1632 to 1820. Minard described it as a "visual register" that he drew "in order to better grasp all the circumstances of the maintenance."[1] The colored graphs visualize several metrics Minard calculated by drawing from historical contracts. The yellow graph indicates the total pavement surface area in Paris, while the blue one shows the total maintenance expenditures per annum. The vertical axis is not labeled; instead, readers have to make do with horizontal scales provided for each graph in the top left section. Punctuated graphs indicate a lack of data sources. The diagram reveals a pattern break after the Revolution of 1789, when the maintenance budget (blue) nosedived for several years. At the same time, the average maintenance price per square meter (rose) grew because the pavement gradually wore out.

MINARD TRANSLATED

Chronological table of Paris pavement maintenance

The horizontal line of the abscissae represents the years and each ordinate indicates the surface area or the corresponding expenditure. Dotted lines were used where information was unavailable. Using the scales above, the reader can find the numerical value of each ordinate.

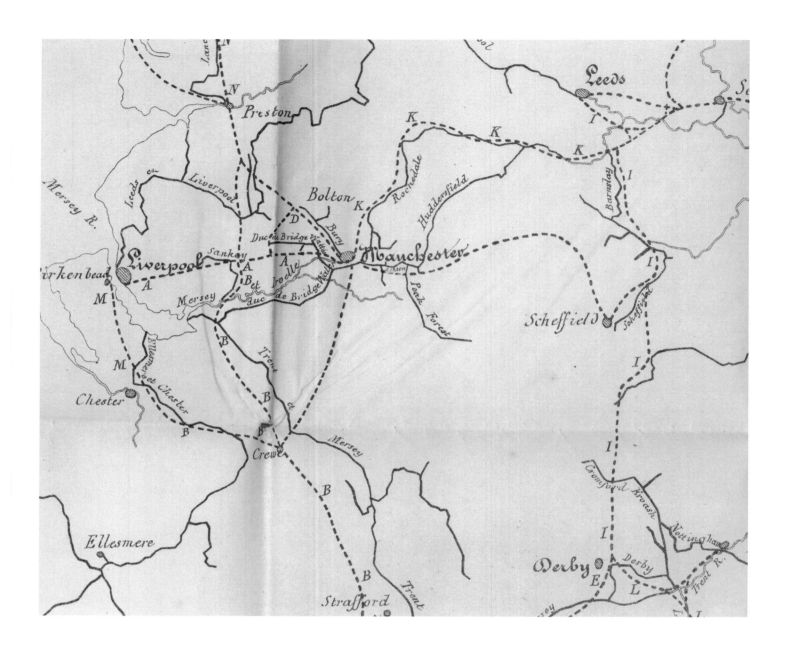

2

Major Canals and Railroads in England

➤ **"Principaux canaux et railways d'Angleterre en concurrence"**
1844. Lithographic print. 52.5 × 66.9 cm. Published in: *Des conséquences du
voisinage des chemins de fer et des voies navigables* (Paris: Fain et Thunot, 1844)

This map shows English waterways and
railroads and was published in a brochure
that discussed the relationship between
existing canals and new railroad routes.
The booklet contained many data tables
to support Minard's argument that railroads should be built along valleys, i.e.,
in the vicinity of existing canals. Like

the majority of his maps, this work is
reduced to the absolute minimum of
graphic means: England's coastlines are
barely distinguishable, and the inner
landscape is not depicted at all except
for a number of location names and
a tangle of traffic routes.

Principaux Canaux et Railways d'Angleterre en concurrence.

dressé par M. Minard Ingénieur en chef divisionnaire des ponts et chaussées.

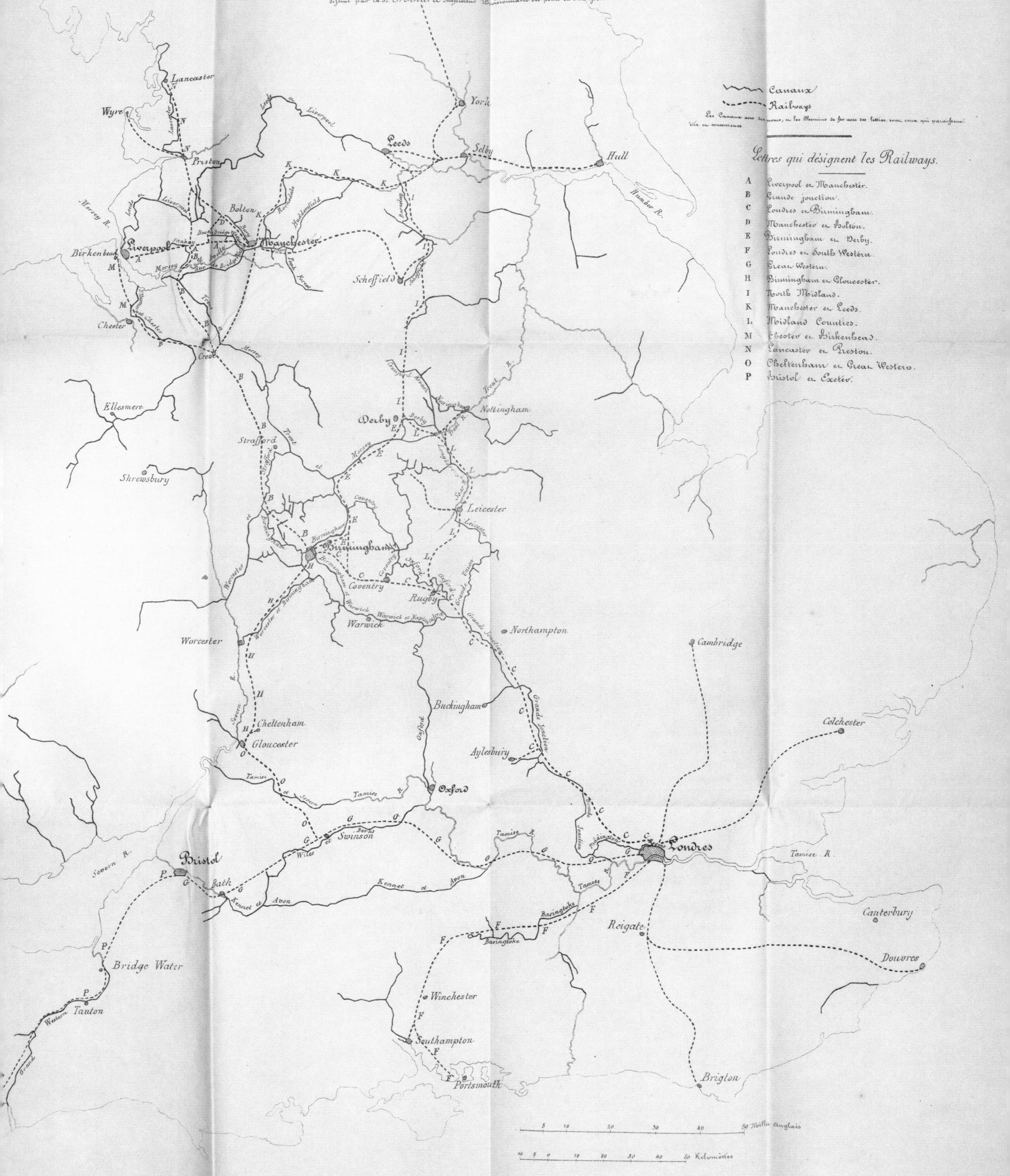

— Canaux
---- Railways

Les Canaux sont desservis, et les Chemins de fer avec des lettres; ceux qui paraîtront être en concurrence

Lettres qui désignent les Railways.

A	Liverpool et Manchester.
B	Grande Jonction.
C	Londres à Birmingham.
D	Manchester et Bolton.
E	Birmingham et Derby.
F	Londres et South Western.
G	Great Western.
H	Birmingham et Gloucester.
I	North Midland.
K	Manchester et Leeds.
L	Midland Counties.
M	Chester et Birkenhead.
N	Lancaster et Preston.
O	Cheltenham et Great Western.
P	Bristol et Exeter.

Lancaster · Wyre · Preston · Bolton · Leeds · York · Selby · Hull
Liverpool · Manchester · Birkenhead · Mersey R. · Chester · Crewe · Sheffield
Ellesmere · Shrewsbury · Stafford · Derby · Nottingham · Leicester
Worcester · Birmingham · Coventry · Rugby · Warwick · Northampton · Cambridge
Cheltenham · Gloucester · Buckingham · Oxford · Aylesbury · Colchester
Bristol · Bath · Swindon · Winchester · Southampton · Portsmouth · Brighton
Bridge Water · Taunton · Basingstoke · Reigate · Londres · Canterbury · Douvres

Humber R. · Mersey · Trent · Severn · Tamise · Kennet et Avon · Thames R.

5 10 20 30 40 50 Milles anglais
10 5 0 10 20 30 40 50 Kilomètres

Tableaux figuratifs de la Circulation de quelques chemins d...

indique, selon l'échelle, le nombre de voyageurs qui ont passé sur les différentes parties d'un chemin. Les...

(Dessiné par M. Minard, Inspecteur divisionn...

Chemins Belges — Circulation de Janvier et Février 1843 dans un seul sens. Les hachur...

Les hachures serrées indiquent les voyageurs échangés entre Bruxelles et Ostende seulemens.

Les hachures serrées indiquent les voyageurs écha... entre Bruxelles et Liège seulemens.

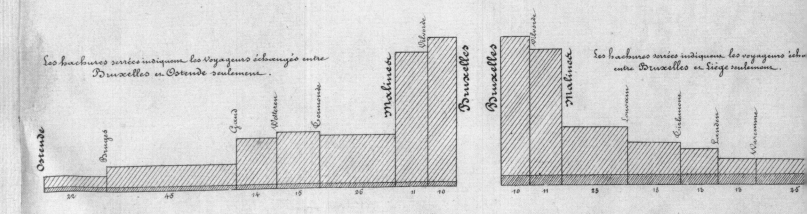

Chemin de Strasbourg à Bâle — Circulation de Mars 1842. Les hachures claires indiquent le...

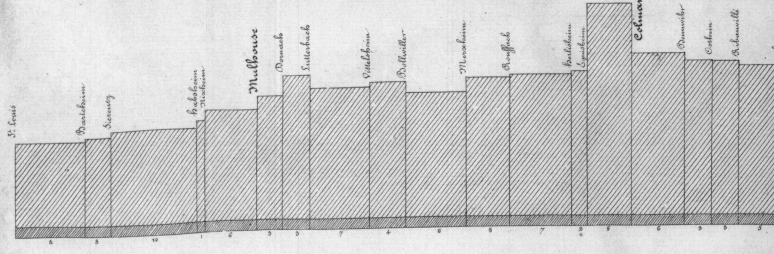

Chemin de Lyon à St. Etienne — Circulation de Mars. Avril

et Mai 1841. Les hachures claires indiquent le parcours partiel, les hachures serrées le parcours total ou le transit.

Chemin de Paris à Orléans —

Les hachures claires indiquent le parcours partiel, les... (y compris moitié les voyageurs communs avec l...

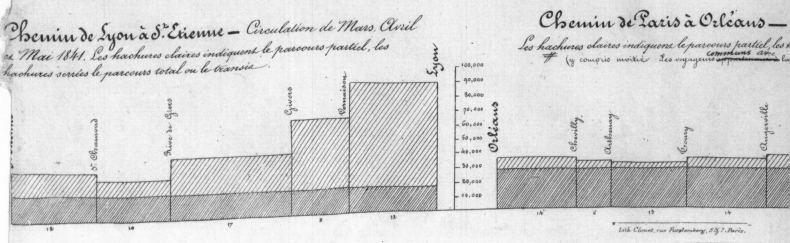

Lith. Clouet, rue Furstemberg, 5 & 7. Paris.

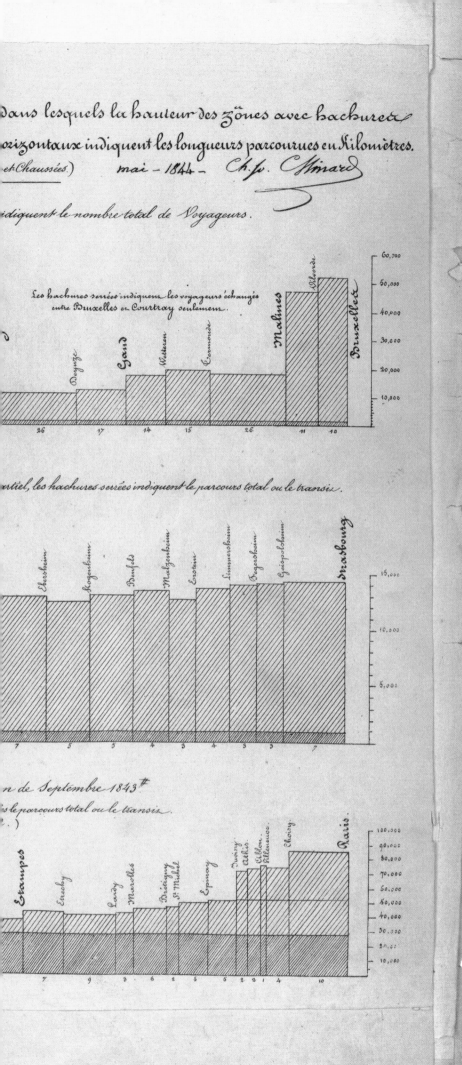

3

Circulation on Several Railroads

◄ **"Tableaux figuratifs de la circulation de quelques chemins de fer"**
May 1844. Lithographic print. 43.4 × 33.7 cm.
Published in: *Des tableaux graphiques et des cartes figuratives* (Paris, 1861)

This is Minard's earliest *tableau graphique.* He was convinced that new railroad lines should not just serve their two end destinations, but also foster regional traffic between towns along the route.[2] Here he analyzed the traffic on several Belgian and French lines. The height of each bar represents the number of passengers traveling along that section, while the width shows the relative distance. The light hachures denominate the passengers per section, while the dark hachures refer to passengers who traveled the full distance. Minard notes that the traffic is shown "in one single direction"; however, there is no indication which direction he means.

4

Circulation of Passengers Between Dijon and Mulhouse

➤ **"Carte de la circulation des voyageurs par voitures publiques sur les routes de la contrée où sera placé le chemin de fer de Dijon à Mulhouse"**
March 1845. Lithographic print, hand-tinted.
71.0 × 45.3 cm. Published in: *Des tableaux graphiques et des cartes figuratives* (Paris, 1861)

In this revolutionary map, created in the middle of a debate about where to project the railroads between Dijon and Mulhouse in eastern France, Minard analyzed the street traffic on preexisting roads in the region. It is the first time that he implemented the flow map method. The width of each section indicates how many passengers annually traveled on the street. The map itself is extremely stripped down; it features barely any landscape details other than a network of local place names and rivers. The graphic survived in two versions: In the earlier one, the flow is colored in one tint only. Later, Minard differentiated between passengers who traveled on only one section of the road (darker tint) and those who traveled longer distances (lighter tint).

MINARD TRANSLATED

Circulation of travelers by public carriage on the roads of the region in which the Dijon–Mulhouse railroad will be built

The width of the zones represents the number of travelers at a rate of half a millimeter per thousand travelers per year.

The darker zone represents travelers moving between two villages without traveling beyond.

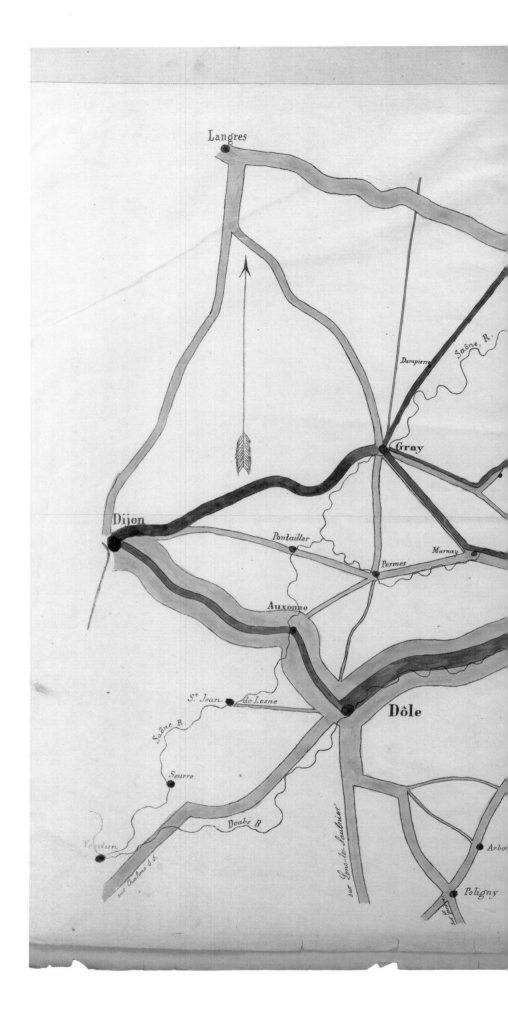

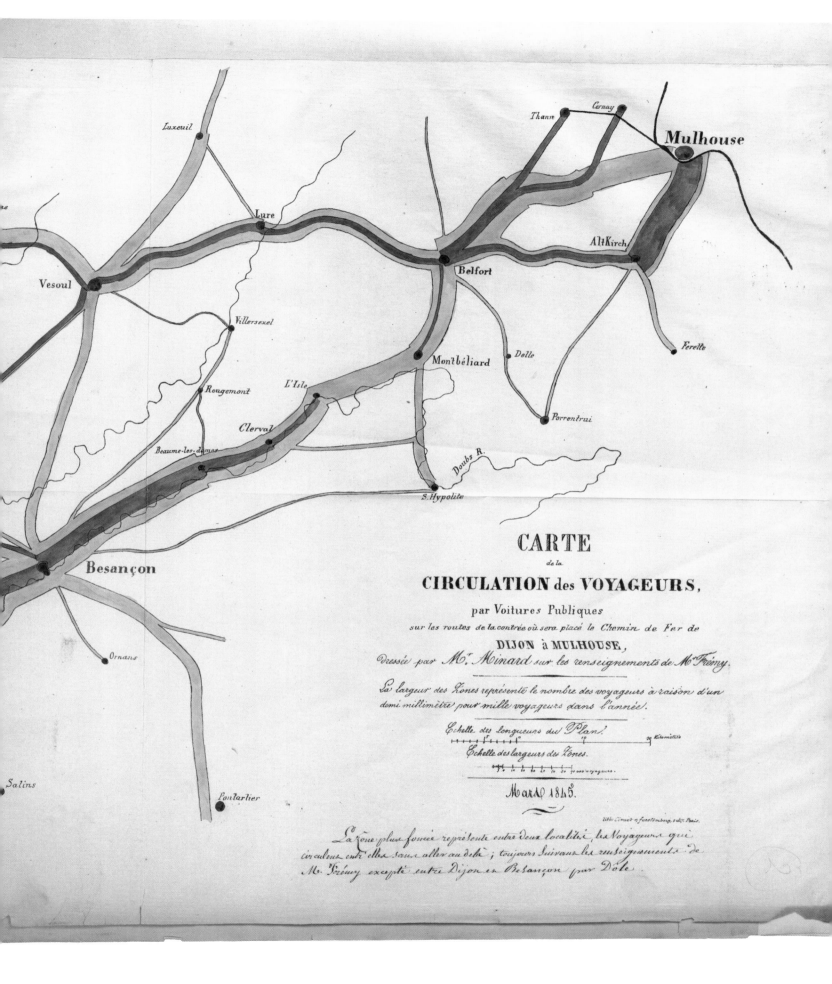

CARTE
de la
CIRCULATION des VOYAGEURS,
par Voitures Publiques
sur les routes de la contrée où sera placé le Chemin de Fer de
DIJON à MULHOUSE,
Dressée par M.ʳ Minard sur les renseignements de M.ʳ Frémy.

La largeur des Zones représente le nombre des voyageurs à raison d'un
demi millimètre pour mille voyageurs dans l'année.

Echelle des longueurs du Plan.
Echelle des largeurs des Zones.

Mars 1845.

Lith. Cornet q. Furstenberg, 5 Seft. Paris.

La Zone plus foncée représente entre deux localités, les Voyageurs qui
circulent entre elles sans aller au delà ; toujours suivans les renseignements de
M.ʳ Frémy excepté entre Dijon et Besançon par Dôle.

41

Tableau figuratif du mouvement commercial

dressé par M.ᵣ Minard sur les renseignements

Le mouvement total équivaut à 131,000 tonneaux parcourant la lo...

Le transit y est compris pour 16,000 tonne...

Extrait des Rapports su...
(page 436)
Ministère de l'O...
A côté des beaux modèles exposés par ...
ressort de la VIII classe : l'atlas...
circulation sur le Canal du Centre en 18...
inspecteur général des Ponts et Chau...
sur des Chemins de fer EN 1844...

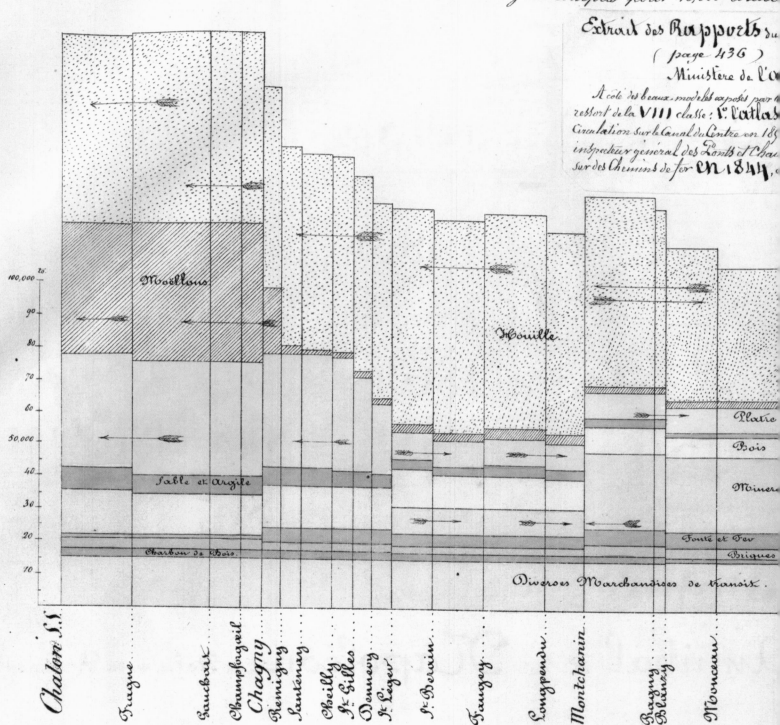

Moëllons

Houille

Plâtre

Bois

Miner...

Sable et Argile

Fonte et Fer

Charbon de Bois

Briques

Diverses Marchandises de transit.

Chalon S.S. — Fragne — Saubois — Champforgeuil — Chagny — Remigny — Santenay — Rceilly — S.ᵗ Gilles — Dennevoy — S.ᵗ Léger — S.ᵗ Berain — Faugay — Longpendu — Montchanin — Ragny Blanzy — Monceaux

100,000 / 90 / 80 / 70 / 60 / 50,000 / 40 / 30 / 20 / 10

Un millimètre pour mille tonneaux — Trois millimè...

On a compris dans le transit les
marchandises allant de Châlon au Canal
latéral à la Loire et réciproquement.

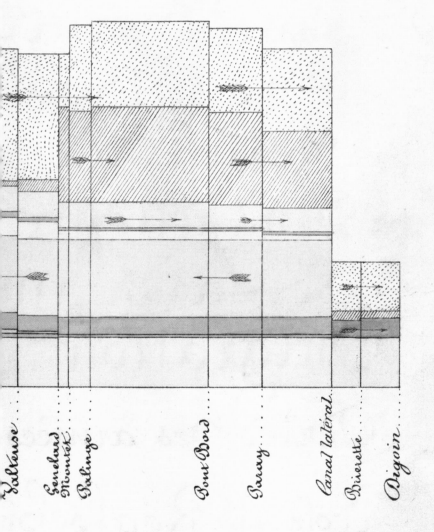

Canal du Centre en 1844

Comoy. x — *1845 Ch. P. Minard*

du Canal ou 117 kilomètres.

te international de l'Exposition Universelle de 1855.

Mention pour Ordre.

re, du Commerce et des travaux publics.

Jes travaux publics se trouvent deux publications importantes qui sont du
de la Loire de l'ing.r en chef J. Couvreu 2°.es les tableaux graphiques de la
Bés par l'ing.r en chef Comoy, d'après le Système que M.r Minard
traite avait imaginé et appliqué aux représentation de la Circulation
ral du Centre en 1845. *Signé M. Wertheim rapporteur*

Valtouse *Genelard Montet Palinge* *Pont Bord* *Paray* *Canal latéral* *Biverette* *Digoin*

un kilomètre.

Commercial Traffic on the Canal du Centre in 1844

◄ **"Tableau figuratif du mouvement commercial du Canal du Centre en 1844"** December 1845. Lithographic print, hand-colored. 43.9 × 33.6 cm. Published in: *Des tableaux graphiques et des cartes figuratives* (Paris, 1861)

In this second *tableau graphique*, Minard analyzed freight traffic on the Canal du Centre. The base line refers to the geographical distances along the canal. The height of each bar shows the amount of goods transported along each section, with both directions considered. Minard differentiated between categories of freight using dotting, hachure, and color. Those are (from the top down): coal, construction stones, plaster, sand and argil, wood, ore, iron, brick stones, charcoal, and "diverse merchandise in transit." Minard tried to indicate directions by including arrows, but he did not execute this systematically. Still, the arrows add some basic stories, indicating, for instance, that minerals (light brown) traveled only along particular sections toward the town of Montchanin (presumably to be delivered to the nearby industrial region of Le Creusot). The handwritten note on the right was added after the Exposition Universelle of 1855, where several diagrams using the same technique had been exhibited without crediting Minard. In the printed publication quoted here, the jury acknowledged the method had originally been invented by Minard (cf. page 28).

MINARD TRANSLATED

Figurative Tableau of the commercial traffic on the Canal du Centre, 1844–1845

Total commercial traffic is equivalent to 131,000 barrels traveling the length of the canal or 117 kilometers. Transit is included for 16,000 barrels.

One millimeter per thousand barrels—Three millimeters per kilometer.

Travelers Passing Through Grenoble Junction

➤ **"Embranchement de Grenoble. Aperçu de la circulation actuelle des voyageurs dans les voitures publics"**
January 1846. Lithographic print, hand-tinted. 34.8 × 47.8 cm.

This map survived in Minard's portfolio of statistical works, but we do not know its original context. It evaluates traffic on several street connections between Lyon, Grenoble, and Valence in southern France. The traffic flows show one thousand traveling passengers with each third of a millimeter. An important variation here is that Minard distinguished the street from the flow of passengers: the street is shown as a black line, while the flow of passengers is tinted gray. Dashed lines indicate existing or projected railroad lines.

EMBRANCHEMENT DE GRENOBLE.

Aperçu de la circulation actuelle des Voyageurs dans les voitures publics.

La largeur des Zônes teintées indique approximativement le nombre annuel des voyageurs, à raison d'un tiers de millimètre pour mille voyageurs et en ne supposant que les deux tiers des places occupés.

Les lignes ponctuées indiquent les chemins de fer exécutés ou projêtés. *(Janvier 1846)*

LYON

Crémieux

Morestel

St Symphorien

Heyrieu

La Verpillières

Bourgoin

La Tour du Pin

Pont-Beauvoisin.

Givors

Vienne

Bournay

Biol

Virieu

Chateaunay

Montrevol

Villeneuve

Champier

Burcin

Les Echelles

La Côte St André

La Frette

Lemp

La Murette

St Laurent

Revel

Mplaine

Voiron

Beaurepaire

St Etienne

Rives

Moirans

Viriville

Tullins

Voreppe

St Rambert

Moras

Roibon

Vinay

St Vallier

St Marcellin

St Donnat

Pont en Royan

Grenoble

Tournon

Tain

Romans

Roche de Glun

Valence

10 ⌐ 5 ⌐ 0 ⌐ 10 ⌐ 20 Kilomètres

Un tiers de millimètre pour mille voyageurs.

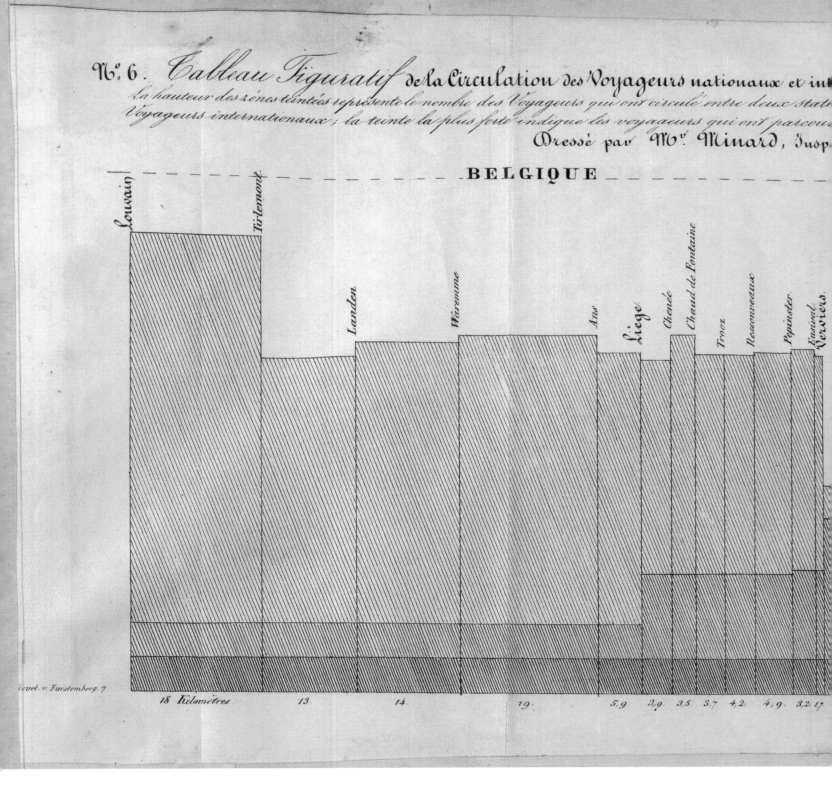

7

**Circulation of Passengers Between
Belgium and Prussia in 1844**

▲ "Tableau figuratif de la circulation des voyageurs
nationaux et internationaux sur le chemin de fer entre
la Belgique et la Prusse en 1844"
May 1846. Lithographic print. 45.7 × 20.6 cm. Published
in: *Des voyageurs internationaux sur le chemin de fer entre
la Belgique et la Prusse* (Paris, 1846)

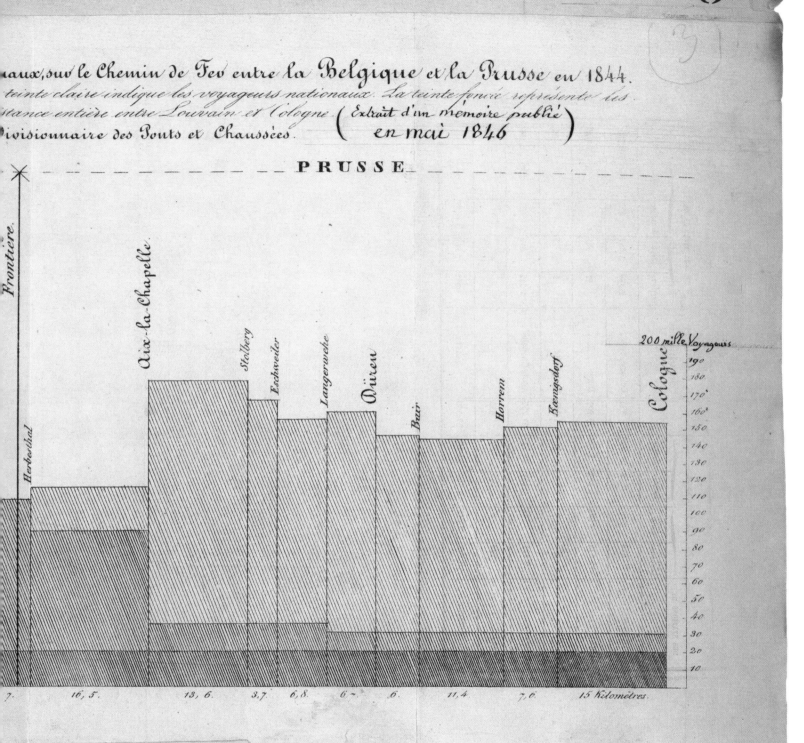

...aux, sur le Chemin de Fer entre la Belgique et la Prusse en 1844.
...teinte claire indique les voyageurs nationaux. La teinte foncée représente les
...stance entière entre Louvain et Cologne (Extrait d'un mémoire publié
...Divisionnaire des Ponts et Chaussées. (en mai 1846)

PRUSSE

This and the following graphic were published in a brochure in which Minard elaborated on how much the new railroad services affected existing traffic and whether they boasted new connections. In particular, Minard looked at the first international railroad between Leuven (Belgium) and Cologne (then Prussia). The border between the two countries is shown in the middle of the diagram. Again, the horizontal baseline represents the route, with distances and intermediary stations noted along the bottom and top respectively. The height of the bars refers to the number of passengers for each section. Three categories are distinguished: national passengers (light hachures), international passengers who have traversed the border (medium hachures), and those who traveled the full distance (darkest hachures).

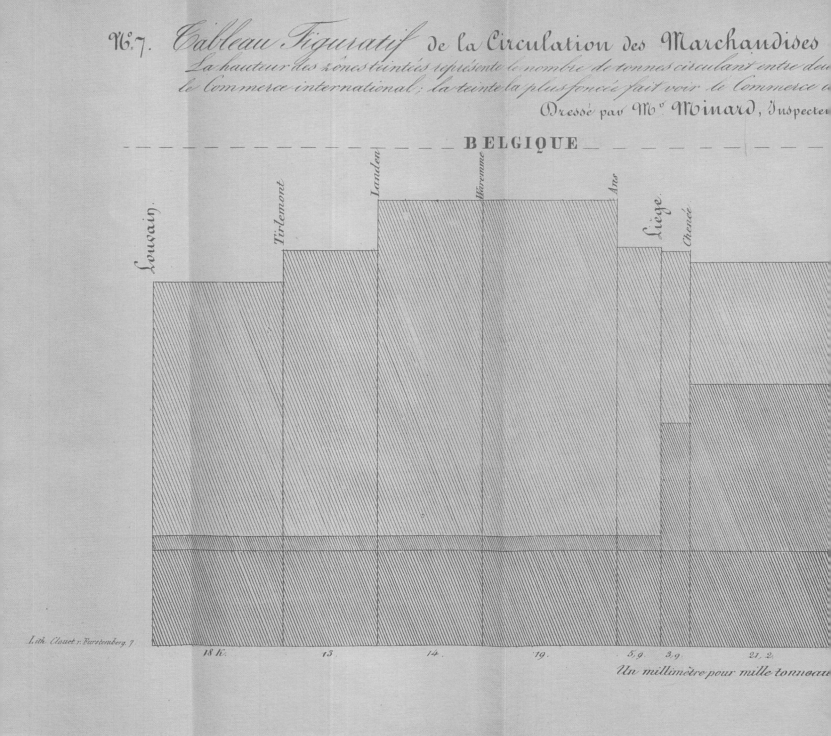

8

**Circulation of Goods Between
Belgium and Prussia in 1844**

▲ "Tableau figuratif de la circulation des marchandises sur
le chemin de fer entre la Belgique et la Prusse, en 1844"
May 1846. Lithographic print. 52.5 × 21.2 cm. Published in: *Des
voyageurs internationaux sur le chemin de fer entre la Belgique et
la Prusse* (Paris, 1846)

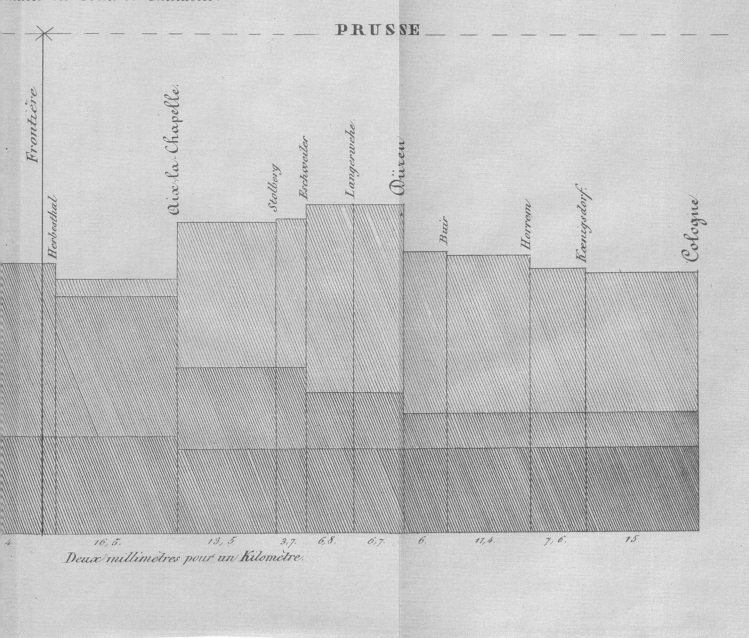

Chemin de Fer, entre la Belgique et la Prusse, en 1844.

...ns. La teinte claire indique le Commerce national, la teinte foncée représente

...it de la Mer sur l'Allemagne.

...maire des Ponts et Chaussées.

PRUSSE

Frontière

Herbesthal

Aix-la-Chapelle.

Stolberg

Eschweiler

Langerwehe

Düren

Buir

Horrem

Koenigsdorf.

Cologne

4   16,5.   13,5   3,7   6,8.   6,7.   6   11,4.   7,6.   15

Deux millimètres pour un Kilomètre.

This piece accompanies [7] and evaluates the freight traffic along the Belgium-Rhineland route. Again, the base line represents the length of the railroads, with distances in kilometers noted along the bottom. The height of bars represents the amount of merchandise transported. Goods are measured in tonnes (one millimeter of height on the original graphic refers to 1,000 tonnes). Minard did not provide a scale for the height but confined himself to a text label explanation at the bottom. Unlike in [5], no categories of goods are distinguished. The light hachure shows internal freight traffic, the medium hachure denotes the goods traveling across the border, and the darkest hachure shows the proportion of merchandise traveling the full distance. This is the last of Minard's early tableaux graphiques. He subsequently focused on other formats in his visualization studies, most prominently the flow map method.

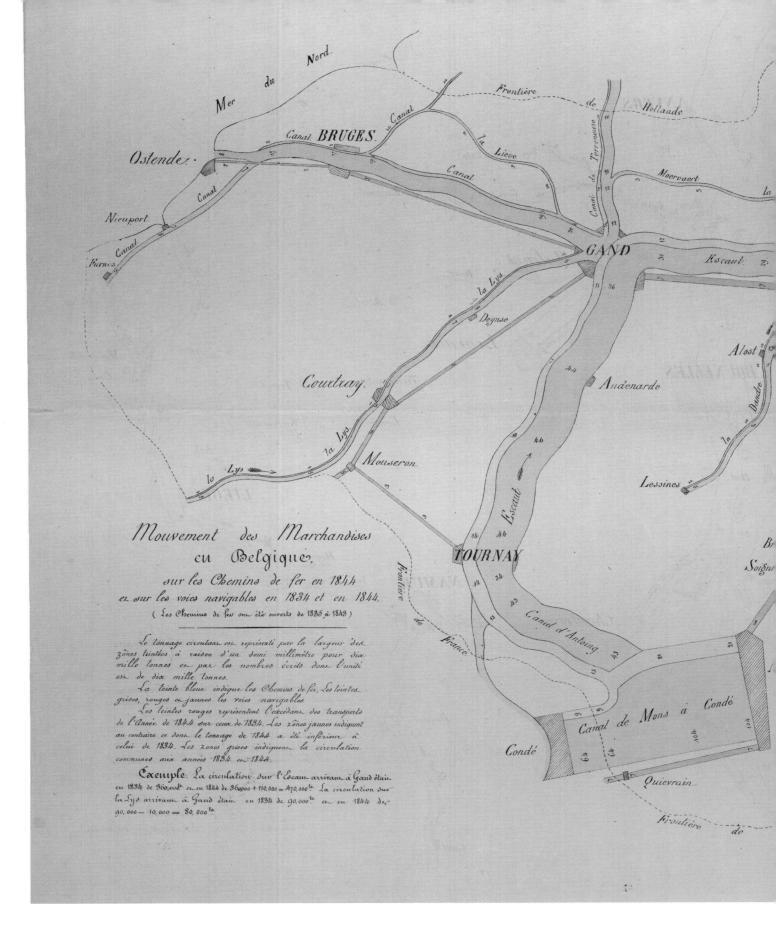

Mouvement des Marchandises
en Belgique,
sur les Chemins de fer en 1844
et sur les voies navigables en 1834 et en 1844.
(Les Chemins de fer ont été ouverts de 1835 à 1843)

Le tonnage circulant est représenté par la largeur des zônes teintées à raison d'un demi millimètre pour dix mille tonnes et par les nombres écrits dont l'unité est de dix mille tonnes.

La teinte bleue indique les Chemins de fer. Les teintes grises, rouges en jaunes les voies navigables.

Les teintes rouges représentent l'excédant des transports de l'Année de 1844 sur ceux de 1834. Les zônes jaunes indiquent au contraire ce dont le tonnage de 1844 a été inférieur à celui de 1834. Les zônes grises indiquent la circulation commune aux années 1834 et 1844.

Exemple. La circulation sur l'Escaut arrivant à Gand était en 1834 de 360,000 et en 1844 de 360,000 + 110,000 = 470,000 tes. La circulation sur la Lys arrivant à Gand était en 1834 de 90,000 tes et en 1844 de 90,000 − 10,000 = 80,000 tes.

9

**Circulation of Goods in Belgium
in 1834 and 1844**

▲ "Mouvement des marchandises en Belgique, sur les chemins de fer en 1844 et sur les voies navigables en 1834 et en 1844"
March 1847. Lithographic print, hand-colored. 87.5 × 61.7 cm.

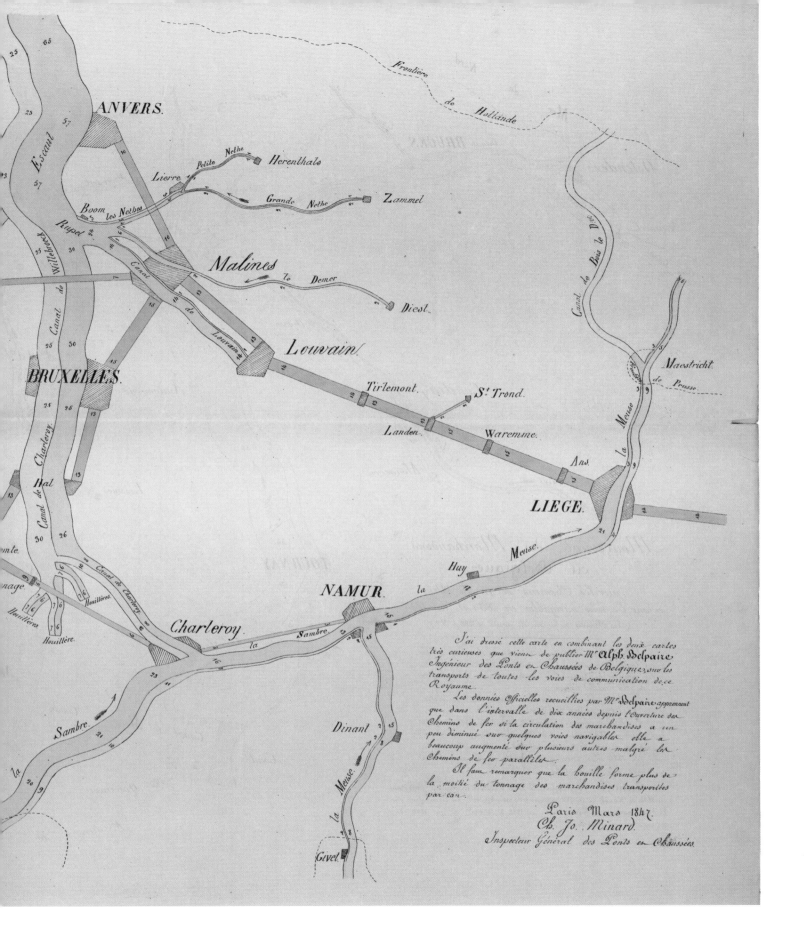

In this visualization, Minard substantially advanced his flow map concept by introducing color and comparing traffic flows over a period of ten years. The map represents freight traffic in Belgium on the railroads in 1844 (blue), as well as along canals in 1834 and in 1844. Gray flows represent a constant volume of waterway traffic over that time. Red flows show where traffic had grown, while yellow flows indicate where it diminished. Minard varied the shapes of flows: the railroads form straight flow segments; waterways are curvy. For the first time, Minard added exact numbers next to the flows.

Transport of Mineral Fuels in France, 1845–1860

After a break of four years, Minard reinitiated his visualization studies with a map about the transportation of mineral fuels within France. Over the following decade, he re-adopted the topic several times, expanding it into a series of six works in total. Color classifies minerals according to their origin. Blue, green, and brown flows are fuel resources imported from Belgium, England, and Germany, respectively. Pink, yellow, and gray flows represent domestic coal from the Loire coal mining basin, the Valenciennes area, and some miscellaneous French mines, respectively. The first map in this series is also the first in which Minard used proportional circles. The surface area of the circles indicates the relative coal production of select French mines; the black dots show the local energy consumption in the respective departments (administrative districts). The combined use of circles and dots delivers an instant local energy summation.

In the second map, Minard employed the same scale and color scheme as the first; however, he dispensed with the proportional circles. Waterways are labeled with their names, while "C." indicates a canal and "Ch." marks short railway lines. A few roads are shown as well, and those flows are marked by dots. Comparison with the earlier map shows that the coal imports from Belgium and Germany (blue and brown) increased substantially. It is interesting to note that Minard opted for a lithographic color print in this second work (and for the first time in his oeuvre), which produced a slightly shifted and more intense color scheme. However,

Minard returned to hand-colored prints for all following updates of the series.

In the third map, Minard used the same colors and scales, except he changed the shade for "miscellaneous French mines" from gray to black. In this map, the layout of the flows is somewhat more refined than in previous ones. However, with the overall traffic volume having increased, Minard struggled to find a good arrangement for the wide flows in northeastern France, comprised of Belgian imports (in blue) and domestic coal production from the region of Valenciennes (in yellow).

This area continued to be a problem in the fourth map leading to some questionable layering and braiding solutions, like in those directly to the north of Paris. Also, some of the pink flows in the Lyon area illustrate another challenge of the flow method: short voluminous flows block a substantial portion of map space and have no precisely located beginning or ending.

The fifth and sixth map contain a data table on the lower right providing the raw figures that Minard had calculated in order to prepare the maps from the series. The tables provide the total amounts of coal transported through France in tonnes per kilometer and year, split by mode of transport.

When updating his visualizations—in this series and in others—Minard made it a priority to keep the scaling and colors of flows consistent where possible. This decision to use a set of fixed elements had consequential effects—it allowed him to create a consistent set of maps, which could be easily compared over the years.

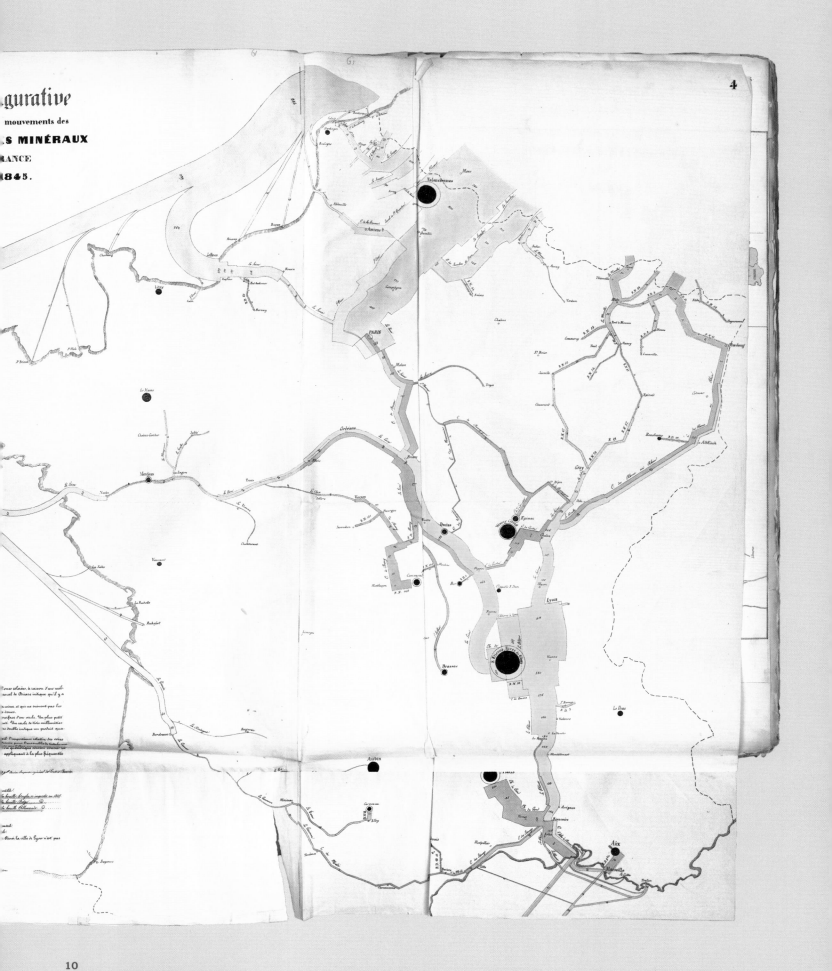

4

10

**Transport of Mineral Fuels
in France in 1845**

1 of 6

▲ "Carte figurative des principaux mouvements des
combustibles minéraux en France en 1845"
June 1851. Lithographic print, hand-colored. 91.5 × 94.3 cm.

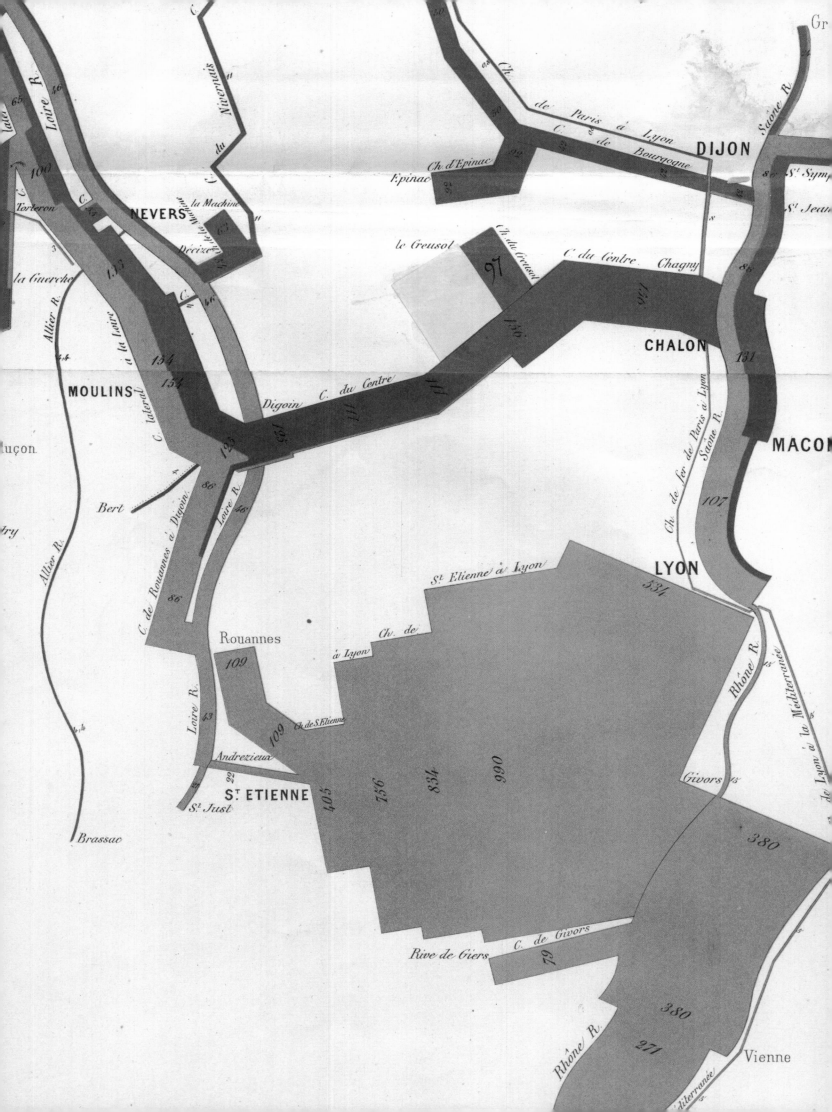

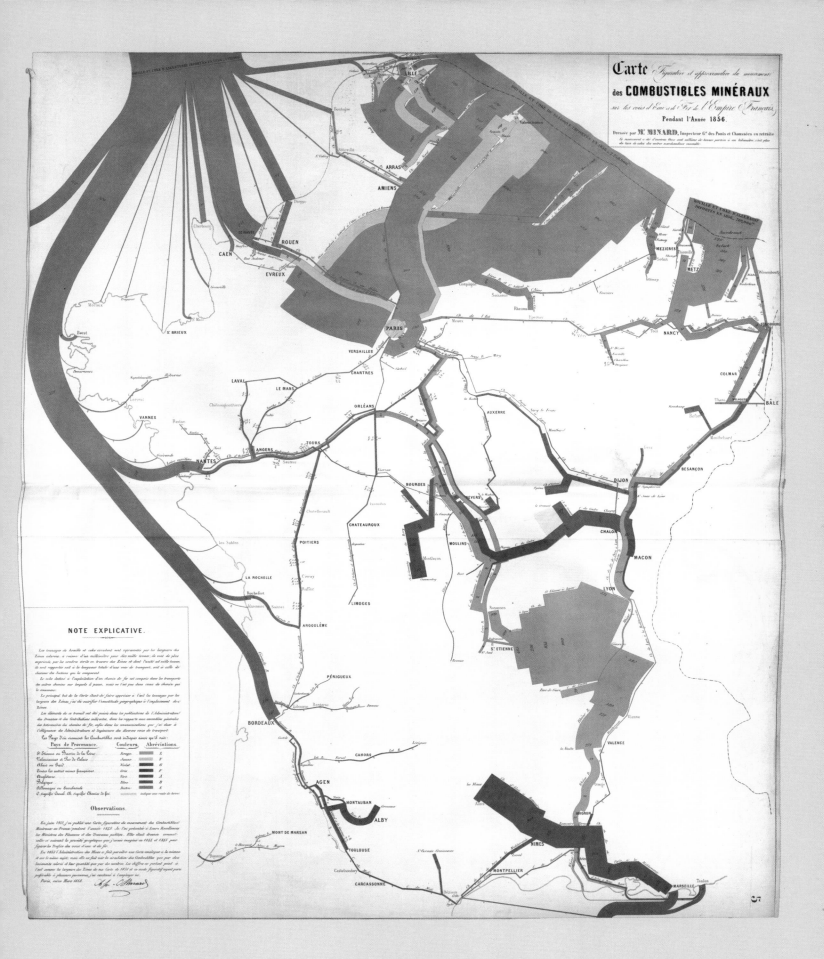

20

**Transport of Mineral Fuels
in France in 1856**

2 of 6

▲ "Carte figurative et approximative du mouvement des
combustibles minéraux sur les voies d'eau et de fer de l'Empire
français pendant l'année 1856"
March 16, 1858. Lithographic color print. 76.2 × 90.2 cm.

NOTE EXPLICATIVE.

Les tonnages de houille et coke circulant sont représentés par les largeurs des zones colorées, à raison d'un millimètre pour dix mille tonnes ; ils sont de plus exprimés par les nombres écrits en travers des zones et dont l'unité est mille tonnes, ils sont rapportés soit à la longueur totale d'une voie de transport soit à celle de chacune des sections qui la composent.

Le coke destiné à l'exploitation d'un chemin de fer est compris dans les transports des autres chemins sur lesquels il passe, mais il ne l'est pas dans ceux du chemin qui le consomme.

Le principal but de la Carte étant de faire apprécier à l'œil les tonnages par les largeurs des zones, j'ai dû sacrifier l'exactitude géographique à l'emplacement des zones.

Les éléments de ce travail ont été puisés dans les publications de l'Administration des Douanes et des Contributions indirectes, dans les rapports aux assemblées générales des Actionnaires des Chemins de fer, enfin dans les communications que j'ai dues à l'obligeance des Administrateurs et Ingénieurs des diverses voies de transport.

Les Pays d'où viennent les Combustibles sont indiqués ainsi qu'il suit :

Pays de Provenance	Couleur	Abréviations
St Étienne ou Bassin de la Loire	Rouge	L
Valenciennes et Pas-de-Calais	Jaune	V
Alais ou Gard	Violet	G
Toutes les autres mines Françaises	Noir	F
Angleterre	Vert	A
Belgique	Bleu	B
Allemagne ou Sarrebrouck	Bistre	S

C. signifie Canal, Ch. signifie Chemin de fer ~~~~~~~ indique une route de terre.

MINARD TRANSLATED

Figurative and approximative map of the movement of mineral fuels on the waterways and railroads of the French empire in 1857

The tonnage of coal and coke in circulation is represented by the width of the colored zones at a rate of one millimeter for every ten thousand tonnes. These values are also recorded, in units of a thousand tonnes, across the zones and correlate to either the total length of the transport route or of each of the sections that compose it.

Coke utilized by a railroad is included in the transport of the other railroads on which it passed, but is not included in the routes that consumed it.

As the purpose of this map is to make the relative tonnages visible to the eye by using the width of the zones, I have sacrificed geographical accuracy for the placement of the zones.

The information used to prepare this map was drawn from the Tax and Customs Administration, from the reports to the General Assembly of Railroad Shareholders, and from communications with the directors and engineers of the various transport routes, to whom I am grateful.

The countries from which the mineral fuels were sent are indicated as follows: [see chart in Note Explicative, above]

Observations:
In June 1851, I published a map of the movement of mineral fuels in France in 1845. I presented it to their Excellencies the Ministers of Finance and Public Works. Like this one here, it was created following a graphic method I devised in 1844 and 1845 to show trade on waterways and railroads.

In 1853, the Department of Mines published a map similar to mine and on the same subject, but it depicted the circulation of fuel only by colored lines, with quantities only in numbers. As the widths of zones speak more clearly to the eye than figures, and this mode having seemed preferable to many, I have continued to use it here.

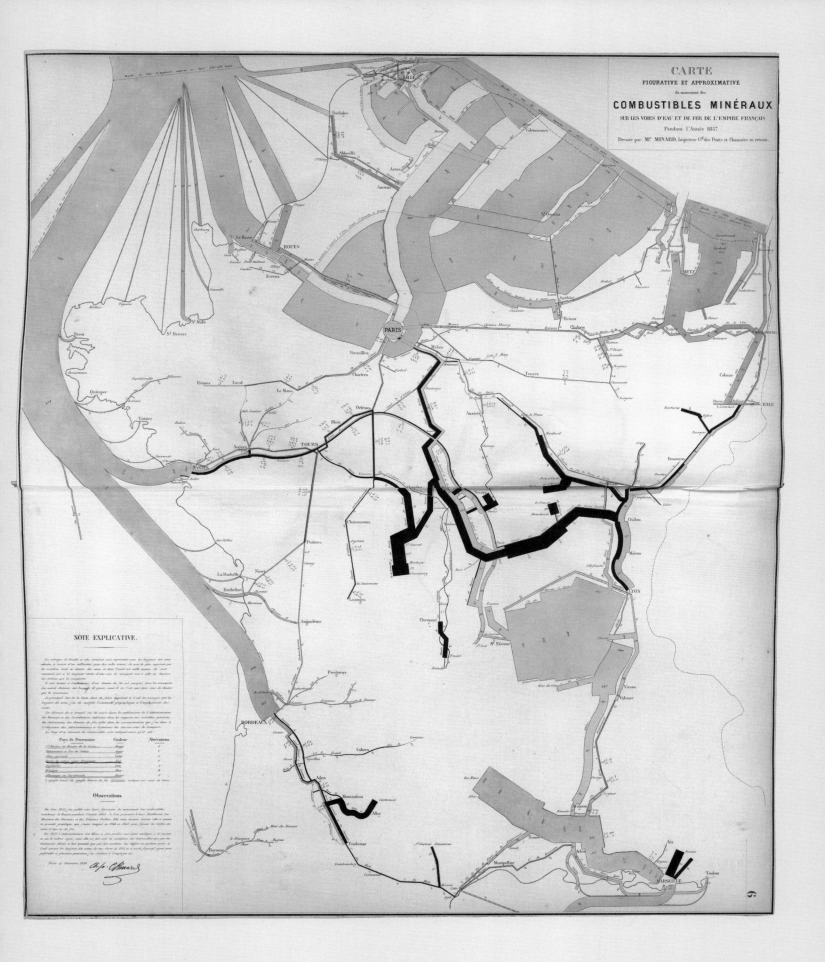

**Transport of Mineral Fuels
in France in 1857**

▲ "Carte figurative et approximative du mouvement des
combustibles minéraux sur les voies d'eau et de fer de l'Empire
français pendant l'année 1857"

December 27, 1858. Lithographic print, hand-colored. 75.3 × 89.5 cm.

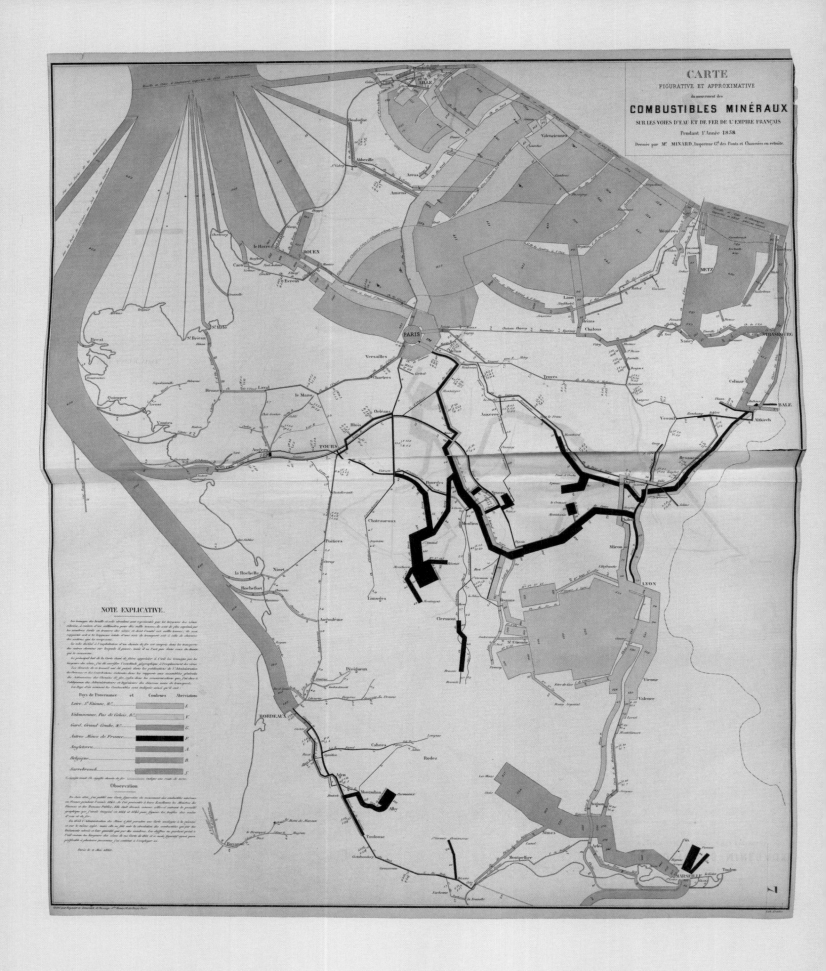

**Transport of Mineral Fuels
in France in 1858**

4 of 6

▲ "Carte figurative et approximative du mouvement des
combustibles minéraux sur les voies d'eau et de fer de l'Empire
français pendant l'année 1858"

May 2, 1860. Lithographic print, hand-colored. 77.0 × 89.2 cm.

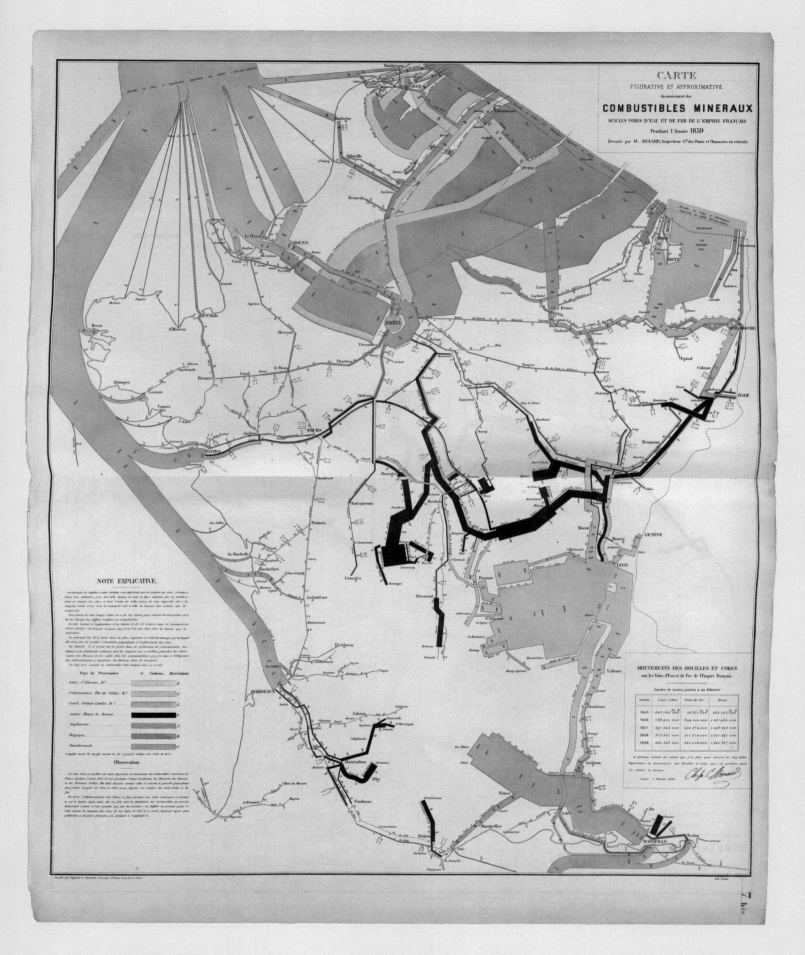

▲ "Carte figurative et approximative du mouvement des
combustibles minéraux sur les voies d'eau et de fer de l'Empire
français pendant l'année 1859"

February 3, 1861. Lithographic print, hand-colored. 76.9 × 95.2 cm.

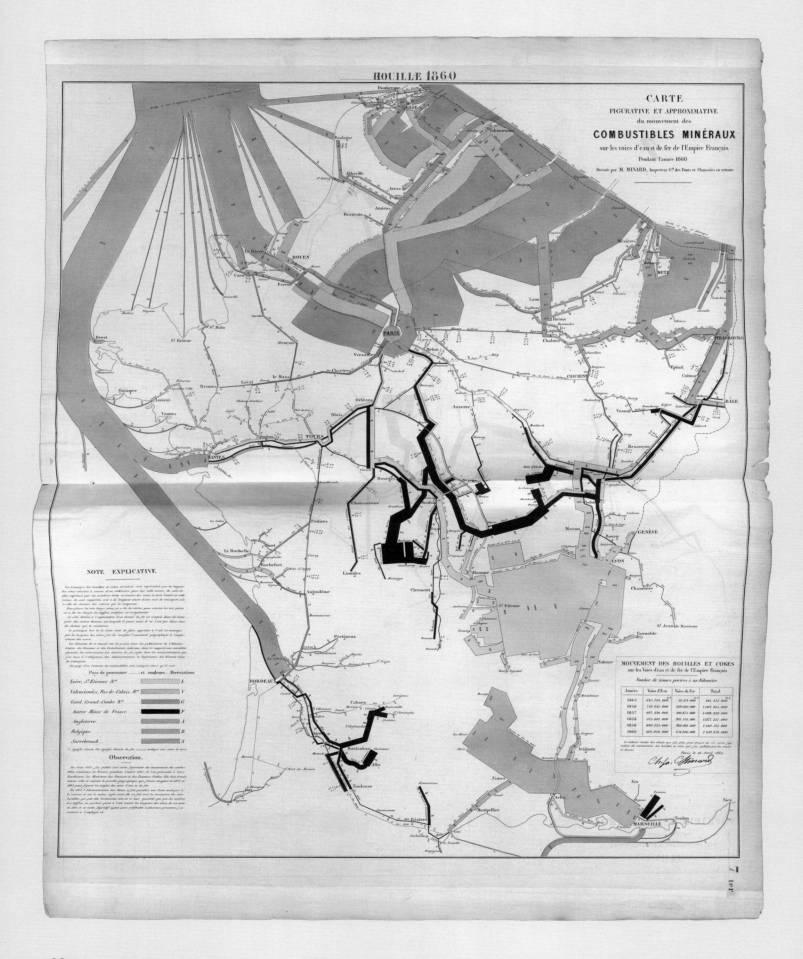

Transport of Mineral Fuels in France in 1860

▲ "Carte figurative et approximative du mouvement des combustibles minéraux sur les voies d'eau et de fer de l'Empire français pendant l'année 1860"

April 23, 1862. Lithographic print, hand-colored. 77.0 × 96.8 cm.

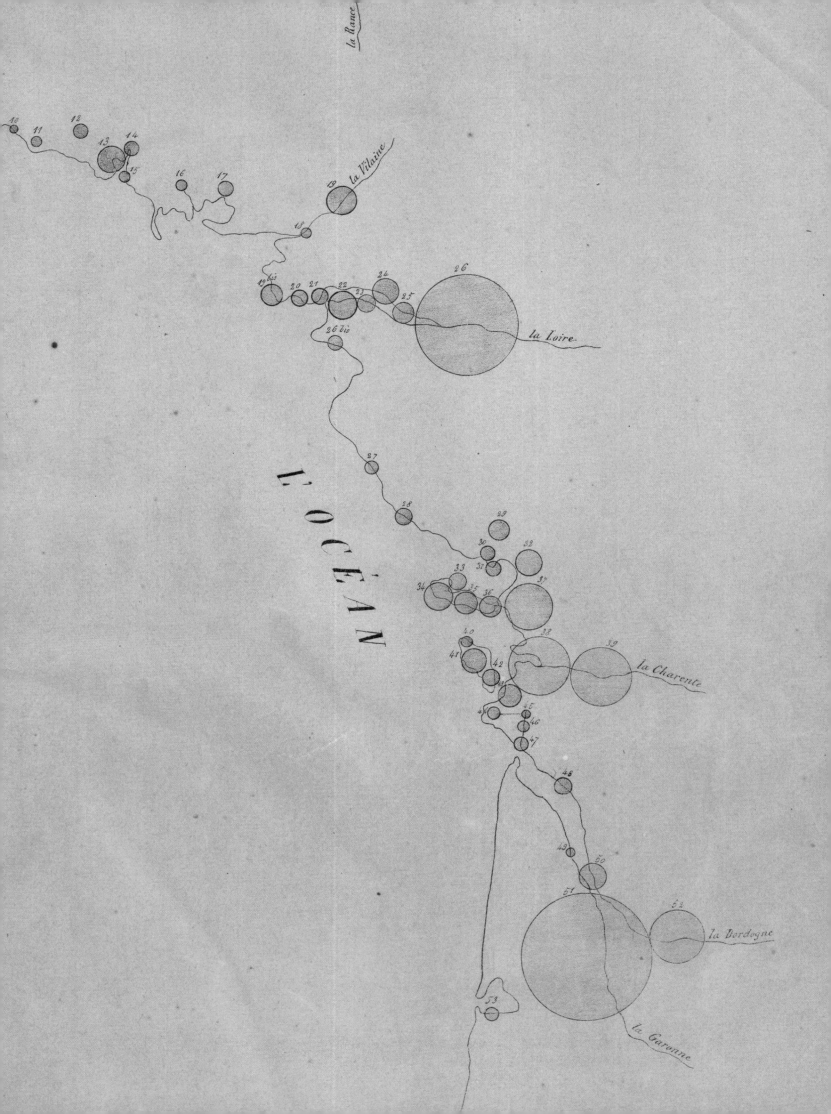

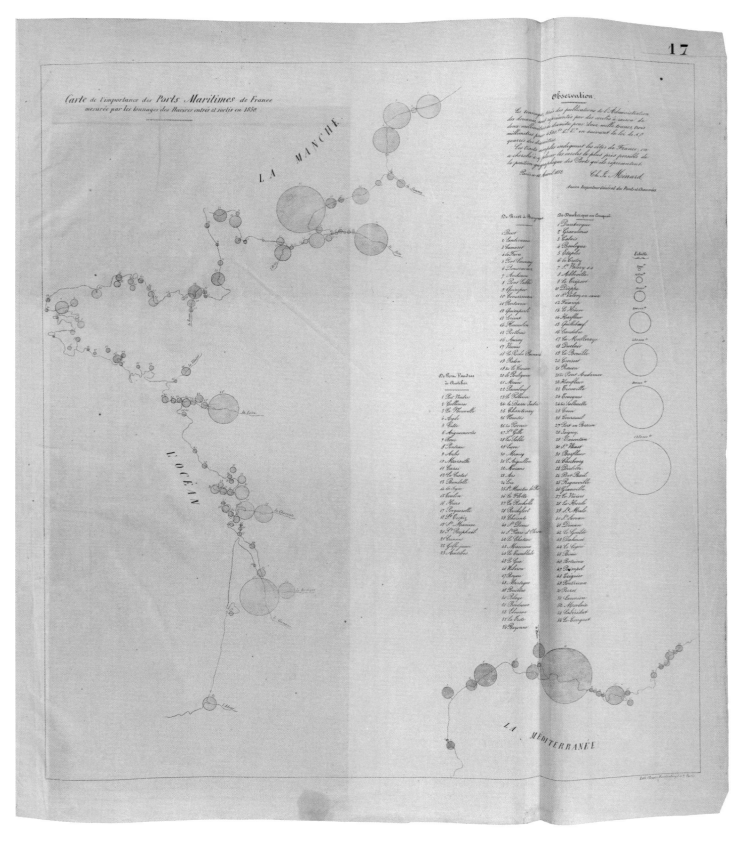

Carte de l'importance des Ports Maritimes de France mesurée par les tonnages des Navires entrés et sortis en 1850

LA MANCHE

L'OCÉAN

LA MÉDITERRANÉE

11

Maritime Ports in France in 1850

▲ "Carte de l'importance des ports maritimes de France mesurée par les tonnages des navires entrés et sortis en 1850"
April 16, 1852. Lithographic print.
63.2 × 73.0 cm.

In this seemingly unfinished work, Minard elaborates on the method of using proportional circles, first employed in [10]. The map seems to defy cartographic representation on a very basic level, as the geography of France is described only by its coastline and a few names of estuaries and seas. Minard calculated the relative importance of French harbors according to their annual turnover of cargo, and represented them by proportional circles. A scale gives an indication of the volumes represented. Minard produced an enhanced version of this map [24] in 1859, and further employed proportional circles in maps [25] and [42].

La ....e.
Saujon Saintes Montignac
Cognac La Charente Angoulème
Sireuil

La Gironde

636
Blaye
L'Isle
Bourg
622 Libourne Montpont
Eaubardemont
96
Bordeaux Branne La Dordogne Bergerac
670
Le Dronn
326 Langon La Garonne
276 Marmande
Le Lot
Le Ciron 186 Aiguillon
Villandraut 166
La Baïse Ag...
Condom

La Midouze
Tartas Mont-de-Marsan
L'Adour Dax L'Adour St Sévère
Bayonne 91
Peyrorade
Cambo

ouanes pour la

u'out bien voulu me

compagnies de

ciculation moyenne

approximativement

à d'autres

thèses (B), mais en

quelques rivières (C),

la représentation

y en a très peu en

souvent des

ser et n'y compren-

'ils indiquent

, exacts au point

port commercial;

ider ou les trains

u une cote mal

des bateaux vides,

le stère pour une

he. Chinary

ecteur général

Chaussées.

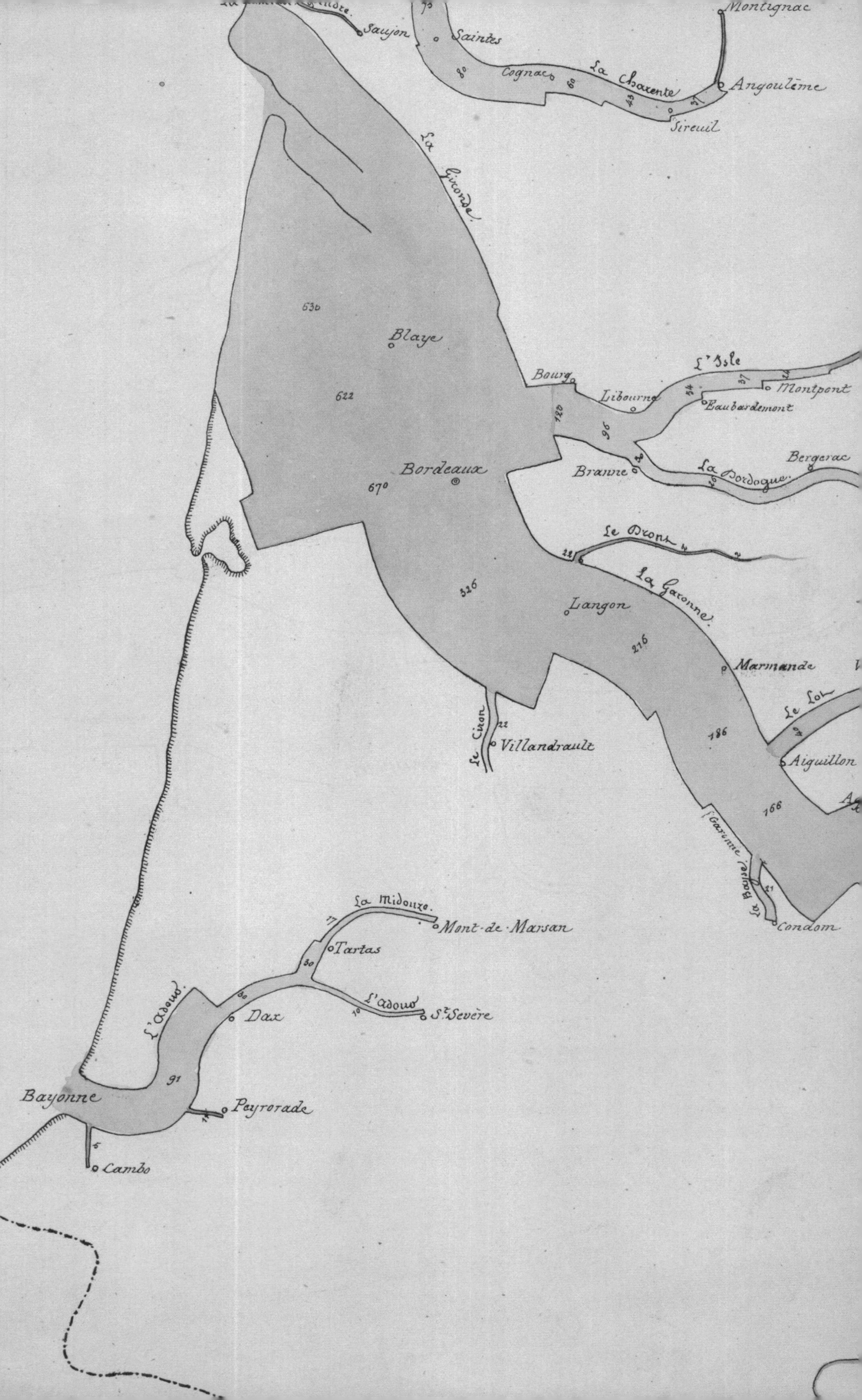

12

Circulation of Goods on French Waterways in 1850

▲ "Carte figurative et approximative
des tonnages de marchandises,
(flottage compris) qui ont circulé sur
les voies navigables de france pendant
l'année 1850"
June 20, 1852. Lithographic print, hand-colored. 84.6 × 116.2 cm.

In this second flow map of France,
Minard sought to estimate the total volume of freight traffic along French waterways in 1850. Across the flows, Minard
added detailed numbers to enable a
more precise reading. He subtly varied
the shape of flows: natural waterways
bend softly, while canals display sharp

edges. While clearly providing an overall impression of traffic volumes, this
piece also reveals the challenges of
placing proportionate flows on a map.
At times, the flows become so wide that
they take up considerable map space.
For instance, the city of Paris is "drown-
ing" in a sea of traffic along the Seine.

Circulation of Goods on French Railroads and Waterways, 1850–1862

This series of ten maps compares the fluctuating freight traffic on waterways and railroads in France from 1850 to 1862. Green flows show transportation volumes on waterways, while rose-colored flows show traffic via the railroads. The shape of the waterway indicates its type: rivers display natural curves, while canals form angled segments. For the first time here, Minard marked Paris with an enormous hatched circle, which works as an anchor in an otherwise rather bare cartographic space. In the first two maps, one millimeter of flow width on the map represents twenty thousand tonnes of goods. Comparison of the first two maps reveals that traffic on the railroad lines had, expectedly, increased substantially between 1850 and 1853. At the same time, the transportation on waterways had— less expectedly—not decreased but risen. Interestingly, the flow of traffic on the river La Marne (just east of Paris), which had wandered curiously around the railway line in the earlier map, is straightened out in the second update.

In the third map, Minard altered the scaling of the flows, with three millimeters of width now representing one hundred thousand tonnes. He explained in the side note that this adaptation was necessary in order to incorporate a significant rise in traffic around the capital, and that he regretted that the first two maps are therefore not directly comparable to later versions. Minard maintained this amended scale for the rest of the series, and with the exception of this change, he kept the layout and colors consistent. In doing so, he enabled his readers to evaluate the gradual changes in freight traffic brought about by the introduction of the railroads.

Through the full series, Minard continually provided raw numbers in the top left box. This data reveals that by 1857 the total volume of railroad freight traffic began to outweigh the freight traffic on waterways. This overall increase in traffic volume entailed challenges for Minard in visually integrating the flows, which in many instances overlap or cross each other. One feature that remains unexplained from Minard's notes is why the flows sometimes cross each other with straight lines and other times with hatched lines. The stenciled short titles at the top of these maps were added in 1870 when Minard assembled and bound his oeuvre in a large portfolio, which he gave to the École nationale des ponts et chaussées.

The regular installments of these maps, published over the course of more than a decade, give a telling picture of how the growing railroad network gradually pervaded France. While the first map displays only a few unconnected lines with just a moderate capacity for carrying freight, the final maps show a developed network that accommodated a substantial share of freight traffic. The changes are particularly evident along the Mediterranean route, from Marseille up to Lyon and Paris. While there had been significant waterway traffic in the early 1850s, by 1861—a mere ten years later—this route was dominated by the new railroad connection. As this series grew, it enabled a systematic investigation of a given dataset changing over time. With his regular updates to this map and its consistent set of elements, Minard not only allowed for a comparison of the respective traffic data but also created a significant cartographic style.

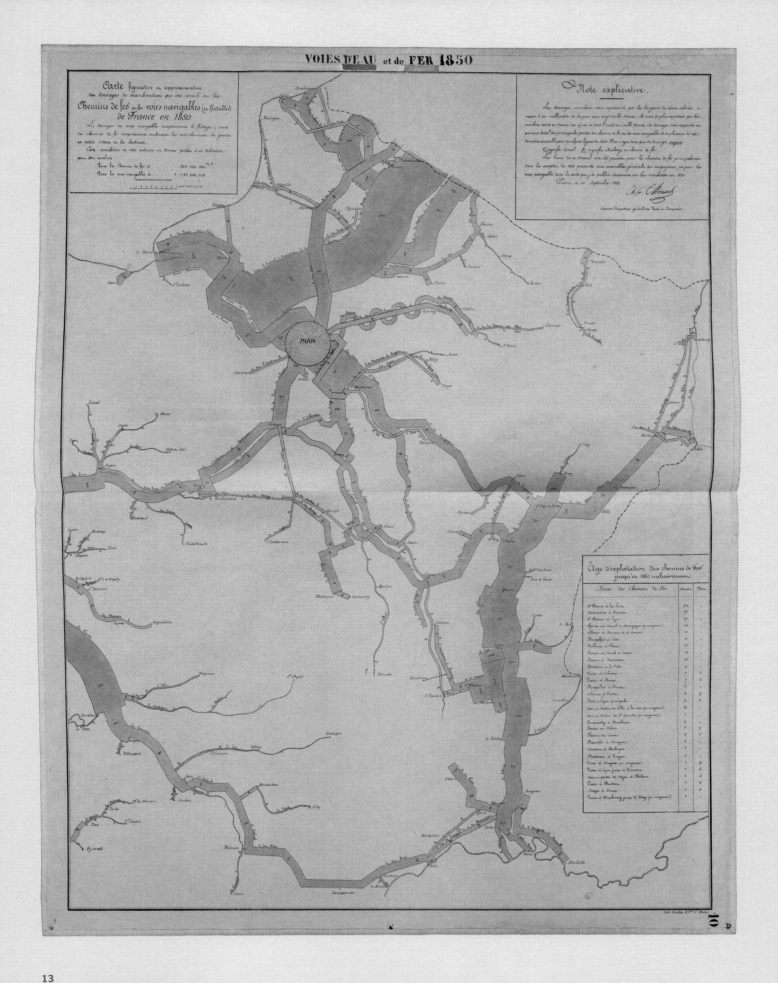

13

**Circulation of Goods
on French Railroads and
Waterways in 1850**

▲ "Carte figurative et approximative des tonnages des
marchandises qui ont circulé sur les chemins de fer et les voies
navigables (en flottables) de France en 1850"
September 20, 1852. Lithographic print, hand-colored. 68.0 × 89.8 cm.

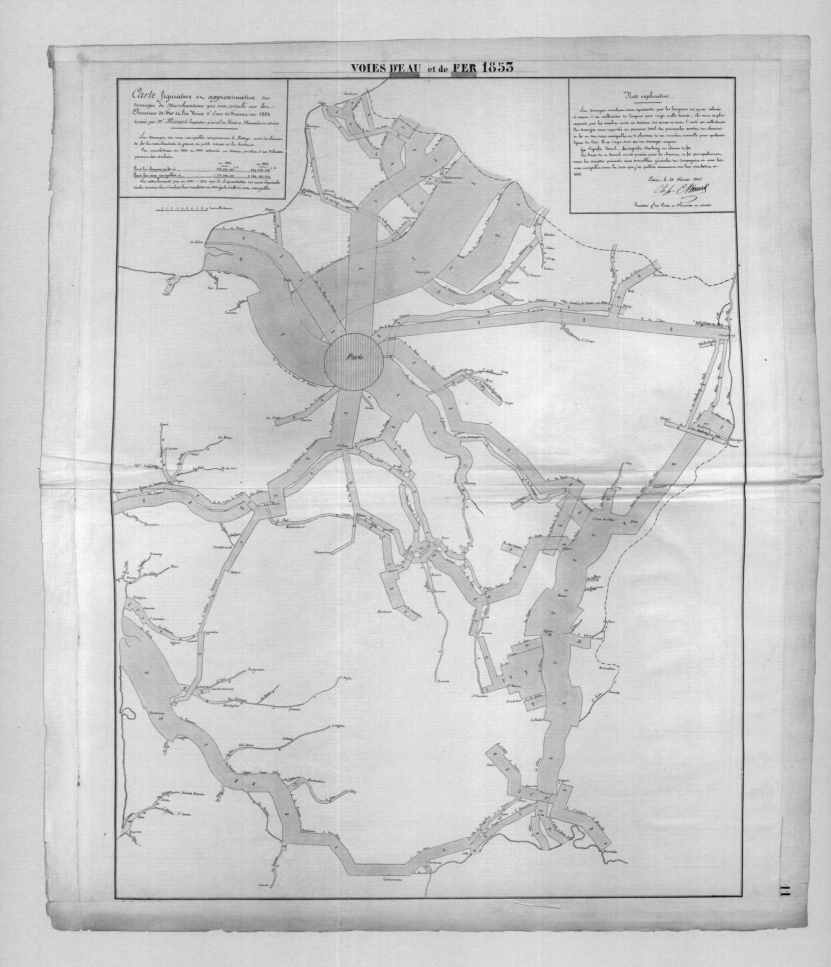

16

**Circulation of Goods
on French Railroads and
Waterways in 1853**

2 of 10

▲ "Carte figurative et approximative des tonnages des
marchandises qui ont circulé sur les chemins de fer et les voies
d'eau de France en 1853"
February 28, 1855. Lithographic print, hand-colored. 70.0 × 87.0 cm.

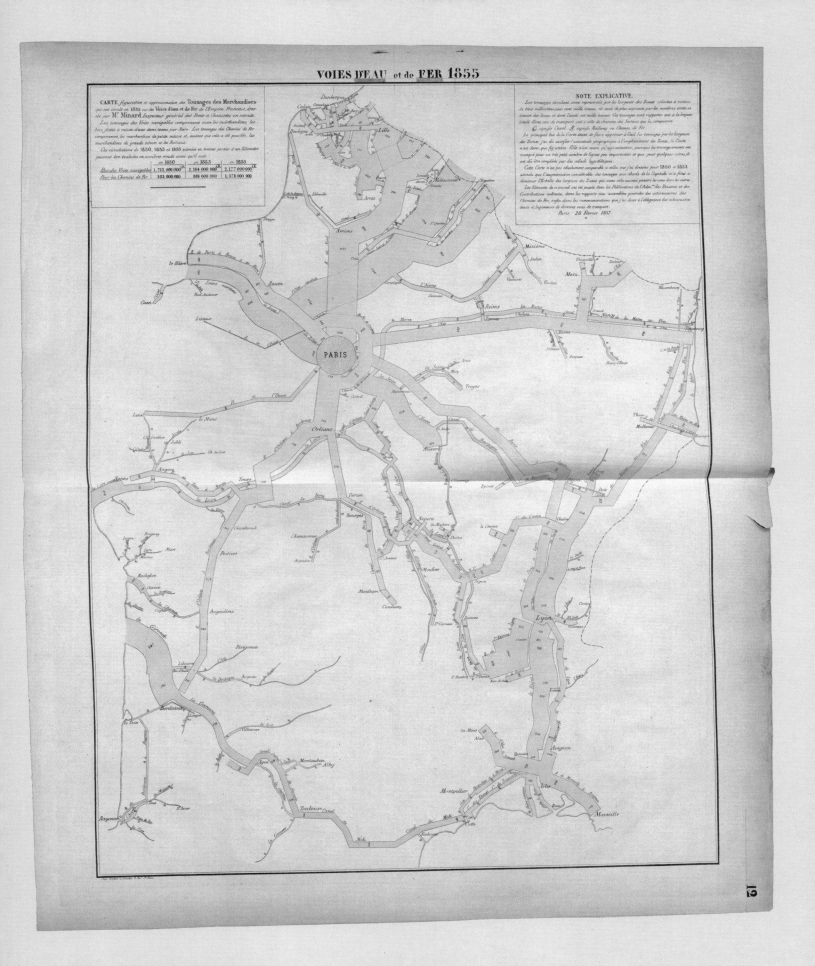

18

**Circulation of Goods
on French Railroads and
Waterways in 1855**

3 of 10

▲ "Carte figurative et approximative des tonnages des
marchandises qui ont circulé en 1855 sur les voies d'eau et
de fer de l'Empire français"
February 28, 1857. Lithographic print, hand-colored. 73.9 × 91.5 cm.

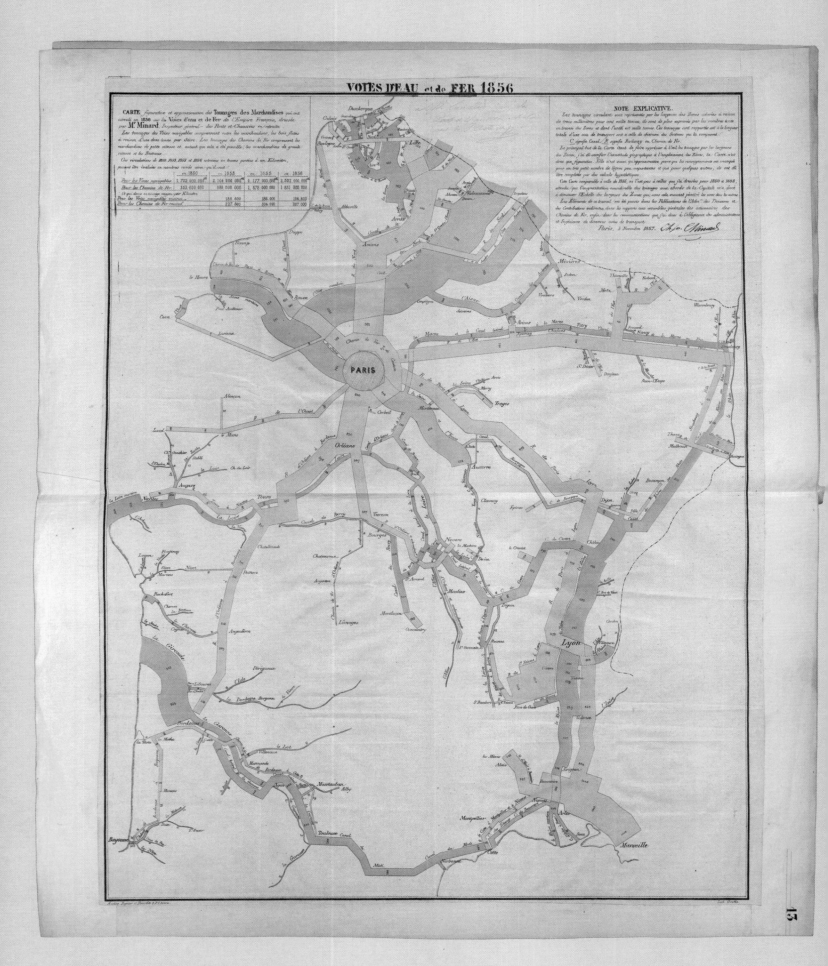

19

**Circulation of Goods
on French Railroads and
Waterways in 1856**

4 of 10

▲ "Carte figurative et approximative des tonnages des
marchandises qui ont circulé en 1856 sur les voies d'eau et
de fer de l'Empire français"
November 5, 1857. Lithographic print, hand-colored. 64.8 × 83.7 cm.

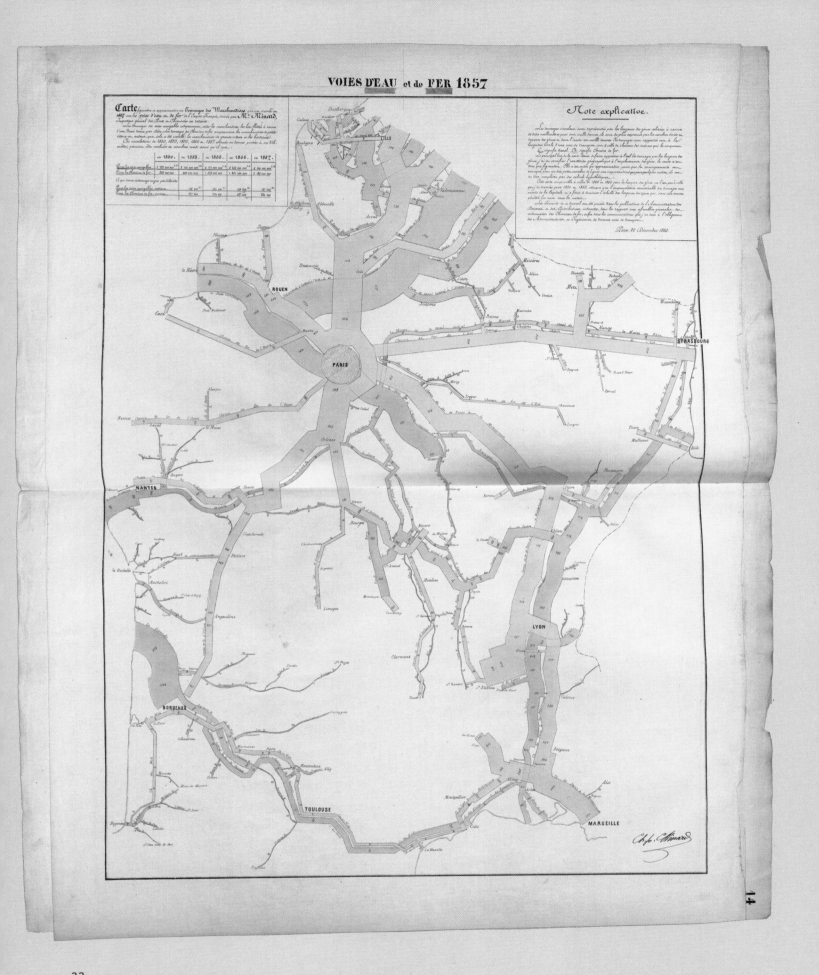

22

**Circulation of Goods
on French Railroads and
Waterways in 1857**

5 of 10

▲ "Carte figurative et approximative des tonnages des
marchandises qui ont circulé en 1857 sur les voies d'eau et
de fer de l'Empire français"
December 22, 1858. Lithographic print, hand-colored. 70.7 × 94.2 cm.

CARTE *figurative et approximative des* **Tonnages des Marchandises** *qui ont circulé en* **1858** *sur les voies d'eau et de fer de l'Empire Français, dressée par* **M. MINARD,** *Inspecteur général des Ponts et Chaussées en retraite.*

Les tonnages des voies navigables comprennent, outre les marchandises, les bois flottés à raison d'une demi-tonne par stère. Les tonnages des chemins de fer comprennent les marchandises de petite vitesse et, autant que cela a été possible, les marchandises de grande vitesse et les bestiaux.

Ces circulations de 1850, 1853, 1855, 1856, 1857, 1858 estimées en tonnes portées à un kilomètre, peuvent être évaluées en nombres ronds ainsi qu'il suit:

	en 1850.	en 1853.	en 1855.	en 1856.	en 1857.	en 1858.
Pour les voies navigables	1.722.000.000 t.k	2.164.000.000 t.k	2.177.000.000 t.k	2.302.000.000 t.k	2.166.000.000 t.k	1.788.000.000 t.k
Pour les Chemins de fer	353.000.000 "	889.000.000 "	1.518.000.000 "	1.851.000.000 "	2.189.000.000 "	2.288.000.000

Ce qui donne en tonnage moyen par kilom.

Pour les voies navigables, environ		185.600 to	186.000 to	196.000 to	187.000 to	154.000 to
Pour les Chemins de fer, environ		227.500 "	314.000 "	327.000 "	320.000 "	311.000 "

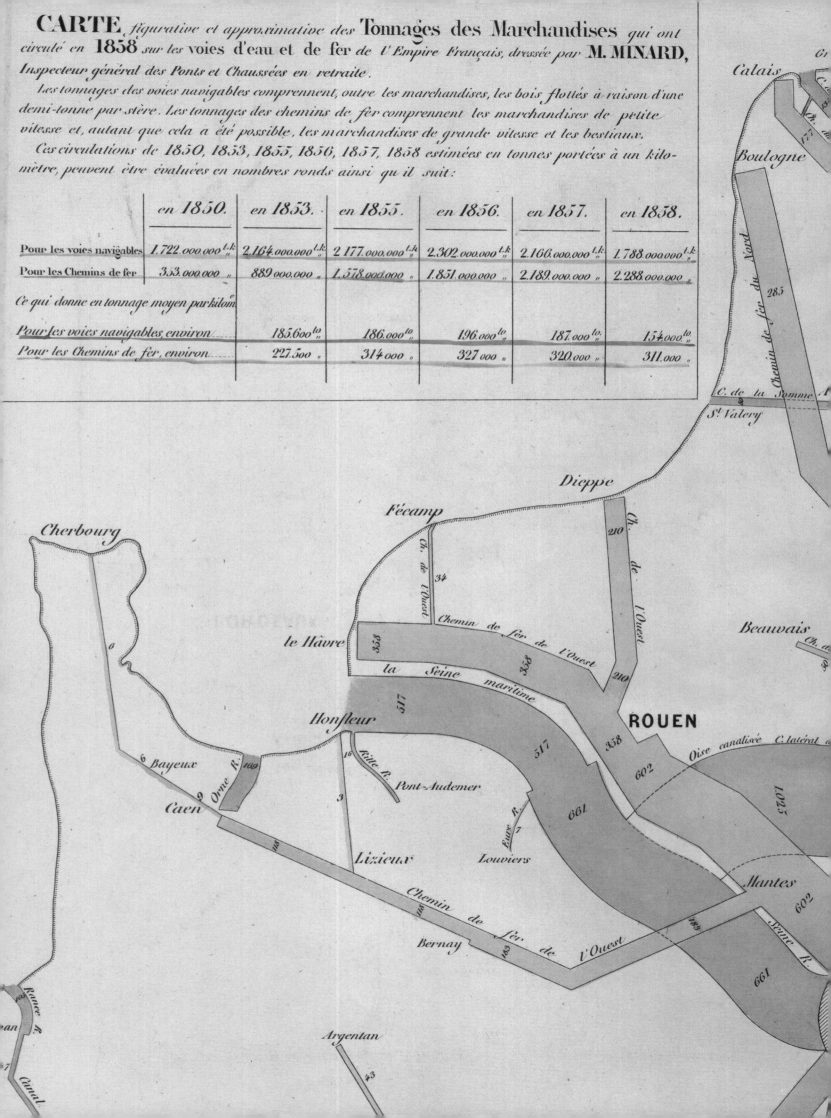

Calais

Boulogne

Chemin de fer du Nord

285

C. de la Somme

St Valery

Dieppe

Fécamp

Ch. de l'Ouest

34

210

Ch. de l'Ouest

Beauvais

le Hâvre

358

Chemin de fer de l'Ouest

358

210

la Seine maritime

Cherbourg

6

517

ROUEN

358

Oise canalisée   C. latéral

Honfleur

517

602

1025

6 Bayeux   Orne R. 169

16   Rille R.

Pont-Audemer

661

Eure R. 7

Caen

3

Louviers

Lisieux

Mantes

Bernay

Chemin   de   fer   de   l'Ouest

602

Seine R.

661

Argentan

43

Rance R.

Canal

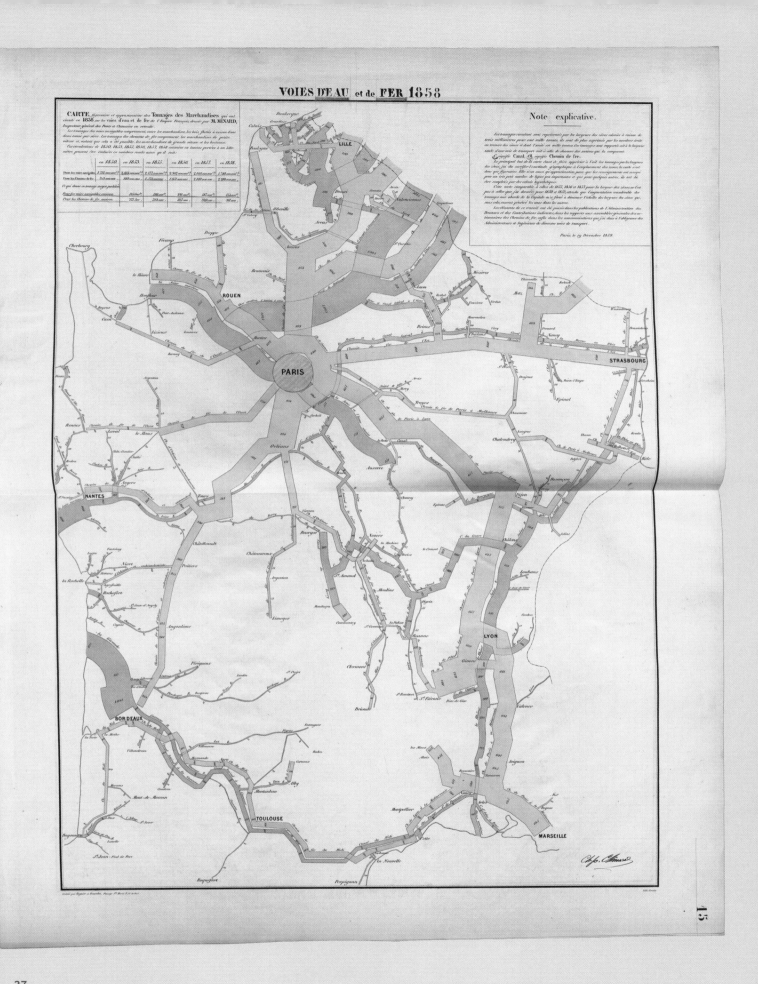

▲ "Carte figurative et approximative des tonnages des
marchandises qui ont circulé en 1858 sur les voies d'eau et
de fer de l'Empire français"
December 19, 1859. Lithographic print, hand-colored. 73.6 × 93.6 cm.

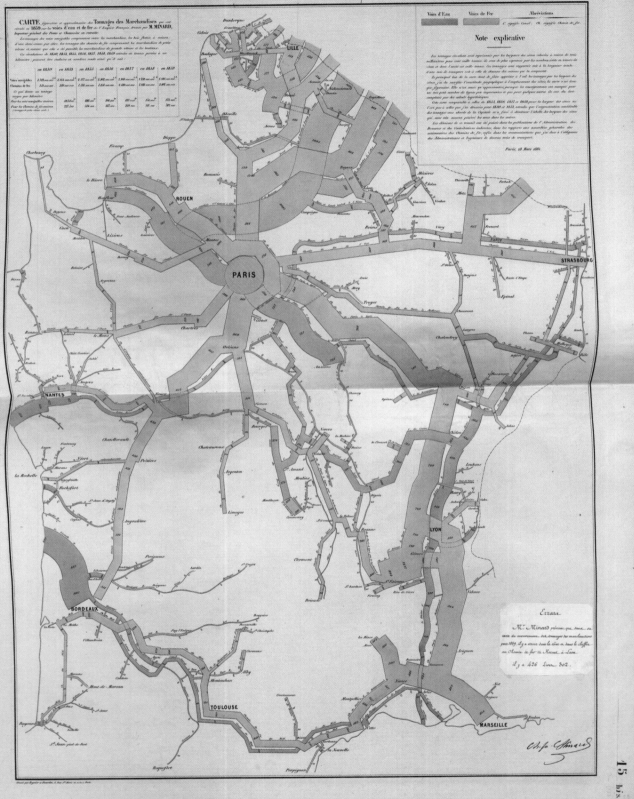

**Circulation of Goods
on French Railroads and
Waterways in 1859**

▲ "Carte figurative et approximative des tonnages des
marchandises qui ont circulé en 1859 sur les voies d'eau et
de fer de l'Empire français"
March 28, 1861. Lithographic print, hand-colored. 71.6 × 92.4 cm.

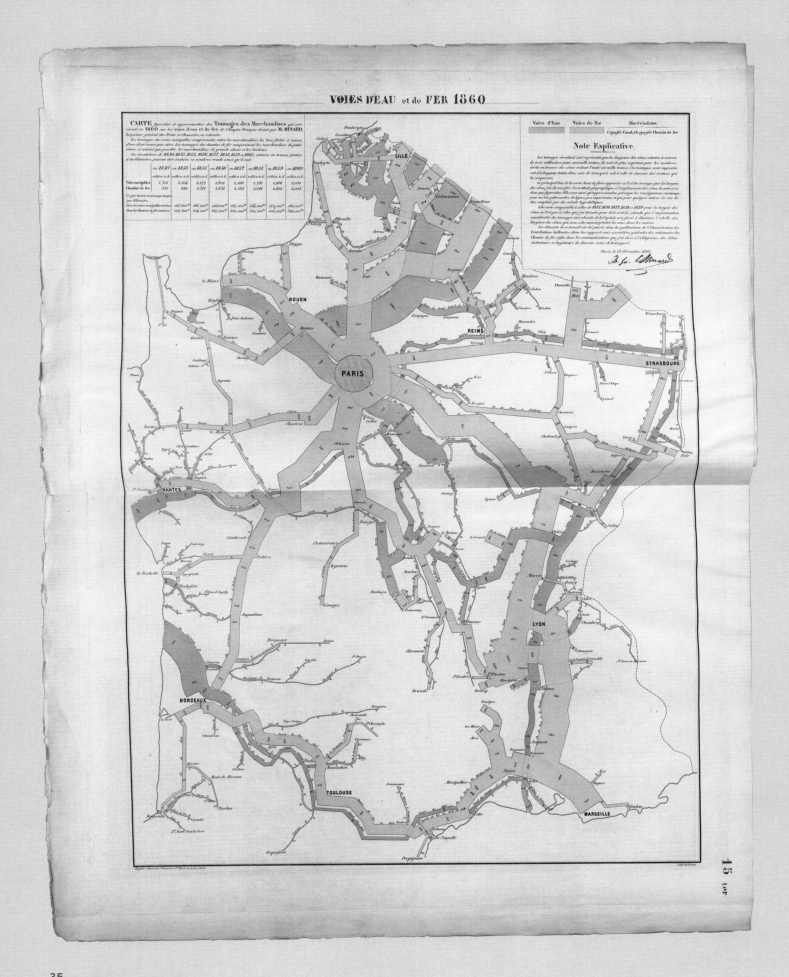

**Circulation of Goods
on French Railroads and
Waterways in 1860**

▲ "Carte figurative et approximative des tonnages des
marchandises qui ont circulé en 1860 sur les voies d'eau et
de fer de l'Empire français"
December 13, 1861. Lithographic print, hand-colored. 74.9 × 97.2 cm.

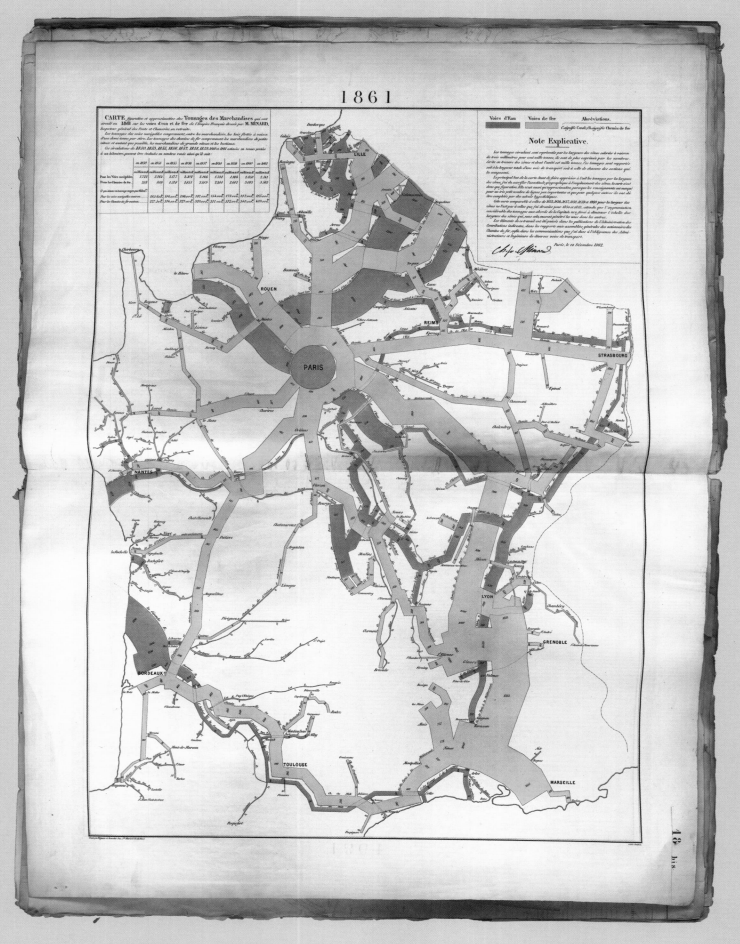

39

Circulation of Goods on French Railroads and Waterways in 1861

▲ "Carte figurative et approximative des tonnages des marchandises qui ont circulé en 1861 sur les voies d'eau et de fer de l'Empire français"
December 12, 1862. Lithographic print, hand-colored. 74.0 × 96.2 cm.

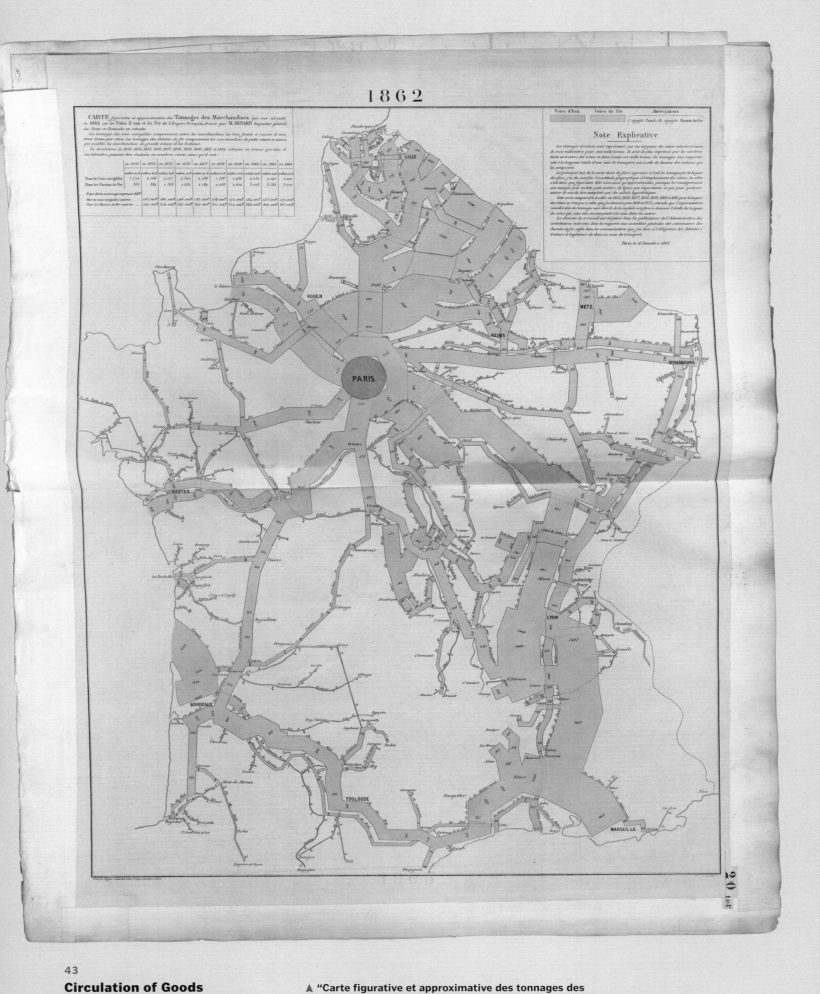

43

**Circulation of Goods
on French Railroads and
Waterways in 1862**

10 of 10

▲ "Carte figurative et approximative des tonnages des
marchandises qui ont circulé en 1862 sur les voies d'eau et
de fer de l'Empire français"
December 16, 1863. Lithographic print, hand-colored. 66.6 × 90.2 cm.

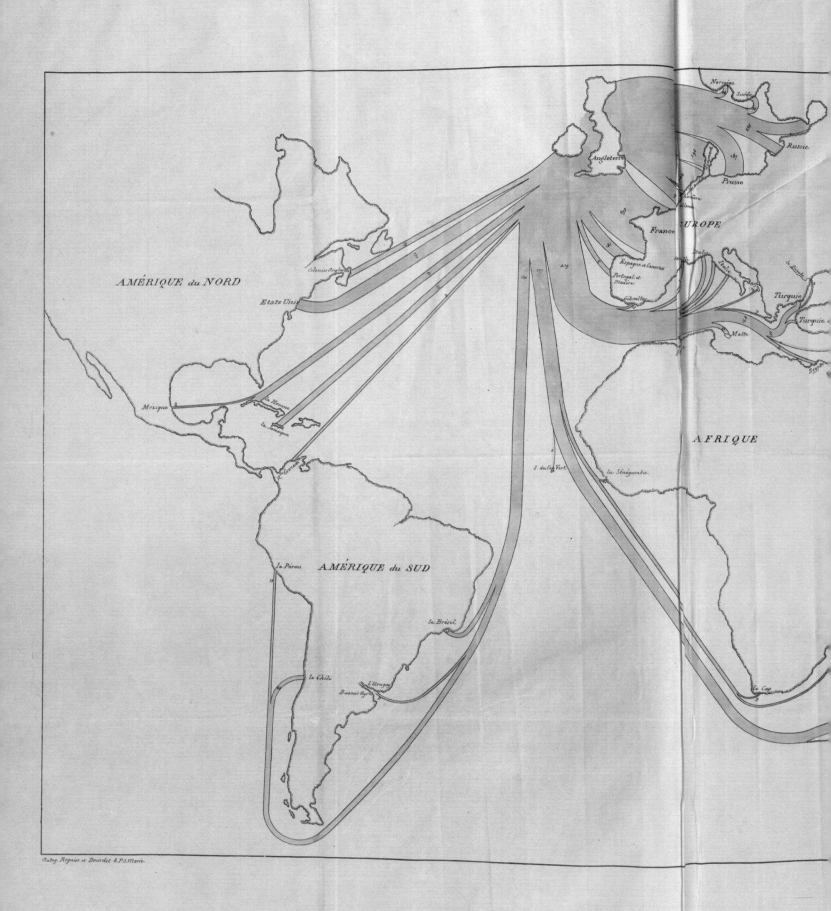

AMÉRIQUE du NORD

AMÉRIQUE du SUD

AFRIQUE

EUROPE

Norwège
Suède
Russie
Angleterre
Prusse
France
Espagne et Canaries
Portugal et Madère
Gibraltar
Turquie
Turquie
Malte

Colonies Anglaises
Etats Unis
Mexique
la Havane
la Jamaïque
N. Grenade
le Pérou
la Brésil
la Chili
l'Uruguay
Buenos Ayres

I. du Cap Vert
la Sénégambie
le Cap

Autog. Régnier et Dourdet 8. P.S. Marie.

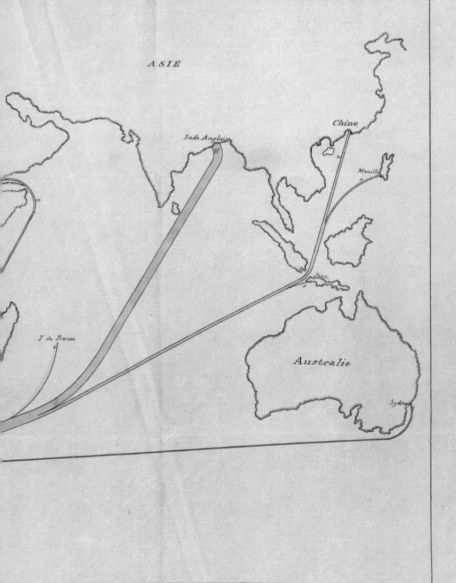

14

English Coal Exported in 1850

◄ "Carte figurative de l'exportation de
la houille anglaise en 1850"
March 1854. Lithographic print, hand-colored.
87.0 × 63.5 cm.

In this map, Minard applies the flow
method to global data for the first time.
It shows the quantities and destinations
of English coal exports. One massive
flow emerges from England and diverges
to various parts of the world, with exact
numbers added for each flow. The base
map is extremely generalized. The continents display crude silhouettes, land-
masses and oceans are not distinguished
visually, and some major islands are
omitted altogether. Instead of delivering a
descriptive world map, Minard created
an impression of the relative importance
of English coal exports. The topic is
later amplified in maps [41] and [53].

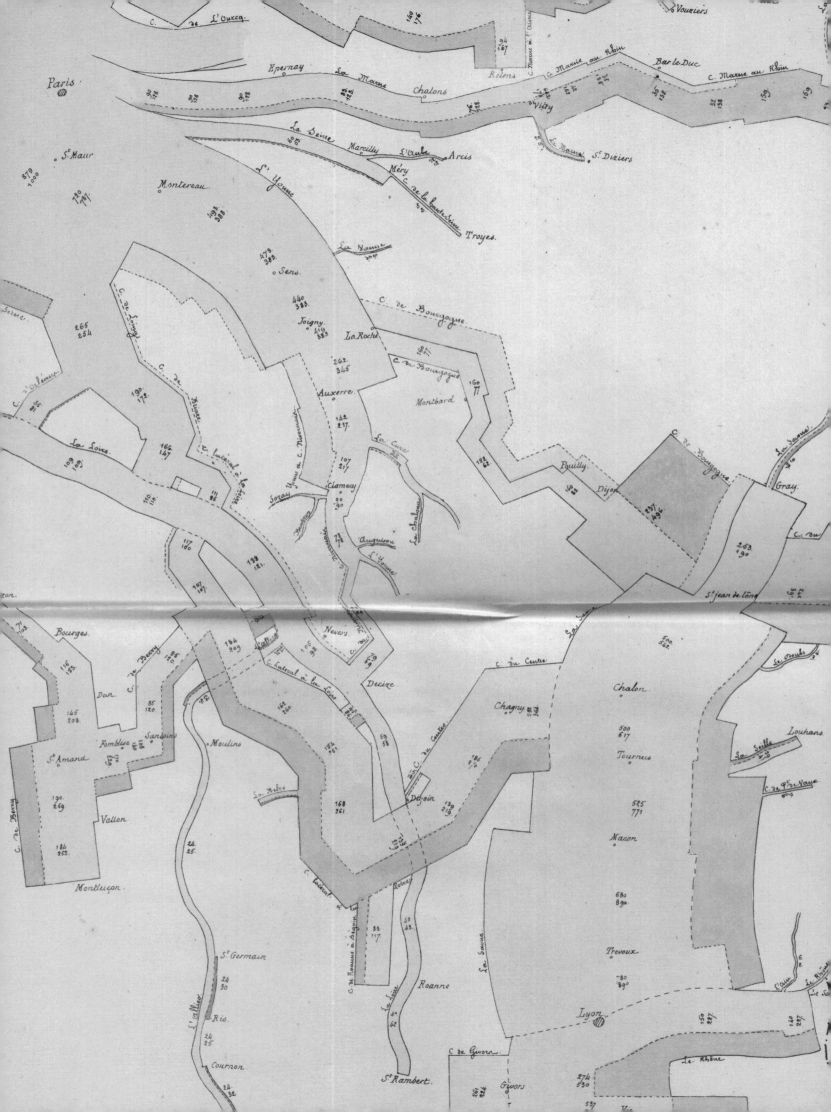

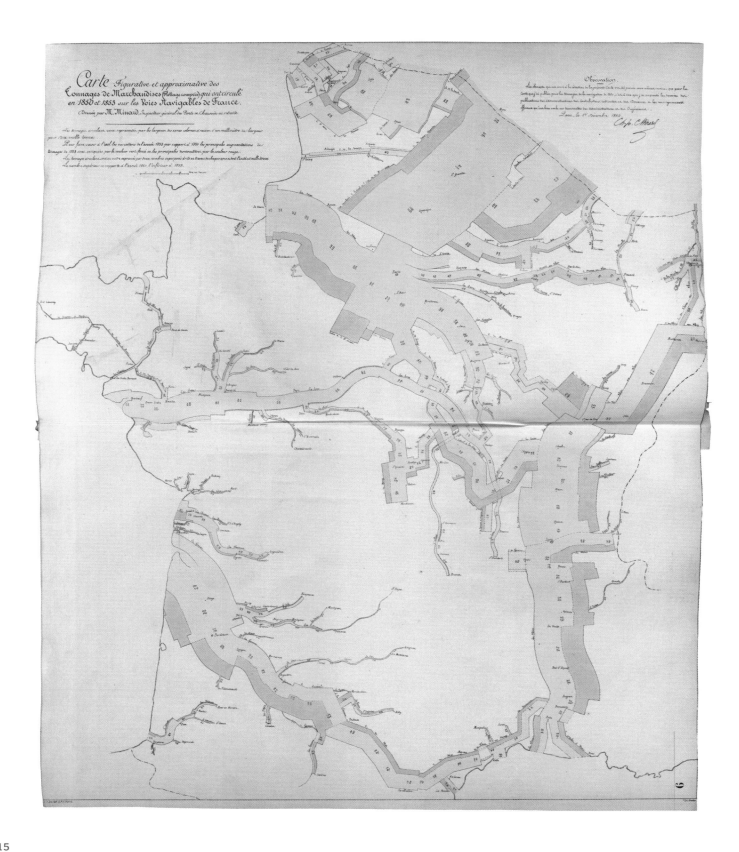

15

Circulation of Goods
on French Waterways
in 1850 and 1853

▲ **"Carte figurative et approximative
des tonnages de marchandises (flottage
compris) qui ont circulé en 1850 et 1853
sur les voies navigables de France"**
December 1, 1854. Lithographic print, hand-
colored. 75.5 × 90.7 cm.

In this map, Minard compared data from
two years through differentiated flows
(a method first employed in [9]). It shows
freight traffic volumes along French
waterways for 1850 and 1853, respectively. Light green designates the constant
volume of traffic for both years. It is
accompanied by either a dark green flow
(where traffic had increased) or a rose

flow (where traffic had decreased in
1853). In some regions, such as in the
northeast, heavy transportation produced
wide flows that were difficult to integrate.
At times, Minard had to sort, bend,
and "braid" the flows to make them all
fit, a challenge he would continue to
contend with in later flow maps.

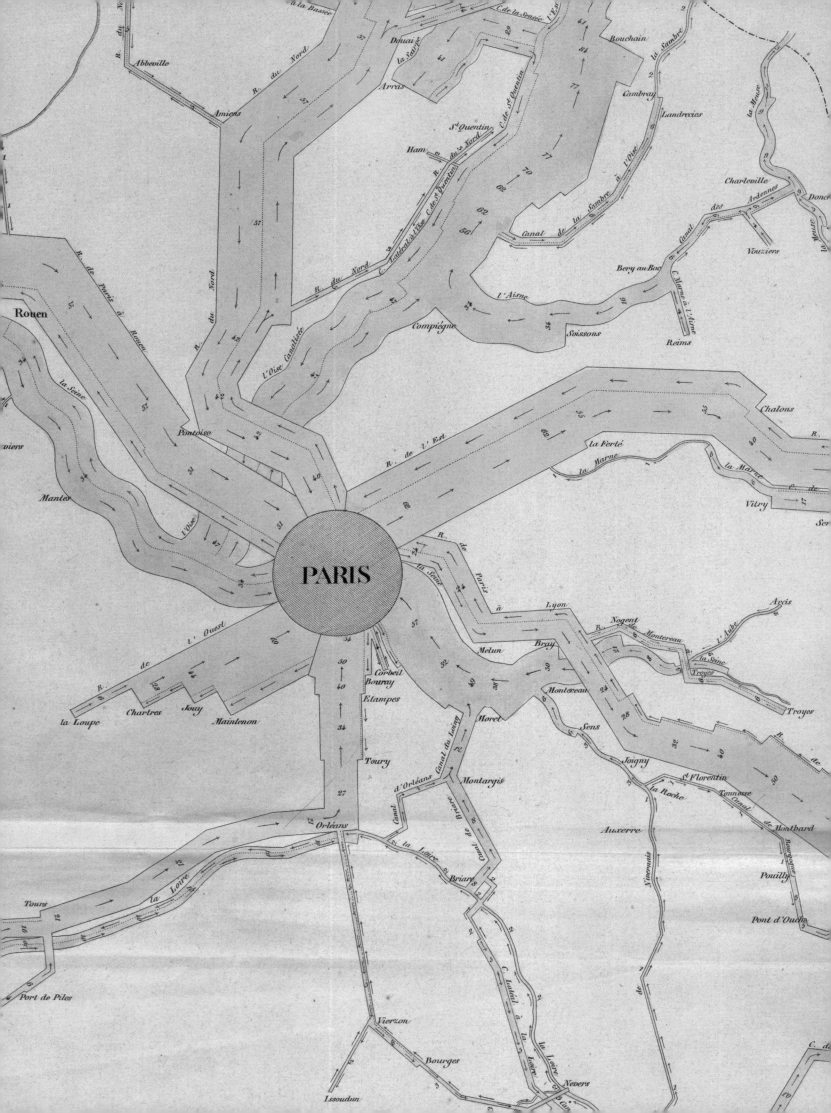

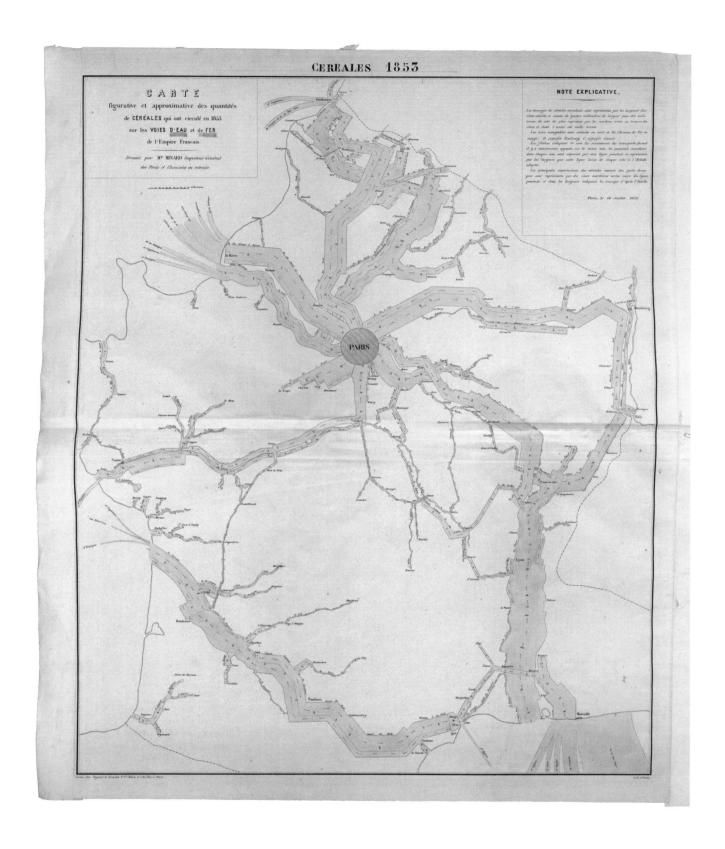

CARTE

figurative et approximative des quantités

de CÉRÉALES qui ont circulé en 1853

sur les VOIES D'EAU et de FER

de l'Empire Français.

Dressée par Mr MINARD Inspecteur Général
des Ponts et Chaussées en retraite.

NOTE EXPLICATIVE.

PARIS

17

Circulation of Cereals on French Waterways and Railroads in 1853

▲ **"Carte figurative et approximative des quantités de céréales qui ont circulé en 1853 sur les voies d'eau et de fer de l'Empire français"**
July 14, 1855. Lithographic print, hand-colored. 68.0 × 83.2 cm.

This map is a variation on two earlier works about freight traffic, [13] and [16], this time focusing on the transport of grain alone. Minard followed the same general layout and color scheme, but included directions for specific shares of traffic. Larger flows are divided longitudinally, and arrows denote the direction of movement. Four millimeters of width represent ten thousand tonnes of grain. Apparently, the volume of traffic was distributed fairly evenly across France. This enabled Minard to calculate wide flows, which he was able to divide and place without much difficulty. However skillful this solution may seem, Minard returned only once to the method of dividing flows for indicating directions [28].

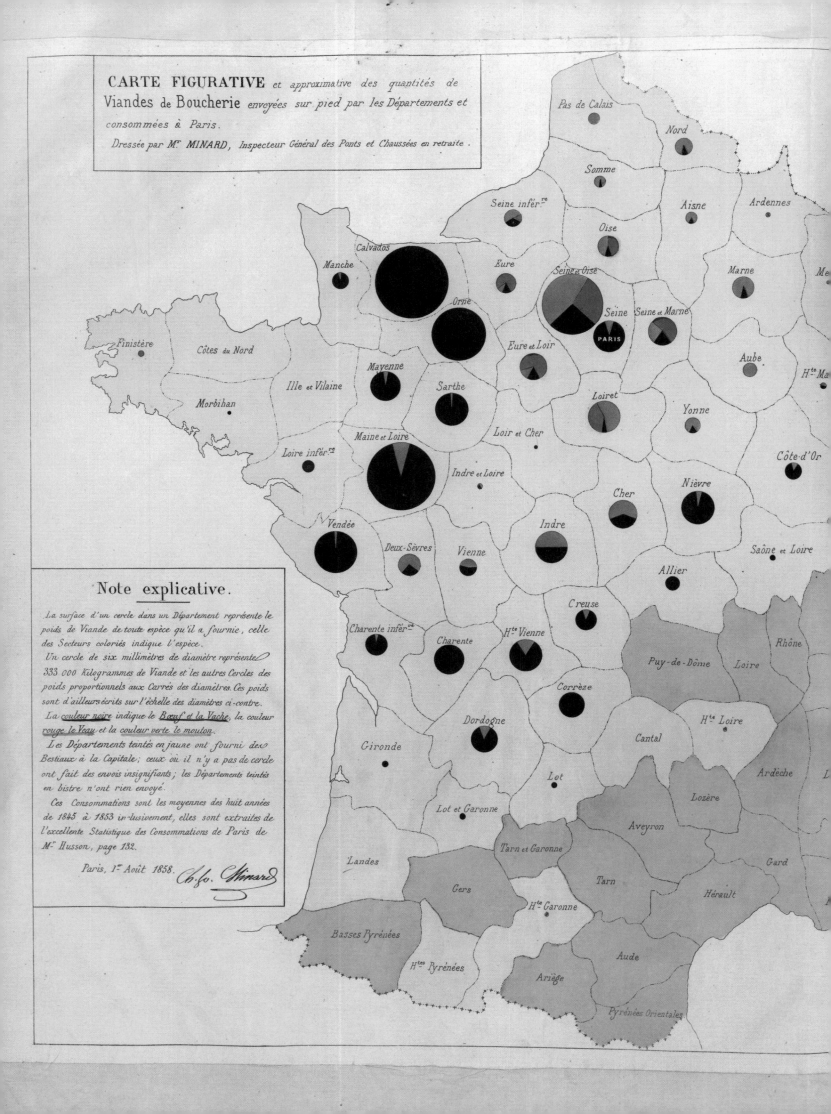

CARTE FIGURATIVE et approximative des quantités de
Viandes de Boucherie envoyées sur pied par les Départements et
consommées à Paris.

Dressée par Mr. MINARD, Inspecteur Général des Ponts et Chaussées en retraite.

Note explicative.

La surface d'un cercle dans un Département représente le poids de Viande de toute espèce qu'il a fournie, celle des Secteurs coloriés indique l'espèce.

Un cercle de six millimètres de diamètre représente 333 000 Kilogrammes de Viande et les autres Cercles des poids proportionnels aux Carrés des diamètres. Ces poids sont d'ailleurs écrits sur l'échelle des diamètres ci-contre. La couleur noire indique le Bœuf et la Vache, la couleur rouge le Veau et la couleur verte le mouton.

Les Départements teintés en jaune ont fourni des Bestiaux à la Capitale; ceux où il n'y a pas de cercle ont fait des envois insignifiants; les Départements teintés en bistre n'ont rien envoyé.

Ces Consommations sont les moyennes des huit années de 1845 à 1853 in-lusivement, elles sont extraites de l'excellente Statistique des Consommations de Paris de Mr. Husson, page 132.

Paris, 1er Août 1858.

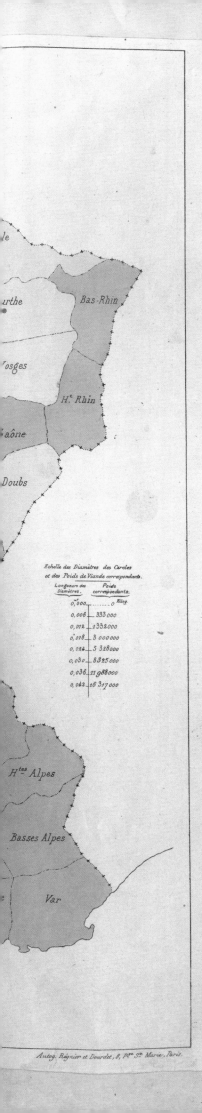

Echelle des Diamètres des Cercles
et des Poids de Viande correspondants.

Longueur des Diamètres.	Poids correspondants.
0,°000	.... 0 Kilog.
0,006	333 000
0,012	1 332 000
0,°018	3 000 000
0,024	5 328 000
0,030	8 325 000
0,036	11 988 000
0,042	16 317 000

Autog. Régnier et Dourdet, 8, Pl.ce S.te Marie, Paris.

21

Quantities of Meat Sent to Paris

◄ "Carte figurative et approximative des quantités de
viandes de boucherie envoyées sur pied par les départements
et consommées à Paris"
August 1, 1858. Lithographic print, hand-colored. 64.9 × 53.6 cm.

This work further elaborated on the use of proportional circles (as begun in [10] and [11]) and introduced sectioned circles as a novelty in Minard's work. The map covers domestic trade in meat by department. For the first time, Minard opted for shading the base map: the departments of France are classified according to whether they had imported meat to the capital or not. Except for a few minor suppliers, proportional circles are included for each supplying department to indicate the relative amount of meat it provided to the capital, with a scale on the right hand side explaining the calcuation. The circle sections distinguish between the different kinds of meat. While Minard does not comment here on his use of proportional circles, he does so explicitly in [24].

MINARD TRANSLATED

Figurative and approximate map of the quantities of red meat sent by the departments and consumed in Paris

Explanatory note: The area of a circle represents the total weight of meat (all species included) supplied by that department; the area of the colored sections indicates the variety.

A circle of six millimeters in diameter represents 333,000 kilograms of meat and the other circles the weight of meat proportional to the diameter squared. These weights are also recorded on the scale opposite.

Areas in black represent beef, red indicates veal, and green is lamb.

The departments colored yellow provided cattle to the capital; those with no circles sent insignificant amounts; tan-colored departments did not supply any meat.

Consumption represented here is the average over the eight years from 1845 to 1853, inclusively. It was drawn from the excellent statistic of consumption in Paris by Mr. Husson, page 132.

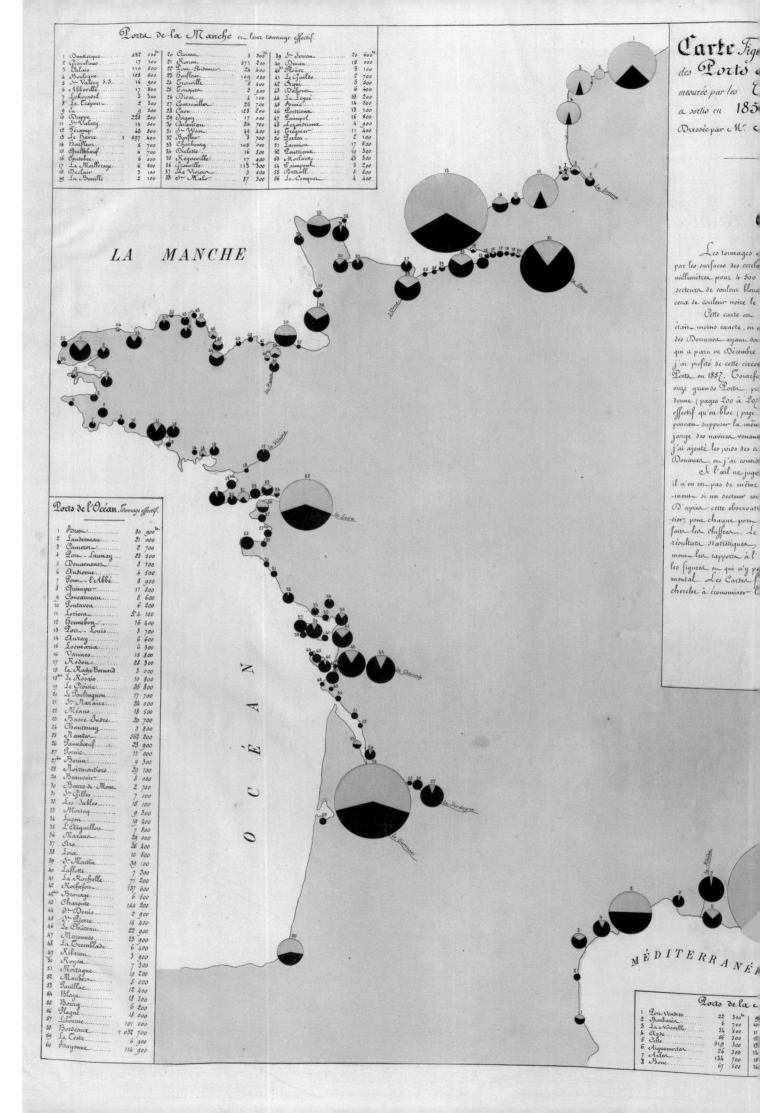

Ports de la Manche en leur tonnage effectif.

1 Dunkerque	552 000	
2 Gravelines	17 100	
3 Calais	110 500	
4 Boulogne	108 500	
5 St Valery S.S.	14 900	
6 Abbeville	17 500	
7 Lehoustel	5 500	
8 Le Crayon	2 500	
9 Eu	9 500	
10 Dieppe	228 200	
11 St Valery	14 500	
12 Fécamp	43 500	
13 Le Havre	1 297 400	
14 Harfleur	5 700	
15 Quillebœuf	4 700	
16 Caudebec	6 000	
17 La Meilleraye	6 500	
18 Duclair	3 100	
19 La Bouille	2 100	
20 Croisset	3 500	
21 Rouen	571 200	
22 Pont-Audemer	24 400	
23 Honfleur	109 000	
24 Trouville	5 400	
25 Touques	2 900	
26 Dives	4 100	
27 Courseulles	25 700	
28 Caen	123 200	
29 Isigny	17 400	
30 Carantan	84 700	
31 St Wast	49 400	
32 Barfleur	3 700	
33 Cherbourg	105 000	
34 Dielette	16 800	
35 Regneville	17 400	
36 Granville	113 300	
37 Le Vivier	3 500	
38 St Malo	87 300	
39 St Servan	20 600	
40 Dinan	15 000	
41 Le Guildo	2 700	
42 Erqui	8 500	
43 Dahouet	6 400	
44 Le Legué	38 200	
45 Binic	14 800	
46 Portrieux	13 100	
47 Paimpol	16 800	
48 Lezardrieux	4 900	
49 Treguier	11 400	
50 Perox	2 100	
51 Lannion	17 500	
52 Pontrieux	10 300	
53 Morlaix	45 300	
54 L'aimpoul	5 200	
55 Portrall	8 800	
56 Le Conquet	4 400	

LA MANCHE

OCÉAN

Ports de l'Océan. Tonnage effectif.

1 Brest	80 900
2 Landerneau	21 000
3 Camaret	2 700
4 Pont-Launay	23 500
5 Douarnenez	8 100
6 Audierne	4 500
7 Pont-l'Abbé	8 900
8 Quimper	11 800
9 Concarneau	8 600
10 Pontaven	6 200
11 Lorient	54 100
12 Hennebon	16 400
13 Port-Louis	3 700
14 Auray	6 600
15 Locmaria	6 300
16 Vannes	15 800
17 Redon	28 300
18 la Roche Bernard	3 000
18bis Le Rossio	10 800
19 Le Croisic	35 800
20 Le Poulinguen	17 700
21 St Nazaire	24 000
22 Méans	18 500
23 Basse Indre	20 700
24 Chantenay	3 800
25 Nantes	582 200
26 Paimbœuf	23 900
27 Pornic	11 000
27bis Bonin	9 300
28 Noirmoutiers	29 100
29 Beauvoir	3 000
30 Barre-de-Mont	2 700
31 St Gilles	7 500
32 Les Sables	18 100
33 Morica	9 300
34 Luçon	19 400
35 L'Eguillon	7 800
36 Marans	29 000
37 Ars	26 400
38 Loix	10 500
39 St Martin	39 100
40 Laflotte	7 300
41 La Rochelle	71 200
42 Rochefort	137 600
42bis Brouage	6 500
43 Charente	144 200
44 St Denis	2 900
45 St Pierre	14 400
46 Le Château	22 900
47 Marennes	23 900
48 La Tremblade	6 400
49 Riberou	3 900
50 Royan	7 300
51 Mortagne	10 200
52 Maubert	5 000
53 Pauillac	12 400
54 Blaye	18 300
55 Bourg	6 200
56 Plagne	18 000
57 Libourne	101 000
58 Bordeaux	1 032 700
59 La Teste	6 900
60 Bayonne	114 900

MÉDITERRANÉE

Ports de la (Méditerranée)

1 Port-Vendres	22 300
2 Barbaira	6 700
3 La Nouvelle	54 500
4 Agde	86 500
5 Cette	319 300
6 Aiguesmortes	26 500
7 Arles	134 700
8 Bouc	67 500

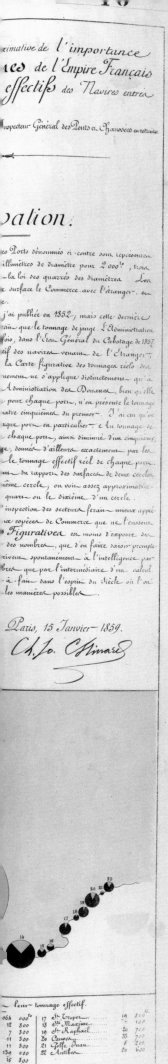

24

Maritime Ports in France in 1857

◄ "Carte figurative et approximative de l'importance des ports maritimes de l'Empire français mesurée par les tonnages effectifs des navires entrés et sortis en 1857"
January 15, 1859. Lithographic print, hand-colored. 59.6 × 74.1 cm.

Continuing Minard's exploration of proportional circles begun in the preliminary map [11], this work examines the relative importance of French sea ports according to the total cargo handled. Again, the ports are numbered and listed in side boxes. The description mentions that the French customs administration—from whom Minard had drawn the data—had recently begun to distinguish between foreign and domestic traffic for each port. Minard visualized these shares by using the circles as pie charts—a method he had first employed some five months earlier in [21]. Blue sections represent international traffic, while black sections refer to domestic shipping. He elaborated on the method in the side note, claiming it was sufficiently easy to judge relative quantities from a sectioned circle.

MINARD TRANSLATED

Figurative and approximate map of the importance of maritime ports of the French Empire measured by the actual tonnage of vessels entering and exiting in 1857

Observation: The actual tonnages written next to the ports referred to here are represented by the area of the circles at a rate of two millimeters diameter per 2,000 tonnes, three millimeters for 4,500 tonnes, etc, etc, following the law of the squared diameters.[3] The blue sections represent foreign trade; black sections, coastal trade.

This map is similar to one I published in 1852 [11], but the previous one was less accurate in that it represented only the tonnage. The Customs Administration having provided, for the first time, in *The State of Cabotage in 1857*, the actual tonnage of vessels coming from abroad, I profited from this circumstance by drawing this map. However, this new information applied only to eleven major ports; for the others, the Customs Administration, although it gives the tonnage for each port, presents the actual tonnage in one block, and finds it four-fifths of the former. I surmised we could assume the same proportion for each port. Thus I added the weight of cargo, which was provided by customs records, to the tonnage of the ships, decreasing at each port by one-fifth, and considered the result the actual tonnage of each port.

While the eye can judge the proportion of the surface area of two circles only with difficulty, this is not the case with sectors of a circle. Whether one sector is, for instance, approximately a quarter or a tenth of the full circle, can easily be seen. Following this observation, I thought the investigation of the sectors would present the share of the two types of trade for each port better than numbers ever could.

The aim of my figurative maps is less to exhibit statistical results, which could be better established by numbers, than to make relationships quickly apparent to the eye, relationships that are instantly grasped where numbers would require the mediation of a mental calculation. The figurative maps are thoroughly in the spirit of the century in which one seeks to save time in all ways possible.

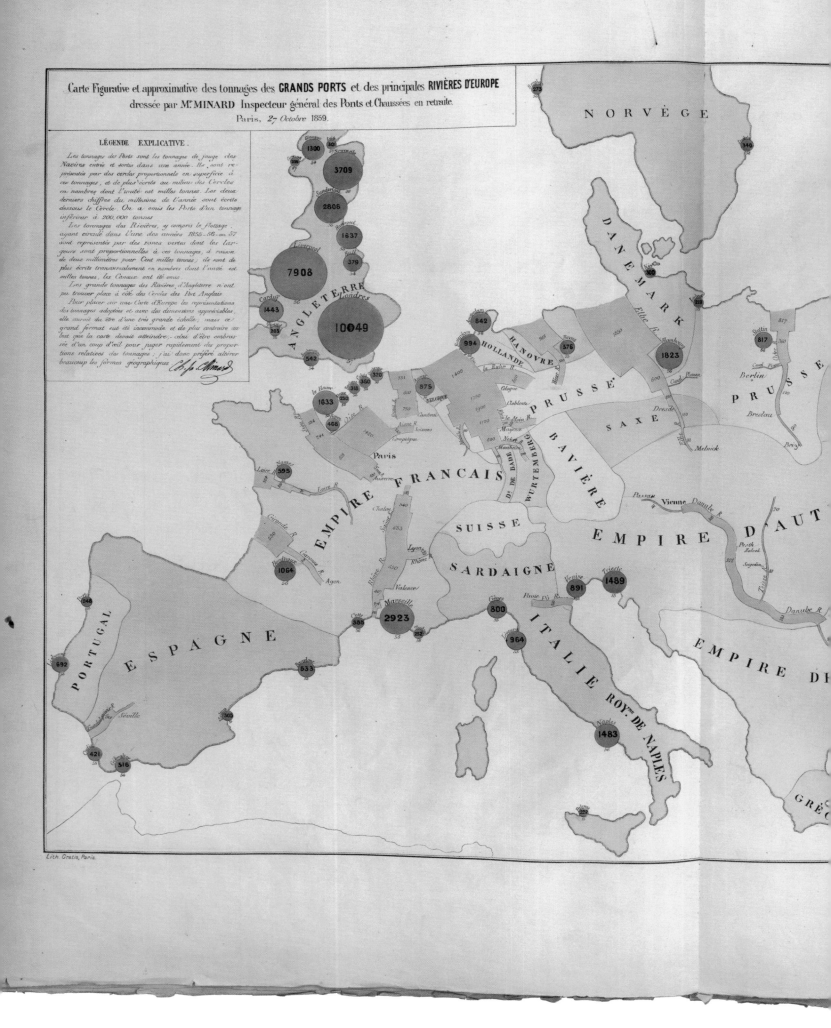

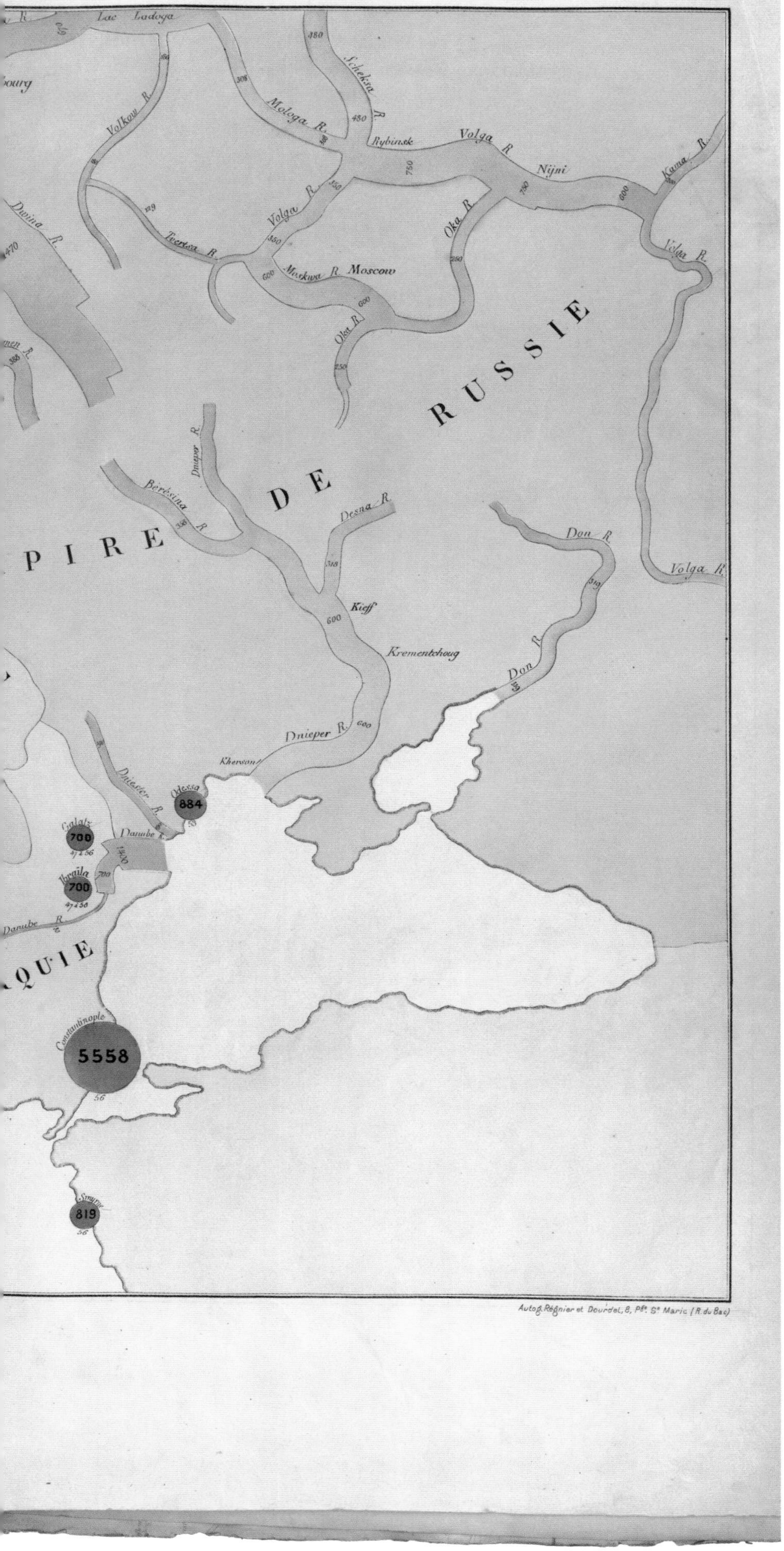

25

Cargo Tonnage of the Major Ports and Rivers of Europe

◄ "Carte figurative et approximative des tonnages des grands ports et des principales rivières d'Europe"
October 27, 1859. Lithographic print, hand-colored. 92.8 × 73.8 cm.

This map investigates traffic capacities of major European ports (shown as proportional circles) and rivers (represented as flows). Raw numbers are included for both, and Minard added numbers beneath each circle to indicate which year of the 1850s the data refers to. Showing both ports and rivers as proportional elements on a map of Europe apparently posed a considerable challenge. This is particularly glaring in Great Britain, where the rivers did not have enough map space beside the enormous port circles and were thus omitted altogether. In other areas, it is difficult to understand that the proportional flows represent rivers. At times, they become so wide that they tend to overshadow other geographic entities; the estuary of the river Rhine, for instance, dwarfs neighboring Belgium.

MINARD TRANSLATED

Figurative and approximate map of the tonnage of the major ports and principal rivers of Europe

Explanatory note: The tonnage of a port is the capacity of the ships entering and exiting in one year. It is represented by a circle with an area proportional to the tonnage, with the amount, in units of a thousand tonnes, noted in the center. The last two digits of the year are written below each circle. Ports with a tonnage of less than 200,000 tonnes were omitted.

Tonnage circulating via the rivers in 1855, 1856, or 1857 is represented by the green zones, with widths proportional to their tonnage at the rate of two millimeters per hundred thousand tonnes. These figures are also recorded transversally in units of a thousand tonnes. Canals were omitted. There was also insufficient space to record the tonnage of English rivers next to the circles representing English ports.

To represent the tonnage across Europe at an appreciable scale would require a map of great size. However, this large format would have been inconvenient and moreover contrary to the purpose of the map—to grasp it at a glance in order to quickly ascertain relative tonnage. I therefore preferred to substantially alter the geographic forms.

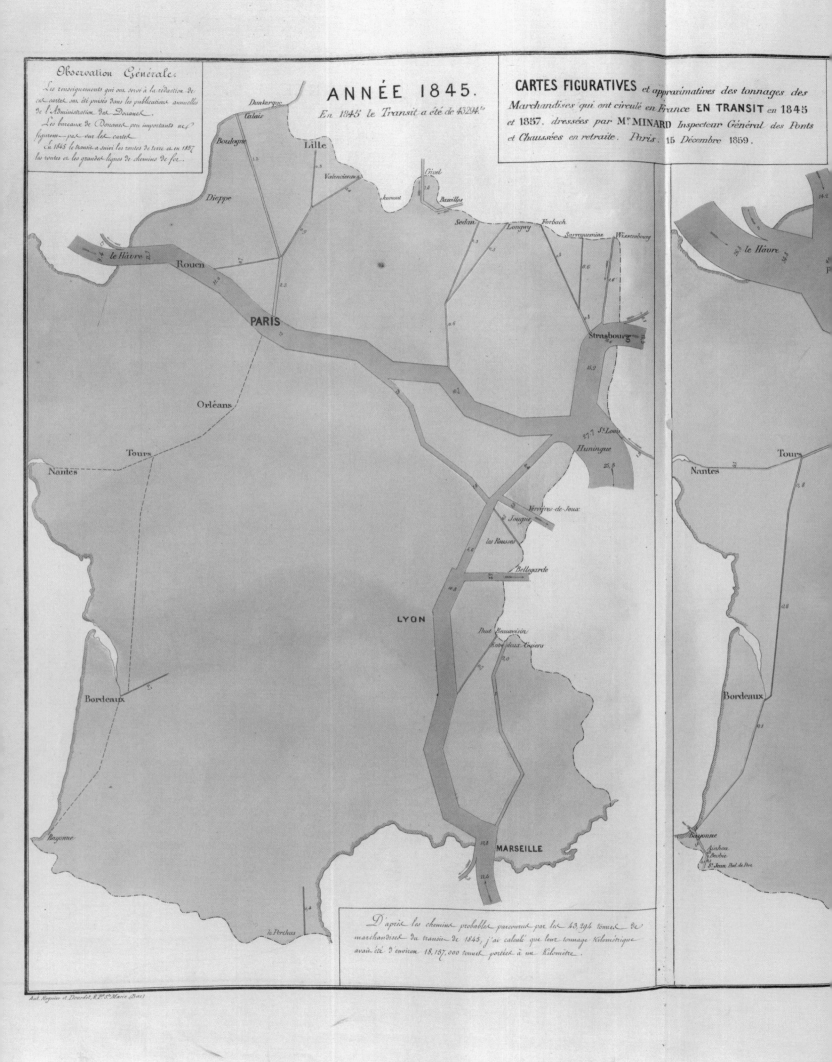

Observation Générale.

Les renseignements qui ont servi à la rédaction de cette carte ont été puisés dans les publications annuelles de l'Administration des Douanes.

Les bureaux de Douanes peu importants ne figurent pas sur cette carte.

En 1845 le transit a suivi les routes de terre et en 1857 les routes et les grandes lignes de chemins de fer.

CARTES FIGURATIVES et approximatives des tonnages des Marchandises qui ont circulé en France EN TRANSIT en 1845 et 1857. dressées par Mr MINARD Inspecteur Général des Ponts et Chaussées en retraite. Paris. 15 Décembre 1859.

D'après les chemins probables parcourus par les 43,294 tonnes de marchandises du transit de 1845, j'ai calculé que leur tonnage Kilométrique avait été d'environ 18,157,000 tonnes portées à un Kilomètre.

Aut. Regnier et Dourdet, 8 Pl. St Marie (Bac).

Dunkerque · Calais · Boulogne · Lille · Valenciennes · Givet · Jeumont · Bazeilles · Sedan · Longwy · Forbach · Sarreguemine · Wissembourg · Dieppe · le Hâvre · Rouen · Strasbourg · PARIS · St Louis · Huningue · Orléans · Tours · Nantes · Verrières-de-Joux · Jougne · les Rousses · Bellegarde · LYON · Pont Beauvoisin · Entre deux Guiers · Bordeaux · Bayonne · MARSEILLE · le Perthus · Ainhoa · Béobie · St Jean Pied de Port

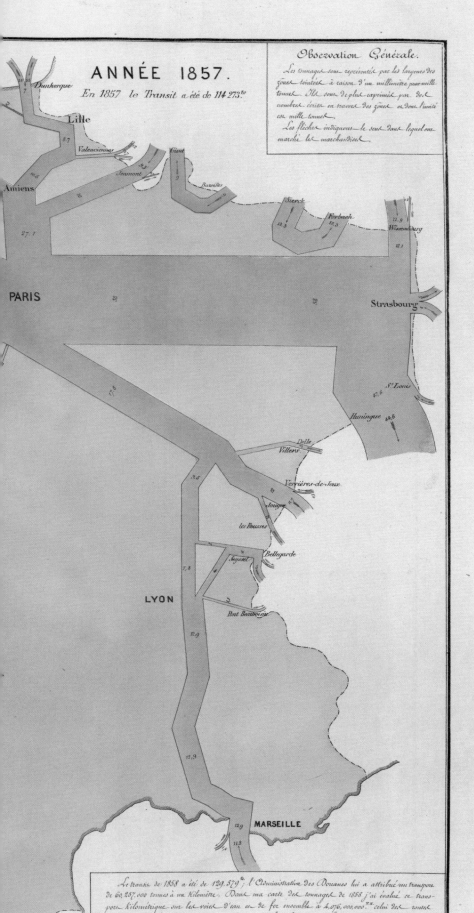

26

Goods in Transit in France in 1845 and 1857

◄ "Cartes figuratives et approximatives des tonnages des marchandises qui ont circulé en France en transit en 1845 et 1857"
December 15, 1859. Lithographic print, hand-colored. 95.9 × 76.8 cm.

This double map compares the amount of freight traffic traversing France on streets in 1845 and on streets and railroads in 1857. In mapping data obtained from the customs administration, Minard apparently merged many distinct movements into continuous flows and assumed a geographic route for the freight. At the exit and entry points, arrows indicate the direction of traffic (incoming or outgoing). This system is not carried out throughout France, however, maybe due to the lack of detailed data. This is the first time Minard juxtaposed two consecutive maps for a chronological comparison. It is interesting that Minard would have chosen the color blue for the flows, as they do not refer to waterways.

MINARD TRANSLATED

Figurative and approximate maps of the tonnage of goods circulating in France in 1845 and 1857

The information used to prepare these maps was drawn from the annual reports of the Customs Administration. Minor customs offices were not included on the maps.

In 1845, transit by road was measured and in 1857 by road and the major railroad lines.

Based on the routes traveled by the 43,294 tonnes of freight in 1845, I calculated a tonne-kilometer of approximately 18,157,000.

General Observation: Tonnages are represented by the width of the colored zones at a rate of one millimeter per thousand tonnes. They are also written across the zones in units of a thousand tonnes. The arrows indicate the direction in which goods traveled.

Transit in 1858 was 129,579 tonnes; the Customs Administration attributed a transport of 60,257,000 tonnes of cargo per kilometer. In my 1858 map of tonnages I estimated the combined tonne-kilometer over waterways and railroad routes at 4,076,000,000. The tonne-kilometer for roads (imperial roads only) can be estimated, based on observations made in 1856–57, at 1,900,000,000. The total for all three means of transport is 5,975,000,000, of which transit makes up only a hundredth.

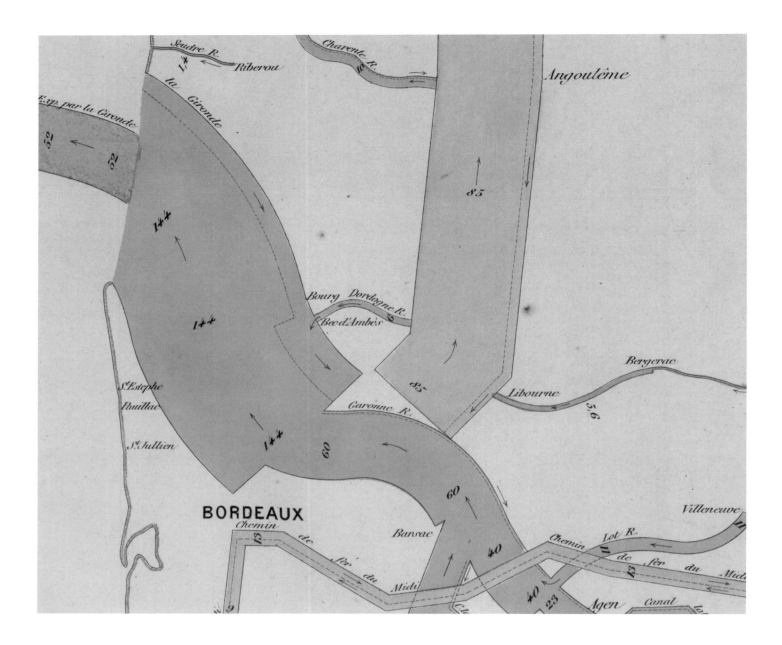

28
Circulation of Wine and Spirits in France in 1857

➤ "Carte figurative et approximative des tonnages des vins, spiritueux etc. qui ont circulé en 1857 sur les voies d'eau et de fer de l'Empire français"
April 18, 1860. Lithographic print, hand-colored. 62.4 × 75.4 cm.

This is a variation on Minard's ongoing series about freight traffic in France (see [13] and following), and it resembles in some instances the map on cereals created five years prior [17]. Minard focused on domestic transport and the export of wine and spirits. The colors follow the scheme of the earlier maps (railroads are rose, and waterways are green). Again, raw numbers are noted across the flows to add detail. As in [17], larger flows are parted by a hatched line, with arrows indicating the direction of movement. Yellow flows indicate an additional type of movement: wine and spirits exports flowing outward from various points along the border of France. Text labels on the map provide further details about these exports.

MINARD TRANSLATED

Figurative and approximate map of the tonnage of wine and spirits circulating in 1857 on the waterways and railroads of the French Empire

Tonnages are represented by the widths of the colored zones at a rate of thirty-three millimeters for every one hundred thousand tonnes. They are also written across the zones in units of one thousand tonnes. The arrows indicate the direction in which the wine and spirits traveled.

The information used to prepare this map was drawn from the publications of the Customs and Tax Administration and from unofficial communications with the directors and engineers of the various transport routes.

The exports represented here include shipments to foreign countries, but not to Algeria nor the colonies.

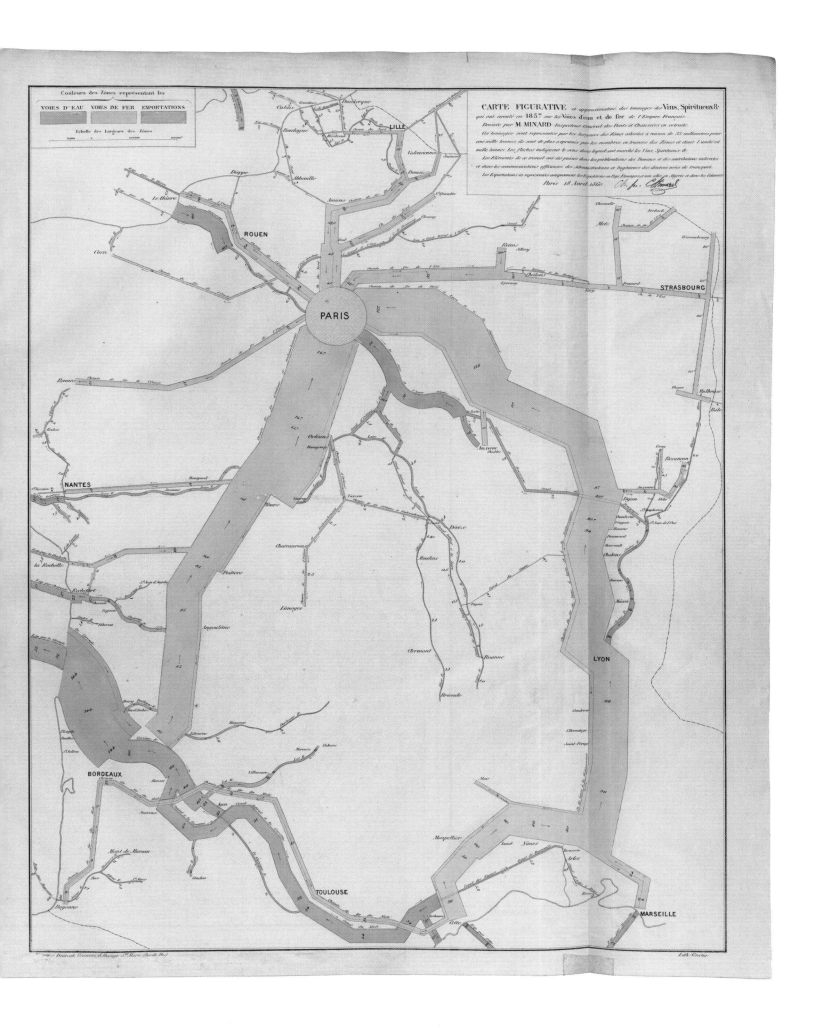

European Cotton Imports, 1858–1865

This series looks at European cotton imports between 1858 and 1865 and refers to the political tensions accompanying the American Civil War. The first map showing the cotton trade in 1858 immediately clarifies why these pressures would spark worries in Europe: the Confederate states supplied the overwhelming share of raw cotton consumed there, and textile businesses all across the continent depended on that supply. One millimeter of flow width represents four thousand tonnes of raw cotton. Color indicates its origin: from the United States (blue), the British colonies in India (yellow), the Middle East (brown), or re-exports from England to other European countries (rose). The base map is rather plain; the east coast of North America is a crude silhouette, and the seven first secessionist states are delineated.

In the second graphic, two consecutive maps compare two moments in time —a method Minard had employed only once before [26]. The map on the right, with data from 1861, portrays a moment when the effects of the American Civil War had not yet kicked in, and Great Britain was already seeking to increase imports from its Indian colonies. In order to fit two maps on one spread, Minard displayed only a part of the world on each and adapted the scaling of the flow width (one millimeter represents five thousand tonnes). Minard included an additional diagram (top left), exhibiting some key figures on global cotton trade over the previous thirty years.

Completed in May 1863, while the American Civil War was raging in full force, the third map draws a dramatic picture, with the exports from the Confederate states having in fact collapsed by 1862. Meanwhile, Great Britain imported substantial amounts from its Indian colonies and the Middle East. Even Cuba and Haiti, which had not even appeared on the earlier maps, now supplied small amounts of cotton to Europe. In the side notes, Minard expressed the expectation that the United States would never regain its dominance in the global cotton market.

The fourth map shows that, as predicted, the Confederate states were not able to sustain their trade volume. The consistent colors and scaling allow for direct comparison with the map's two predecessors, [37] and [40]. In the center box, Minard used the color legend to craft a comprehensive data story. Beneath the color rectangle for each country of origin, Minard included their respective trade volumes from 1858 through 1863. For some outliers among these, he provided additional commentary. For instance, US exports had plummeted from 548,000 tonnes in 1861 to a mere 26,000 tonnes the following year.

In the fifth installment, the previous trend is further enforced: when US exports collapsed, European countries diversified their supply sources. As a new feature, Minard included a map of India, showing where cotton was cultivated as well as the railway lines carrying it to the harbors. The precautions Great Britain took against a shortage of cotton included building a railroad network of more than five thousand kilometers in India between 1860 and 1864.

Minard completed one final map after the war was over in which he showed how profoundly the war had transformed the global trade of cotton, allowing several new producers to enter the market. The crude application of cartography is particularly conspicuous in this work, such as in the Baltic Sea, where Minard dispensed with Scandinavia to make room for the map's titles. In aiming to compose an integrated view of international trade, the base map only serves as a general spatial reference. Coastlines, islands, or even parts of continents were adapted or omitted to generate an undisturbed view of the cotton flows.

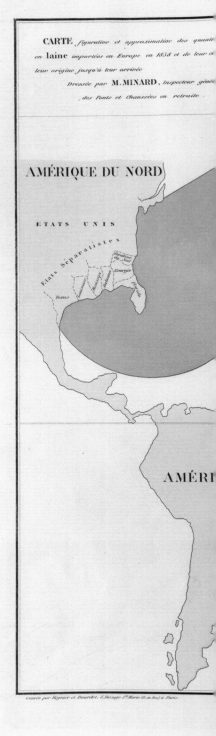

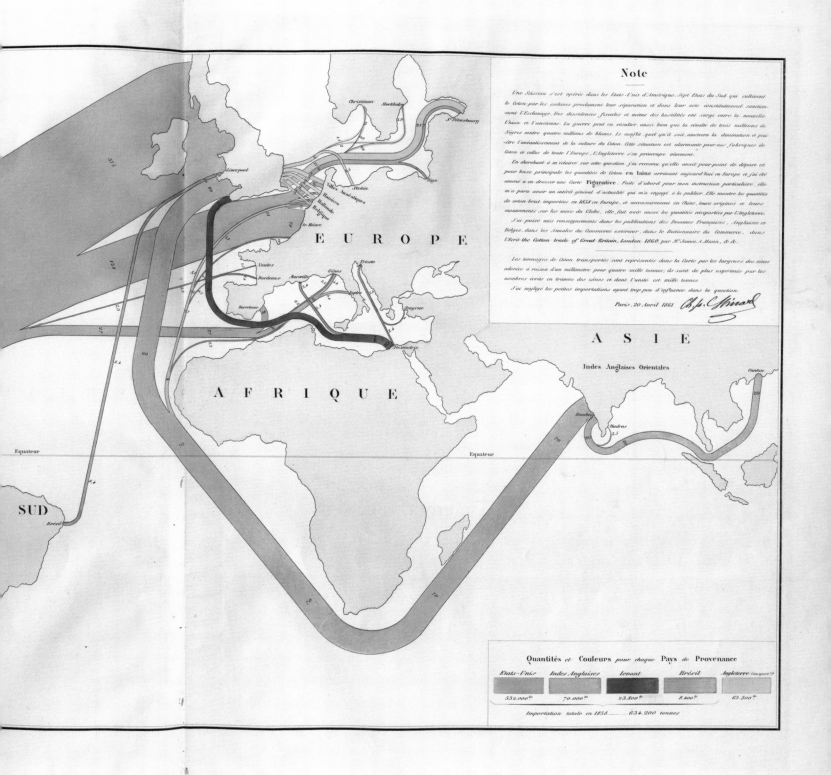

**European Cotton Imports
in 1858**

▲ "Carte figurative et approximative des quantités de coton
en laine importées en Europe en 1858 et de leur circulation depuis
leur origine jusqu'à leur arrivée"
April 20, 1861. Lithographic print, hand-colored. 87.6 × 61.4 cm.

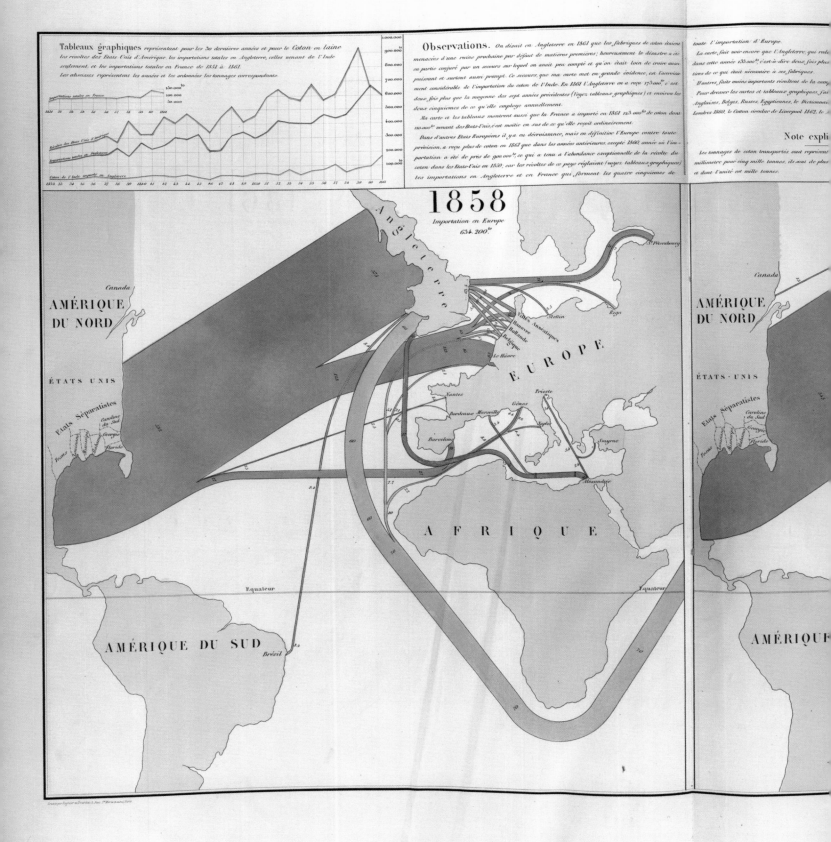

Tableaux graphiques representant pour les 30 dernières années et pour le Coton en laine les récoltes des États Unis d'Amérique, les importations totales en Angleterre, celles venant de l'Inde seulement, et les importations totales en France de 1851 à 1861.

Les abscisses représentent les années et les ordonnées les tonnages correspondants.

Observations. On disait en Angleterre en 1861 que les fabriques de coton étaient menacées d'une ruine prochaine par défaut de matières premières; heureusement le désastre a été en partie conjuré par un secours sur lequel on avait peu compté et qu'on était loin de croire aussi puissant et surtout aussi prompt. Ce secours, que ma carte met en grande évidence, est l'accroissement considérable de l'importation du coton de l'Inde. En 1861 l'Angleterre en a reçu 175.000^t, c'est deux fois plus que la moyenne des sept années précédentes (Voyez tableaux graphiques) et environ les deux cinquièmes de ce qu'elle emploie annuellement.

Ma carte et les tableaux montrent aussi que la France a importé en 1861 125.000^t de coton dont 110.000^t venant des États-Unis, c'est moitié en sus de ce qu'elle reçoit ordinairement.

Dans d'autres États Européens il y a eu décroissance, mais en définitive l'Europe contre toute prévision, a reçu plus de coton en 1861 que dans les années antérieures, excepté 1860, année où l'importation a été de près de 900.000^t, ce qui a tenu à l'abondance exceptionnelle de la récolte du coton dans les États-Unis en 1859, car les récoltes de ce pays réglaient (voyez tableaux graphiques) les importations en Angleterre et en France qui forment les quatre cinquièmes de toute l'importation d'Europe.

La carte fait voir encore que l'Angleterre, qui reçoit dans cette année 435.000^t, c'est-à-dire deux fois plus que la France, ..., tiers de ce qui était nécessaire à ses fabriques.

Note explicative

Les tonnages de coton transportés sont représentés ... millimètre pour cinq mille tonnes, ils sont de plus ... et dont l'unité est mille tonnes.

1858
Importation en Europe
634.200^t

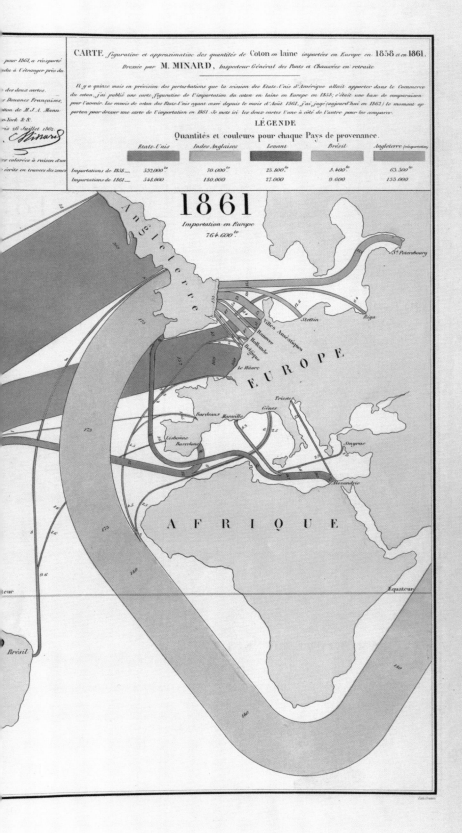

Figurative and approximate map of quantities of cotton imported into Europe in 1858 and 1861

Graphic tables representing cotton crops in the United States of America over the last thirty years, total cotton imported to England, cotton imported to England from India only, and total cotton imported to France from 1851 to 1861. The abscissae represent the years and the ordinates the corresponding tonnage.

Observations. It was said in England in 1861 that the cotton mills were threatened with near ruin because of a lack of raw materials. Fortunately, the disaster was partially averted by assistance we had not counted on and that we were far from believing would be as effective. This relief, which my chart underscores, was the considerable increase of cotton imported from India. In 1861, England received 173,000 tonnes, double the average of the preceding seven years (see the table) and approximately two-fifths of what it uses annually.

My map and tables also show that in 1861 France imported 123,000 tonnes of cotton, of which 110,000 tonnes came from the United States, another half on top of the amount received ordinarily.

In other European countries there was a decrease, although ultimately Europe, against all forecasts, received more cotton in 1861 than in the preceding years except 1860, when importation was around 900,000 tonnes due to the exceptional abundance of the cotton crop in the United States in 1859, and as the crops in that country determined imports to England and France, which constitute four-fifths of all imports to Europe.

Moreover, the chart shows that England, which feared a cotton shortage in 1861, re-exported in that year 133,000 tonnes, or twice as much as in 1858, and sold abroad almost a third of what was needed in its mills.

Other, less significant observations result from a comparison of the two maps.

To draft these maps and graphic tables, I consulted customs documents for France, England, Belgium, Russia, and Egypt; *The Dictionary of Commerce*; *The Cotton Trade*, by M. J. A. Mann, London, 1860; *The 1862 Liverpool Cotton Circular*, the *New York Merchant's Magazine*; etc.

Explanatory note: tonnages of transported cotton are represented by the width of the colored zones at a rate of one millimeter for every five thousand tonnes, and also by the numbers recorded across the zones in units of a thousand tonnes.

Fifteen months ago, in anticipation of the disruption the splitting of the United States of America would bring to the cotton trade, I published a chart of the importation of cotton to Europe in 1858. It was a basis of comparison for the future. Since shipments of cotton ceased in August 1861, I judged it (now 1862) the right moment to draft a chart of the importation in 1861. I have placed the two charts side-by-side to compare them.

37

European Cotton Imports in 1858 and 1861

2 of 6

▲ **"Carte figurative et approximative des quantités de coton en laine importées en Europe en 1858 et en 1861"**
July 26, 1862. Lithographic print, hand-colored. 94.5 × 73.6 cm.

CARTE *figurative et approximative des quantités de* Coton en laine *importées en Europe en* 1858 *et en* 1862
Dressée par Mr. MINARD, *Inspecteur Général des Ponts et Chaussées en retraite.*

Observation. *La présente Carte représente les importations du coton brut en Europe années 1862 et 1858. L'importation de 1858 pouvant être considérée comme moyenne années avant la Guerre Civile d'Amérique, servira de base de comparaison.*

Ma Carte précédente, montrait qu'en 1861 l'exportation des États Unis différait très p de 1858, mais celle-ci indique une énorme réduction en 1862, laquelle est due principalement des Ports des États du Sud. Je dis principalement, parceque ces ports eussent-ils été libres ayant entravé les récoltes, réduit au quart la plantation de 1862 et brulé ou détruit 40.00 approvisionné, les expéditions de 1862 auraient été bien inférieures aux précédentes.

Cette Carte, fait voir que les envois considérables de l'Inde en 1861 se soutiennent et même augmenté (voir tableau graphique.)

Elle montre aussi que les importations d'Égypte et du Brésil en 1862 ont été presque doubl de 1858.

Enfin elle fait voir que l'importation en Angleterre a diminué tandis que la réexportation a au malgré l'accroissement de misère des ouvriers du Lancashire et les blames sévères infligé pu les Ministres Anglais à des marchands et à des filateurs, ceux ci, en 1862, n'en ont pas moins vendu 96.000 to de matière première sur une importation totale de 239.000 to, tandis qu'en 1858 ils n'en av que 63.000 to sur une importation de 460.000 to

Le Commerce du coton brut des États Unis est déplorable pour le présent, pour un avenir un peu é croire, quelque soit l'issue de la guerre, que le travail libre remplacera la culture par les esclaves dé

LÉGENDE.

Les tonnages de coton transportés sont représentés par les largeurs des zones colorées à raison d'un millimètre pour cinq mille tonnes, ils sont des plus exprimés par les nombres écrits en travers des zones et dont l'unité est mille tonnes.

Les Cartes et les tableaux figuratifs ont été dressés sur les documents des Douanes Françaises, Anglaises, Belges, Italiennes, Égyptienne le Dictionnaire du Commerce, le Trade of coton de Mr. J.A.Mann, le coton circulaire et la publication Stotterfoht de Liverpool, le Marchant's Magazine de New -York &c. &c.

Quantités et couleurs pour chaque Pays de provenance.

	États Unis	Indes Anglaises et Asie	Égypte et Syrie	Brésil, Haïti, Mexique &c.	Angleterre (réexportation)
Importations de 1858	532.000 to	70.000 to	23.800 to	8.400 to	63.500 to
Importations de 1862	26.000 to	209.000 to	37.200 to	19.100 to	96.000 to

1858
Importation en Europe
634.200 to

Angleterre

AMÉRIQUE DU NORD

ÉTATS-UNIS

États-Séparatistes
Caroline du Sud
Géorgie
Texas
Floride

Cuba   Haïti

EUROPE

Riga
Stettin
Villes Anséatiques
Hanovre
Hollande
Belgique
Le Hâvre
Nantes
Bordeaux   Marseille   Gênes   Trieste
Barcelone   Naples   Smyrne
Alexandrie

AFRIQUE

Équateur

AMÉRIQUE DU SUD
Brésil

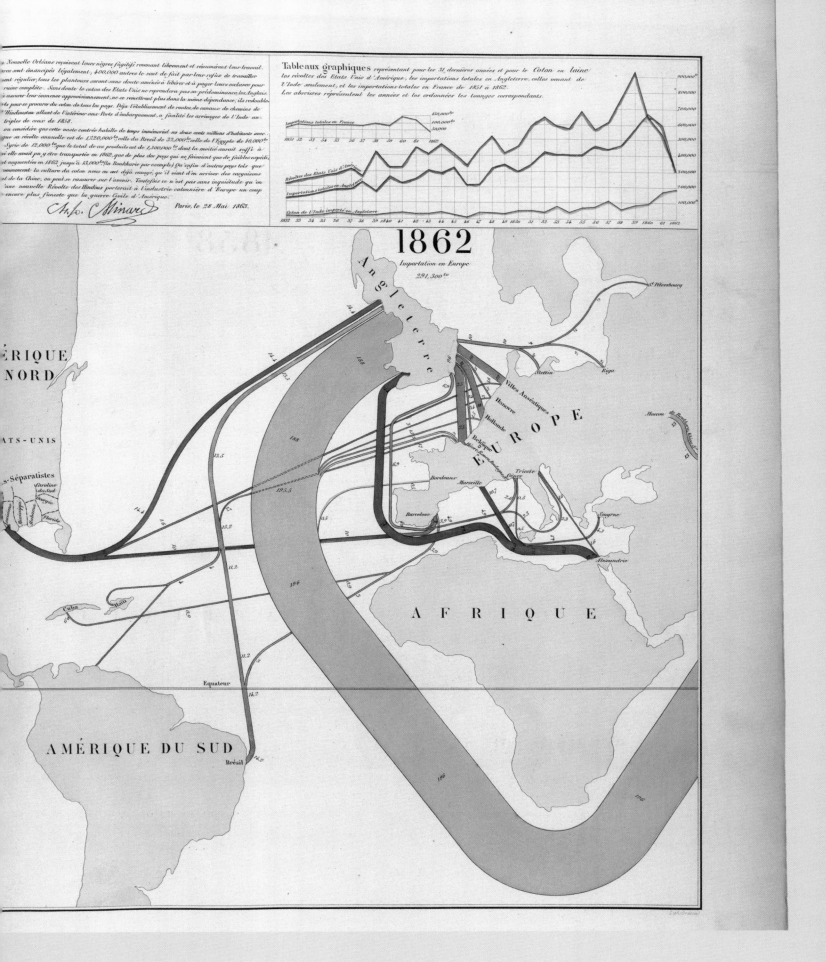

40

**European Cotton Imports
in 1858 and 1862**

3 of 6

▲ "Carte figurative et approximative des quantités de coton
en laine importées en Europe en 1858 et en 1862"
May 28, 1863. Lithographic print, hand-colored. 95.2 × 74.0 cm.

CARTE figurative et approximative des quantités de **COTON** en laine importées en Europe en **1858** et en **1863**

Dressée par M.ʳ MINARD, Inspecteur Général des Ponts et Chaussées en retraite..

Paris, 4 Mai 1864.

Les tonnages de coton transportés sont représentés par les largeurs des zones colorées à raison d'un millimètre pour cinq mille tonnes, ils sont de plus exprimés par les nombres écrits en travers des zones et dont l'unité est mille tonnes.

Les Cartes ont été dressées sur les documents des Douanes Françaises, Anglaises, Belges, Espagnoles Hollandaises, le Dictionnaire du Commerce, le Trade of cotton de M. J. A. Mann, le cotton circular et la publication Stolterfoht de Liverpool, le Marchant's Magasine de Newyork, etc.

Quantités et couleur

		Etats Unis.	Ind
Importations de	1858	532.000 ᵗ	
	1861	543.000 A	
	1862	26.000 B	
	1863	25.800	

A. Importation plus forte que celle de 1858, malgré les

B. Enorme diminution due à la guerre Civile et qui est et

C. Augmentation due à la crainte extrême de la pénurie

D. Augmentation due en partie à la Chine expédiant ses co

E. Accroissement considérable qu'on doit attribuer aux né

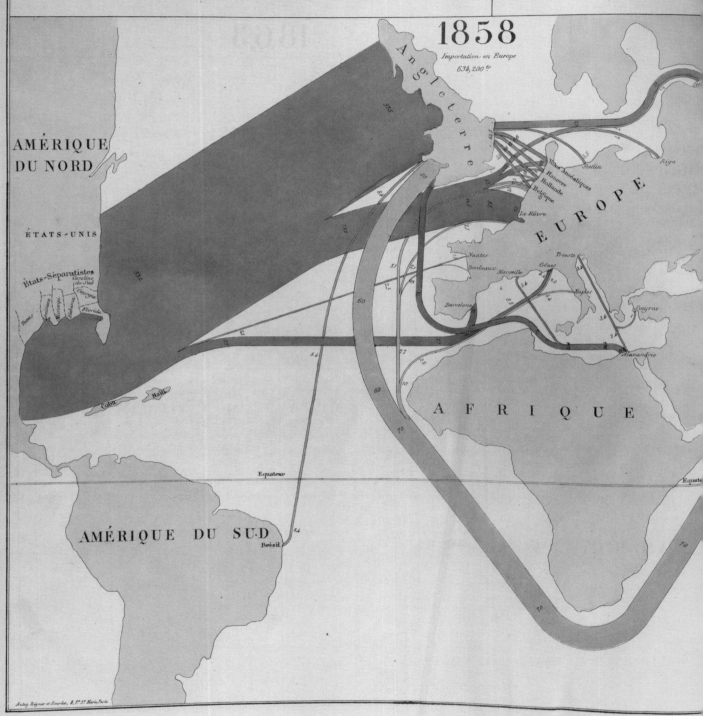

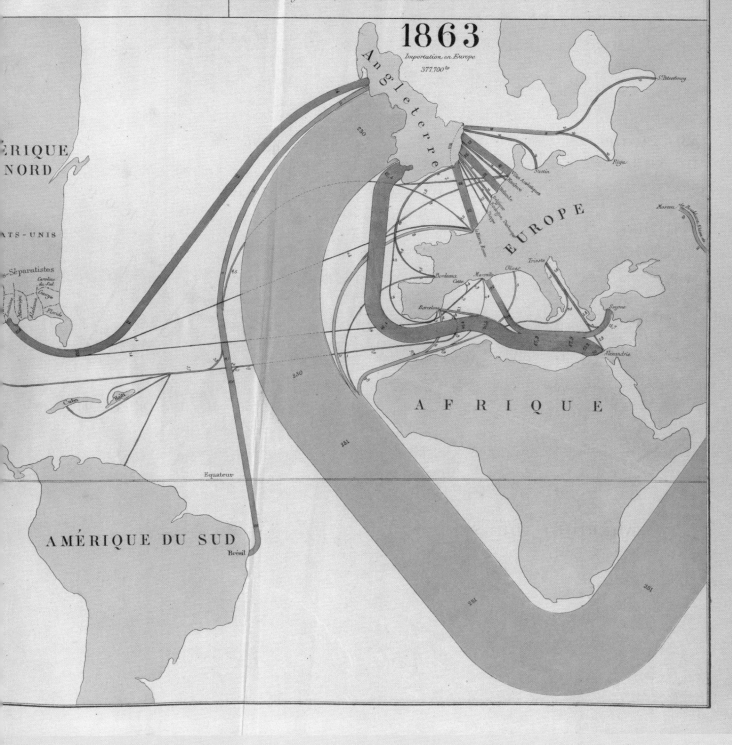

E.

Pays de provenance.

Egypte, Syrie.	Brésil, Indes Occid^les etc.	Angleterre, (réexportation)
23.800^to	8.400^to	63.500^to
27.000	9.600	133.000
37.200	19.100	96.000
71.700 E	19.200	102.000

...e la Guerre Civile, à cause de la vente de tous les stocks
...quelques navires n'avaient échappé aux Blocus.
...dont on ne présumait pas les stocks aussi importants
...fois en Europe.
... Vice-Roi.

Observations. La suspension des arrivages en Europe du Coton des Etats-Unis d'Amérique est l'évènement le plus considérable du Commerce moderne. On ne s'étonnera donc pas qu'ayant fait paraître trois Cartes figuratives du coton brut importé en Europe en 1858, 1861 et 1862, j'en publie une quatrième pour l'importation de 1863.

J'ai continué de mettre en regard l'importation de 1858, parce qu'étant à peu près la moyenne de quelques années avant les troubles d'Amérique, elle sert de comparaison avec les importations des années qui suivent la Guerre Civile.

Mes Cartes font voir la marche progressive des approvisionnements de Coton que l'Europe a tirés des diverses parties du Globe pour remplacer le Coton des Etats-Unis.

L'immense Commerce Maritime actuel a rendu les peuples de la terre solidaires. Une guerre Civile dans l'Amérique du Nord a amené un désastre industriel en Europe par la disette du coton, celle-ci par contre coup a fait augmenter la culture du Cotonnier en Egypte, dans les Indes Occidentales et Orientales. Ces contrées ont plus que triplé leurs expéditions de Coton en Europe ; la solidarité avait fait le mal, elle a donné le remède.

45

European Cotton Imports in 1858 and 1863

4 of 6

▲ "Carte figurative et approximative des quantités de coton en laine importées en Europe en 1858 et en 1863"
May 4, 1864. Lithographic print, hand-colored. 94.9 × 60.1 cm.

CARTE *figurative et approximative des quantités de* **Coton brut**
importées en Europe en 1858 *et en* 1864

Dressée par M. MINARD, *Inspecteur Général des Ponts et Chaussées en retraite*

Paris, le 24 Avril 1865.

Les tonnages de coton transportés sont représentés par les largeurs des zones colorées à raison d'un millimètre pour cinq milles tonnes, et de plus exprimés par les nombres écrits en travers des zones et dont l'unité est mille tonnes.

Les Cartes ont été dressées sur les documents des Douanes Françaises, Anglaises, Belges, Espagnoles, Hollandaises, Italiennes, Autrichiennes, Le Dictionnaire du Commerce, le Trade of cotton de M. J. A. Mann, le cotton circular et la publication Stolterfoht de Liverpool, le Marchant's Magazine de Newyork, l'Economist de Londres etc.

Les Exportations au-dessous de 500ᵀ ne figurent pas sur les Cartes.

LÉGENDE. — Quantités et couleurs pour chaque Pays de provenance.

Importations des années	Etats-Unis	Indes Orientales, Chine etc.	Egypte, Syrie	Brésil, Indes Occidentales etc.	Angleterre (réexport)
1858	532.000ᵗ	70.000	23.800ᵗ	8.400ᵗ	63.500
1861	548.000 A	150.000 C	27.000	9.600	133.000
1862	26.000 B	209.000	37.200	19.100	96.000
1863	25.800 F	261.000 D	71.700 E	19.200	102.000
1864	39.600 F	299.000	96.000	27.500	94.700

A. Importation plus forte que celle de 1858, malgré les entraves naissantes de la guerre civile, à cause de la vente de tous les Stocks
B. Enorme diminution due à la guerre civile et qui eut été encore plus forte si quelques navires n'avaient échappé aux Blocus
C. Augmentation due à la crainte extrême de la pénurie du coton américain dont on ne présumait pas les Stocks aussi importants
D. Augmentation due en partie à la Chine expédiant ses cotons pour la première fois en Europe
E. Accroissement considérable qu'on doit attribuer aux nouvelles plantations du Vice Roi
F. Augmentation due au transit par le Mexique et à l'emploi de petits bâtiments échappant plus facilement aux blocus
G. ___ idem ___ due à de nouveaux chemins de fer et de nouvelles plantations de coton dans l'Inde et aux premiers envois du Japon.

Observation. — La suspension des arrivages en Europe du coton des Etats-Unis d'Amérique est l'événement le plus considérable du Commerce moderne. On ne s'étonnera donc pas qu'ayant fait paraître quatre Cartes figuratives du Coton importé en Europe en 1858, 1861, 1862 et 1863, j'en publie une cinquième pour l'importation de 1864.

J'ai continué de mettre en regard l'importation de 1858, parcequ'étant à peu près la moyenne de quelques années avant les troubles d'Amérique, elle sert de comparaison avec les importations des années qui suivent la guerre civile.

Mes Cartes font voir la marche progressive des approvisionnements de coton que l'Europe a tirés des diverses parties du Globe pour remplacer celui des Etats-Unis.

L'immense Commerce maritime actuel a rendu les peuples de la terre solidaires. Une guerre civile dans l'Amérique du Nord a amené un désastre industriel en Europe par la dureté du coton, celle-ci par contre coup a fait augmenter la culture du cotonnier en Egypte, dans les Indes Occidentales et Orientales. Ces contrées ont plus que triplé leurs expéditions de coton en Europe. La solidarité avait fait le mal, elle a donné le remède.

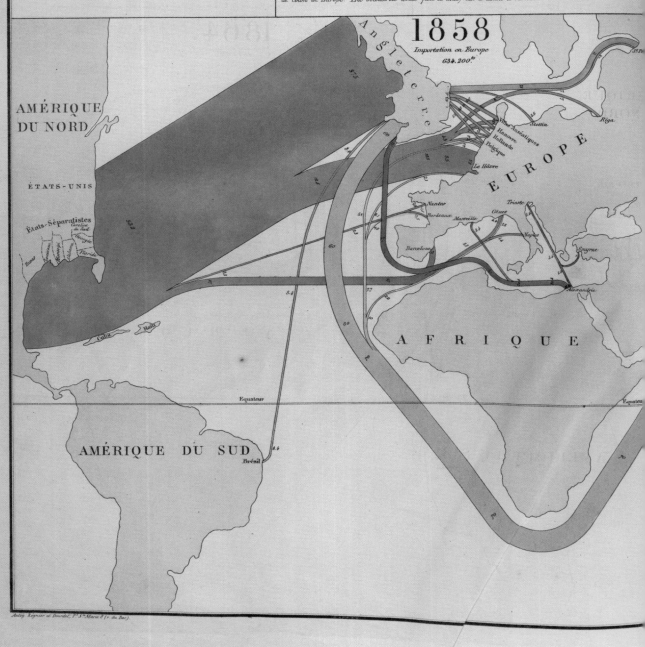

1858
Importation en Europe
634.200ᵗ

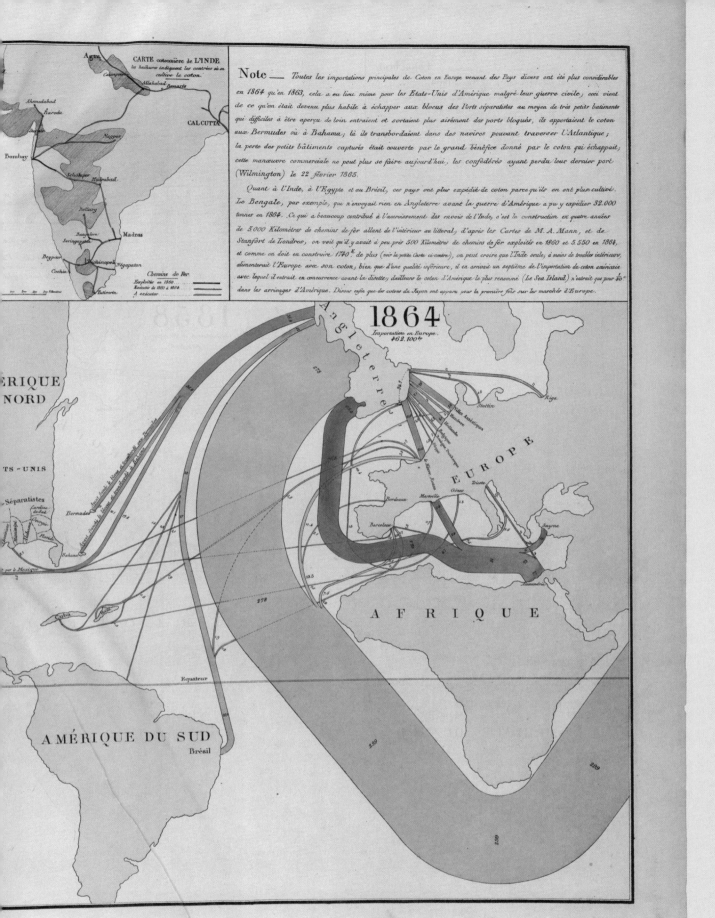

▲ "Carte figurative et approximative des quantités de coton
brut importées en Europe en 1858 et en 1864"
April 24, 1865. Lithographic print, hand-colored. 94.9 × 67.8 cm.

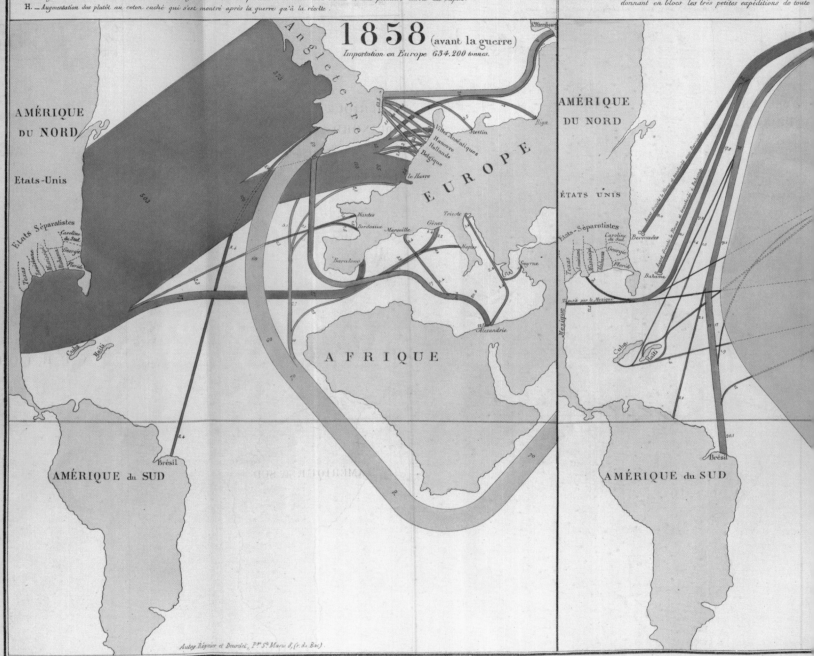

LÉGENDE.—Quantités et couleurs pour chaque Pays de provenance.

CARTE figurative et approximative d...
en 1858 e...
Dressée par M^r. MINARD, Inspec...

		Etats-Unis.	Indes Orientales, Chine etc.	Egypte, Syrie.	Brésil, Indes Occidentales etc	Angleterre. réexportation.
Importations des années	1858	532.000 ^{ta}	70.000 ^{ta}	23.300 ^{ta}	8.400 ^{ta}	63.500 ^b
	1861	548.000 ^A	180.000 ^c	27.000	9.600	133.000
	1862	26.000 ^b	209.000	37.200	19.100	96.000
	1863	25.800	261.000 ^D	71.700 ^E	19.200	102.000
	1864	39.600 ^F	299.000 ^G	96.000	27.500	94.700
	1865	84.900 ^H	266.000	129.600	50.700	119.600

A.—Importation plus forte que celle de 1858, malgré les entraves naissantes de la guerre civile, à cause de la vente de tous les Stocks.
B.—Enorme diminution due à la guerre civile, et qui eut été encore plus forte si quelques navires n'avaient échappé aux Blocus.
C.—Augmentation due à la crainte extrême de la pénurie du coton Américain dont on ne présumait pas les Stocks aussi importants.
D.—Augmentation due en partie à la Chine expédiant ses cotons pour la première fois en Europe.
E.—Accroissement considérable qu'on doit attribuer aux nouvelles plantations du Vice Roi.
F.—Augmentation due au transit par le Mexique et à l'emploi de petits bâtiments échappant plus facilement aux blocus.
G.—Augmentation due à de nouveaux chemins de fer et de nouvelles plantations de coton dans l'Inde et aux premiers envois du Japon.
H.—Augmentation due plutôt au coton caché qui s'est montré après la guerre qu'à la récolte.

Les tonnages de coton transportés sont représentés par les ...
tonnes, ils sont de plus exprimés par les nombres écrits en ...
Les Cartes ont été dressées sur les Documents des Douanes Fr...
Le Dictionnaire du Commerce, le Trade of cotton de M.J.A. ...
le Marchant's Magazine de Newyork, l'économist de Londres ...

Observation : Les importations sont un peu plus fortes que ce...
donnant en bloc les très petites expéditions de toute...

1858 (avant la guerre)
Importation en Europe 634.200 tonnes.

AMÉRIQUE DU NORD

Etats-Unis

Etats Séparatistes

Angleterre

EUROPE

AFRIQUE

AMÉRIQUE du SUD

Brésil

AMÉRIQUE DU NORD

ÉTATS UNIS

Etats Séparatistes

Brésil

AMÉRIQUE du SUD

Autog. Régnier et Dourdet, P.^{te} St Marie 8, (r. du Bac).

104

s de **COTON BRUT** importées en Europe

en 1865,

s Ponts et Chaussées en retraite.

is, *le 14 Mai 1866*.

nes colorées à raison d'un millimètre pour cinq milles
r et dont l'unité est mille tonnes.

ses, Belges, Hollandaises, Italiennes, Autrichiennes,
circular et la publication *Stolterfoht de Liverpool*,
arpi d'Alexandrie etc.

arce que j'ai négligé celles d'une demie tonne et que les Douanes
ai su à laquelle les rapporter.

De l'importation du Coton en 1865. ___ La question

Commerciale du coton entre dans des phases nouvelles depuis que la guerre civile
des États-Unis d'Amérique a cessé.

Toutes les parties du Globe qui envoyaient du coton en Europe en ont expédié
plus en 1865 qu'en 1864, à l'exception de l'Inde et de la Chine; même des contrées
méridionales de l'Europe ont cultivé plus de coton qu'ordinairement et en ont
envoyé près de six mille tonnes à Marseille et à Trieste. Il y a donc aujourd'hui
un surcroît d'activité générale pour la production de cette plante textile.

Toutes fois l'importation de 1865 est encore d'un sixième au-dessous de ce
qu'elle était avant la guerre.

Au milieu des importations diverses, un fait remarquable a lieu. Des cotons
sont expédiés aujourd'hui de Bombay à Liverpool par la Mer Rouge, le
chemin de fer de Suez à Alexandrie, la Méditerranée et l'Océan. La vapeur est
l'unique moteur des mouvements sur les rails et sur les mers; ces transports
sont indépendants de ceux de la Compagnie Péninsulaire Orientale et de la
Compagnie des Messageries Impériales.

Cette voie insolite qui devance le Canal de l'Isthme de Suez, sera-t-elle
encore suivie après l'exploitation du Canal? Indique-t-elle d'autres voies

semblables pour le coton de l'Asie centrale traversant la Mer Noire et la Mer
Caspienne? C'est ce qu'on ne peut dire.

En attendant nous assistons à la lutte opiniâtre des trois Pays grands producteurs
de coton. 1.º Les États-Unis qui cherchent à reconquérir le marché, mais dont le génie si
actif et si entreprenant est singulièrement entravé par l'irrésolution et l'indolence des
nègres affranchis qu'ils ne pourront peut-être plus employer; 2.º l'Égypte qui abandonne
peu à peu sa culture si ancienne du blé pour celle du coton; 3.º l'Inde qui donnant une
nouvelle impulsion aux plantations de coton, existant chez elle de temps immémorial,
voudra à toute force se payer des énormes sacrifices qu'elle a faits en ouvrant des
voies de terre, d'eau et de fer pour relier ses districts cotonniers avec ses ports
maritimes.

Voilà les grandes forces productives, quant aux débouchés consommateurs,
qui se résument presqu'à l'Angleterre, il n'est pas probable que ce pays retombe
dans la même faute d'avoir tiré d'une seule source la matière première indispensable
à la vie de quatre millions de ses habitants. Sans doute il entretiendra entre
les producteurs rivaux une concurrence si utile pour lui et pour l'Europe
et nous pouvons espérer de la voir continuer longtemps.

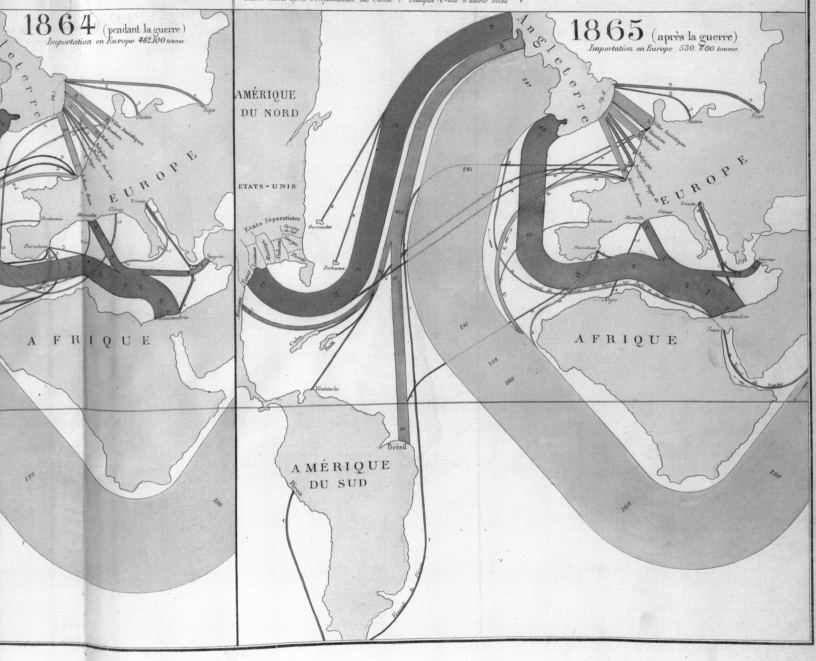

1864 (pendant la guerre)
Importation en Europe 462.100 tonnes

1865 (après la guerre)
Importation en Europe 530.800 tonnes

▲ "Carte figurative et approximative des quantités de coton
brut importées en Europe en 1858 en 1864 et en 1865"
May 14, 1866. Lithographic print, hand-colored. 111.2 × 71.8 cm.

33

Foreign Coal and Coke Markets in France in 1858

➤ "Carte approximative de l'étendue des marchés des houilles et cokes étrangers dans l'Empire français en 1858"
June 17, 1861. Lithographic print, hand-colored. 47.6 × 75.0 cm.

In the context of accelerating industrialization, the reliable supply of coal became crucial for all European countries. To supplement its faltering domestic production, France imported coal from several countries. This map investigates where this coal was consumed: mostly near the harbors or along the waterways and railroad lines through which it entered France. A small fraction was reloaded onto road carriages and further distributed. This is the only map in which Minard shaded regions according to qualitative data. Regions consuming English coal are green, Belgian are blue, and German are brown. Areas that consume English and Belgian or Belgian and German coal are shaded with a mixed tone, while unshaded areas do not utilize any foreign coal.

MINARD TRANSLATED

Approximate map of the extent of foreign coal and coke in the French Empire in 1858.

Areas without color receive almost no foreign fuel.

Note: Foreign coal arrives in France via our ports, our waterways, and our railroads. A very small amount, around 1/50, enters by road.

The greatest quantity is consumed in the ports and in the very places where the waterways and railroads pass. The other portion is reloaded onto carriages and taken to nearby destinations. In order to account for this extension of the market, I have assumed that the coal thus transported is not taken any farther than 25 kilometers in each direction from the place of its first arrival.

The market is therefore ascertained and represented on this map on the basis of information about the movement of coal in our ports, on our waterways, on our railroads, and following the hypothesis that cargo is transported 25 kilometers in every direction.

I have not included very small dispatches reaching remote frontiers by rail, as this map shows only the locations that received at least 400 to 500 tonnes of coal in 1858.

CARTE APPROXIMATIVE d
dans l'Empire Fr

COULEURS des MARCHÉS
des HOUILLES et COKES.

Anglais

Belges

Allemands

Anglais et Belges

Belges et Allemands

Les parties sans couleur ne reçoivent presque pas de combustibles étrangers.

FINIST

Note :

Les houilles étrangéres arrivent en France par nos ports d'eau et nos chemins de fer. Une très petite partie, $\frac{1}{50}$ env. pénètre par les routes de terre.

La plus grande quantité est consommée dans les ports les lieux mêmes où passent les voies d'eau et de fer. L' reprise par voiture, va à des destinations peu éloignées compte de cette extension du marché, j'ai supposé que voiturées ainsi se répandaient en tous sens à 25 Kilomèt de leur première arrivée.

La surface du marché est donc déterminée et représe ma Carte par suite de renseignements certains du mouve houilles dans nos ports, sur nos voies navigables, sur de fer et par l'hypothèse d'un charroi à 25 Kilométres c tous sens.

De très-petites expéditions parviennent par les Chemi à des points fort éloignés des frontières que je n'ai p dans l'étendue des marchés, laquelle ne renferme que les il est arrivé en 1858 au moins 4 à 500 tonnes.

Paris, le 17 Juin 1861.

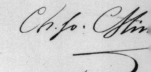

ÉTENDUE des MARCHÉS des HOUILLES et COKES ÉTRANGERS

n 1858, dressée par M.ʳ MINARD inspecteur général des Ponts et Chaussées en retraite.

PAS DE CALAIS

NORD

SOMME

SEINE INFR.ᵉ

AISNE

ARDENNES

OISE

MOSELLE

MANCHE   CALVADOS

EURE

SEINE ET OISE

MARNE

MEUSE

MEURTHE

BAS-RHIN

ORNE

SEINE ET MARNE

DU NORD

EURE et LOIR

AUBE

VOSGES

ILLE ET VILAINE

MAYENNE

SARTHE

Hᵗᵉ MARNE

Hᵗ RHIN

RBIHAN

LOIRET

YONNE

HAUTE - SAÔNE

LOIRE INFÉRIEURE   MAINE et LOIRE

INDRE et LOIRE

LOIR-ET-CHER

CÔTE D'OR

DOUBS

CHER

NIÈVRE

VENDÉE

DEUX-SÈVRES

VIENNE

INDRE

SAÔNE et LOIRE

JURA

ALLIER

AIN

CREUSE

RHÔNE

CHARENTE-INFᵣₑ

CHARENTE

Hᵗᵉ VIENNE

PUY ᴅᴇ DÔME

LOIRE

CORRÈZE

ISÈRE

DORDOGNE

CANTAL

HAUTE LOIRE

ARDÈCHE

DROME

Hᵗᵉˢ ALPES

GIRONDE

LOT

LOZÈRE

LOT et GARONNE

AVEYRON

BASSES - ALPES

TARN ET GARONNE

GARD

VAUCLUSE

LANDES

GERS

TARN

HÉRAULT

BOUCHES ᴅᴜ RHÔNE

VAR

BASSES PYRENÉES

Hᵗᵉ GARONNE

HAUTES PYRÉNÉES

AUDE

ARIÈGE

PYRÉNÉES ORIENTALES

Echelle de 200 Kilomètres.
0 20 40 60 80 100   200

34

Great Ports of the Globe, 1861

➤ **"Carte figurative et approximative
des grands ports du globe"**
August 25, 1861. Lithographic color print.
93.5 × 62.5 cm.

In 1861, Minard again compared the
relative importance of harbors (in the
method employed in [11], [24], and
[25]), this time on a global level. Harbors
are represented as proportional circles,
scaled according to the total annual
cargo they handled. This number is also
inscribed in each circle, while the single
digit number below each circle indicates the year the cargo data refers to
(e.g., 8 = 1858). A text label above each
circle indicates the city. As usual, Minard
used the side note to elaborate on
the origin of his data set, explaining
the laborious process of obtaining and
cleaning the data.

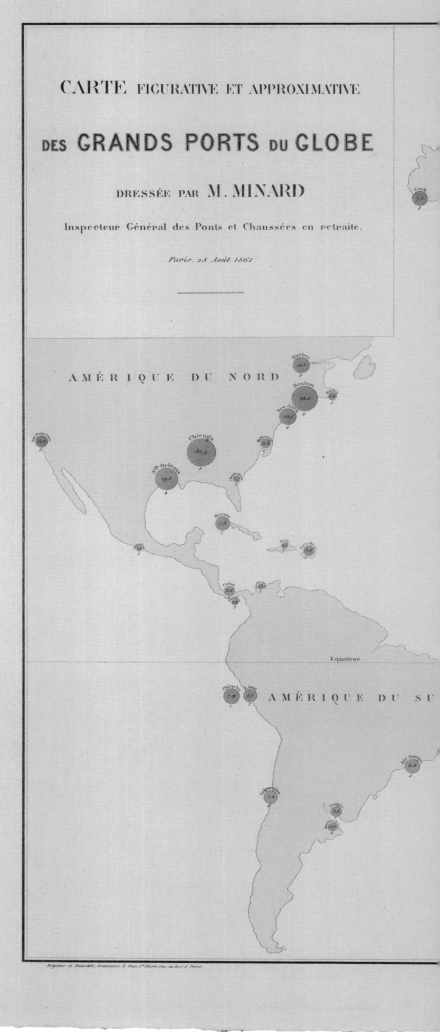

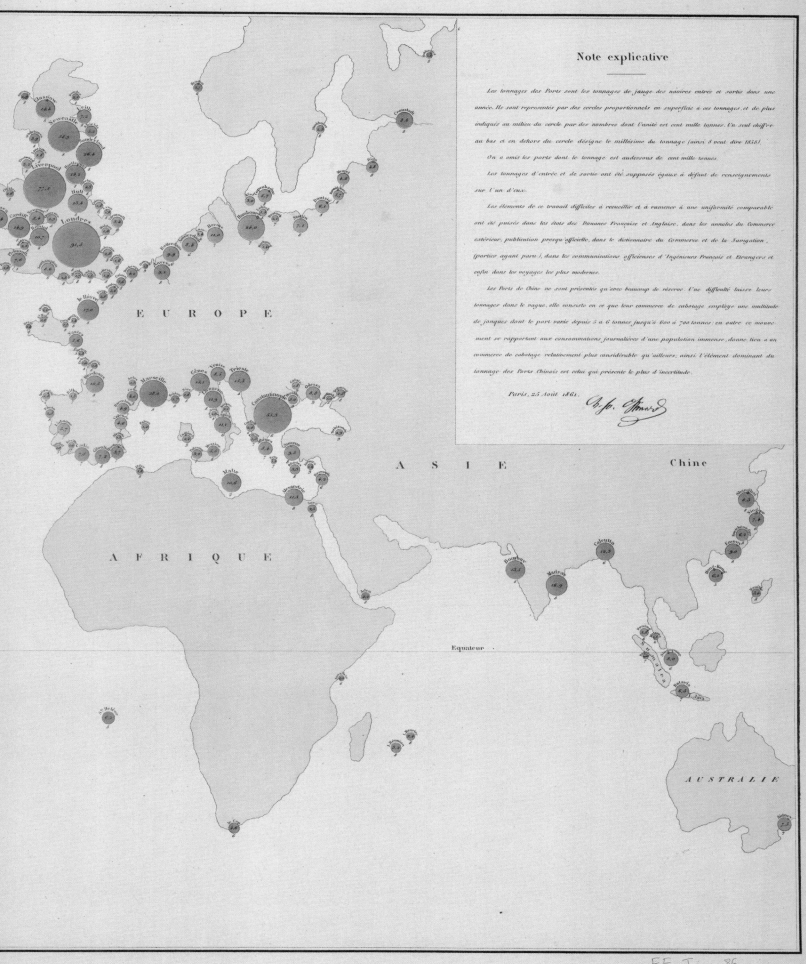

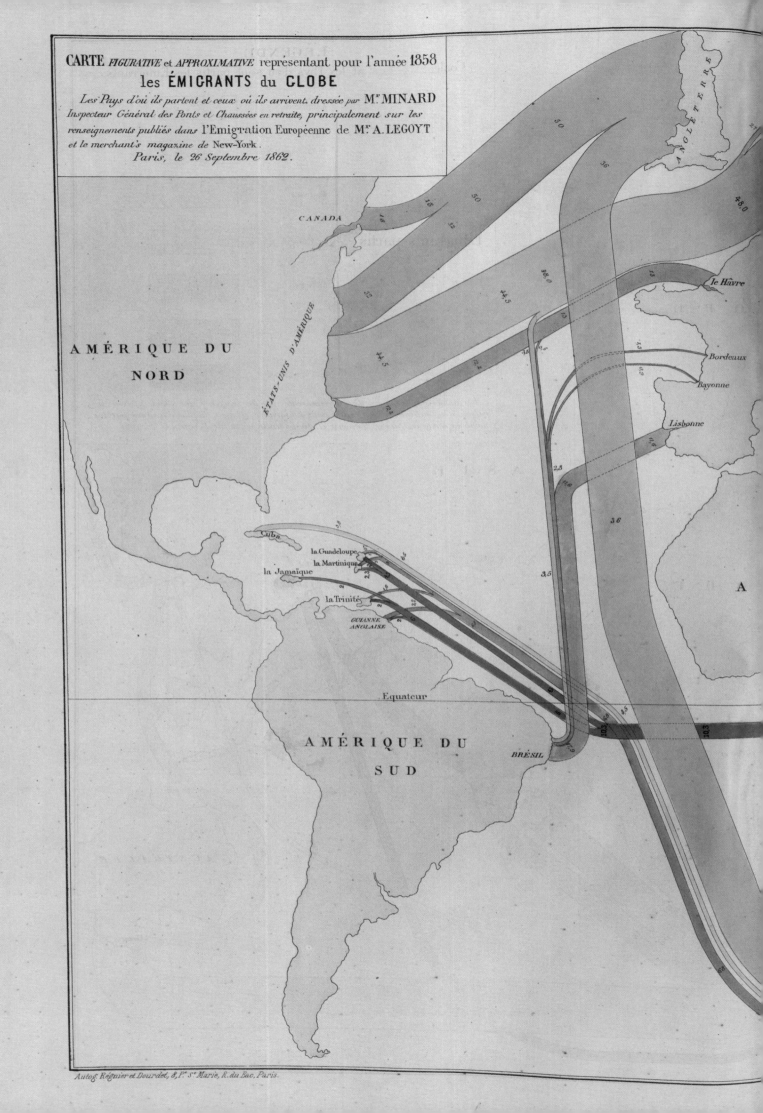

CARTE *FIGURATIVE* et *APPROXIMATIVE* représentant pour l'année 1858
les ÉMIGRANTS du GLOBE
Les Pays d'où ils partent et ceux où ils arrivent. dressée par M. MINARD
Inspecteur Général des Ponts et Chaussées en retraite, principalement sur les
renseignements publiés dans l'Emigration Européenne de M. A. LEGOYT
et le merchant's magazine de New-York.
Paris, le 26 Septembre 1862.

CANADA

AMÉRIQUE DU
NORD

ÉTATS-UNIS D'AMÉRIQUE

ANGLETERRE

le Hâvre

Bordeaux

Bayonne

Lisbonne

Cuba

la Guadeloupe
la Martinique
la Jamaïque

la Trinité

GUIANNE
ANGLAISE

Equateur

AMÉRIQUE DU
SUD

BRÉSIL

Autog. Régnier et Dourdet, 8, r. S.ᵗᵉ Marie, R. du Bac, Paris.

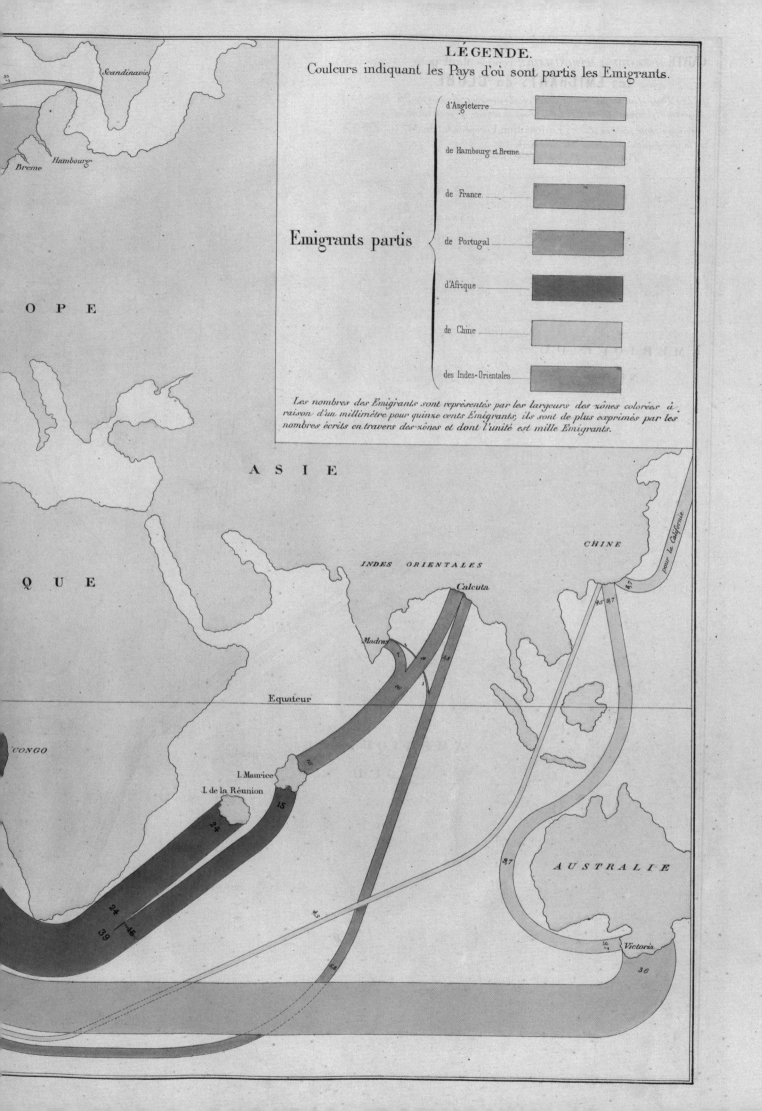

LÉGENDE.

Couleurs indiquant les Pays d'où sont partis les Emigrants.

d'Angleterre

de Hambourg et Breme.

de France.

Emigrants partis { de Portugal

d'Afrique

de Chine

des Indes-Orientales

Les nombres des Emigrants sont représentés par les largeurs des zônes colorées à raison d'un millimètre pour quinze cents Emigrants, ils sont de plus exprimés par les nombres écrits en travers des zônes et dont l'unité est mille Emigrants.

Scandinavie

Breme   Hambourg

OPE

ASIE

QUE

INDES   ORIENTALES

Calcuta

Madras

Equateur

CONGO

I. Maurice

I. de la Réunion

CHINE

pour la Californie

AUSTRALIE

Victoria

38

Migrants of the Globe in 1858

◀ **"Carte figurative et approximative représentant pour l'année 1858 les émigrants du globe"**
September 26, 1862. Lithographic print, hand-colored.
86.4 × 62.0 cm.

This is the first time Minard mapped a social issue, albeit one related to traffic data. The work depicts global migrant flows, colored according to the country of departure (migrants from England are in green, Germany in rose, etc.). Unfortunately, the side note does not explain what motivated Minard to create this work, or the causes or circumstances of the various migration movements. He obviously strived to create a convincing image of global migration patterns. To this end he liberally adapted the base map. For instance, he substantially enlarged the islands of La Réunion and Mauritius in the Indian Ocean, while omitting the much bigger neighboring island of Madagascar altogether. Apparently, there was no data for Madagascar, so he decided to dispense with it. He thus deliberately transformed the world map into a narrative reference frame for his story.

MINARD TRANSLATED

Figurative and approximate map representing emigrants around the world in 1858

The countries from which they left and to which they arrived, based on information published in *European Immigration* by Mr. A. Legoyt and in *New York Merchant's Magazine*.

Colors indicating the countries from which the emigrants left…

The number of emigrants is represented by the widths of the colored zones at a rate of one millimeter for every fifteen hundred emigrants, and also by the numbers written across the zones in units of one thousand emigrants.

41

English Coal Exported in 1860

➤ **"Carte figurative et approximative de la houille anglaise exportée en 1860"**
August 29, 1863. Lithographic print, hand-colored.
105.4 × 68.7 cm.

This work covers global coal exports from England, and updates a map from almost a decade before [14]. Minard would reinitiate the topic again three years later [53]. Notably, the total export rises from 3.5 million tonnes [14] to 7.1 million tonnes (here) to 8.1 million tonnes [53]. Given that Minard kept the original scaling of the flows (one millimeter represents five thousand tonnes), this massive rise poses a major challenge for fitting the flows into the world map. Therefore, Minard made substantial cartographic sacrifices in the outlines of northern Europe and the Mediterranean, where he widened the Strait of Gibraltar and redrew the northern African coastline.

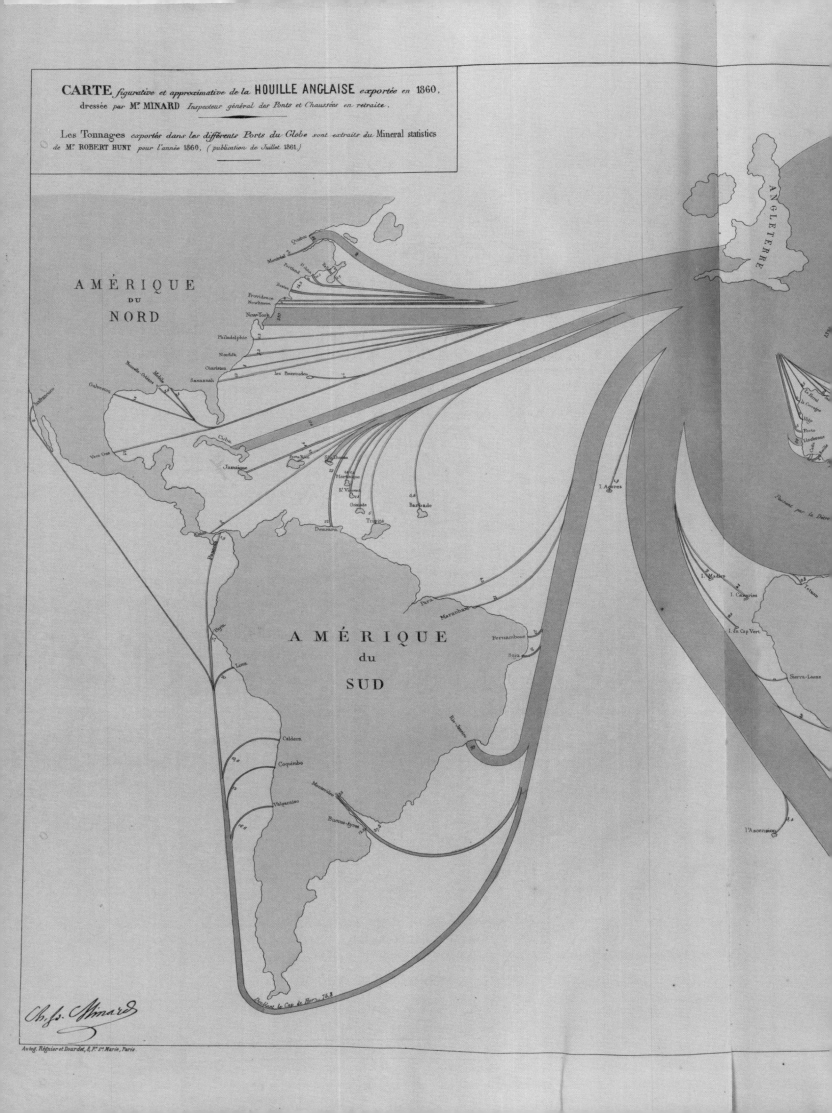

CARTE *figurative et approximative de la* HOUILLE ANGLAISE *exportée en* 1860.
dressée par M. MINARD *Inspecteur général des Ponts et Chaussées en retraite.*

Les Tonnages *exportés dans les différents Ports du Globe sont extraits du Mineral statistics*
de M. ROBERT HUNT *pour l'année 1860, (publication de Juillet 1861.)*

AMÉRIQUE
DU
NORD

AMÉRIQUE
du
SUD

ANGLETERRE

Doublant le Cap de Horn, 75,8

Ch. Js. Minard

Autog. Régnier et Dourdet, 8, R. Ste Marie, Paris.

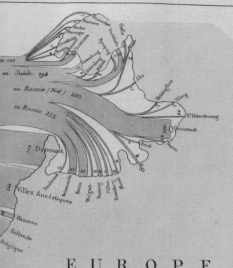

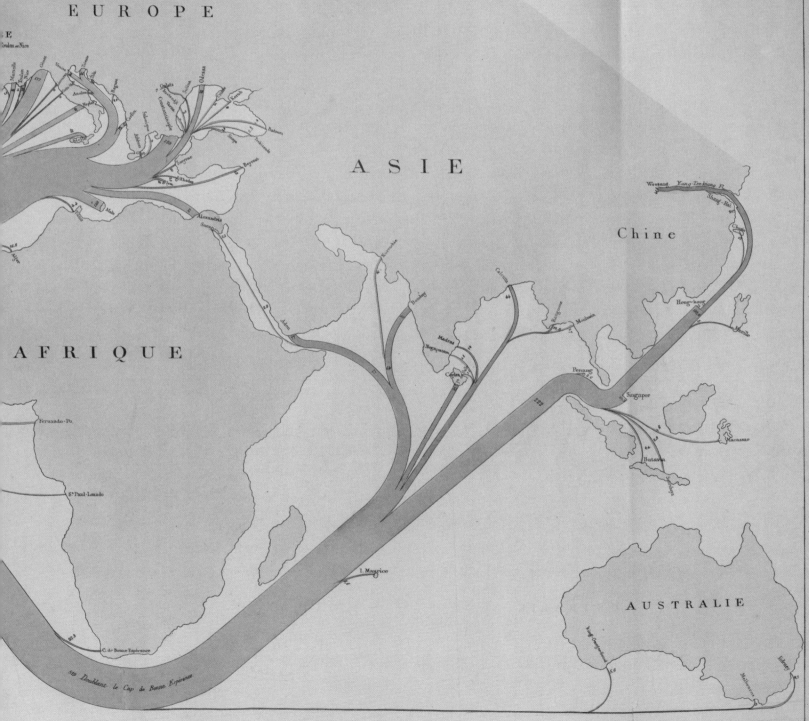

E U R O P E

A S I E

A F R I Q U E

Chine

A U S T R A L I E

Observation.

Les largeurs des Zônes colorées de cette Carte représentent à peu près les quantités de houille exportées à raison d'un millimètre pour vingt mille tonnes. Ces quantités sont de plus exprimées en nombres écrits en travers des Zônes et dont l'unité est mille tonnes.

Les grands totaux, pour chaque contrée ou pour chaque mouvement maritime, sont toujours plus considérables que la somme des tonnages détaillés, parce que sur plus de sept cent lieux d'exportation désignés par M.ʳ Robert Hunt, je ne pouvais faire figurer que les principales exportations au dessus de 500 tonnes.

Dans une carte semblable que j'ai dressée pour l'année 1850, l'exportation totale de la Houille Anglaise était alors de 3,352,000 tonnes, elle s'est élevée en 1860 à 7,100,000 tonnes.

Paris, le 29 Août 1863.

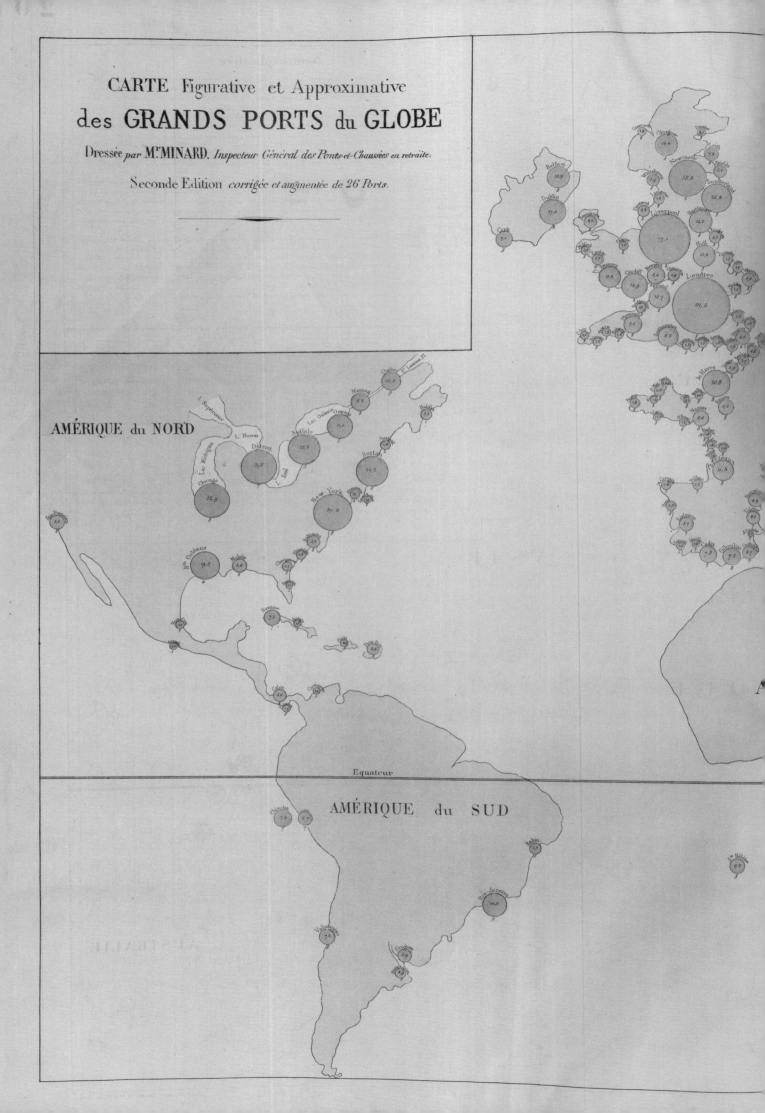

CARTE Figurative et Approximative
des GRANDS PORTS du GLOBE

Dressée par M. MINARD, Inspecteur Général des Ponts-et-Chaussées en retraite.

Seconde Edition *corrigée et augmentée de 26 Ports.*

AMÉRIQUE du NORD

Equateur

AMÉRIQUE du SUD

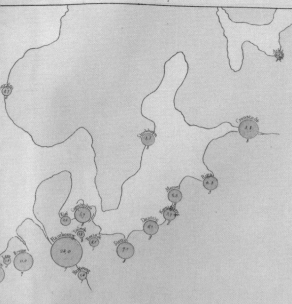

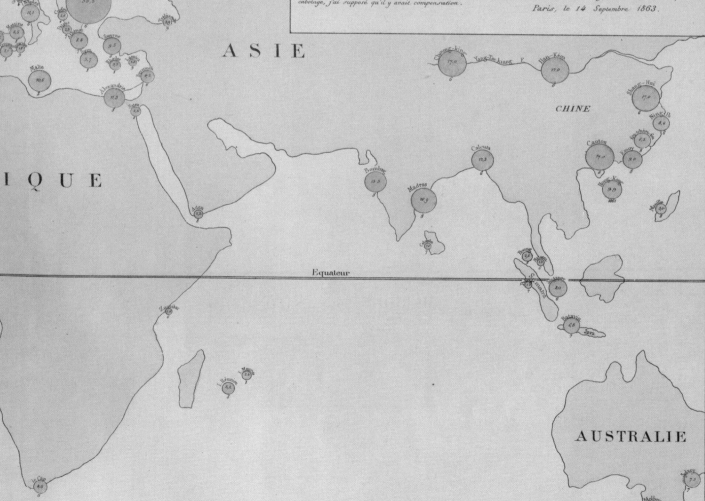

Note explicative.

Les tonnages des ports sont les tonnages de jauge des navires entrés et sortis dans une année. Ils sont représentés par des cercles proportionnels en superficie à ces tonnages, et de plus indiqués au milieu du cercle par des nombres dont l'unité est cent mille tonnes. Un seul chiffre au bas et en dehors du cercle désigne le millésime du tonnage avant 1860. (ainsi 8 veut dire 1858).

On a omis les ports dont le tonnage est au dessous de cent mille tonnes.

Les tonnages d'entrée et de sortie ont été supposés égaux à défaut de renseignements sur l'un d'eux.

Les éléments de ce travail difficiles à recueillir et à ramener à une uniformité comparable ont été puisés dans les états des Douanes Françaises et Anglaises, dans les annales du Commerce extérieur, publication presqu'officielle, dans le dictionnaire du Commerce et de la Navigation, dans les communications officieuses d'Ingénieurs Français et Étrangers et enfin dans les voyages les plus modernes.

Les Ports de Chine ne sont présentés qu'avec beaucoup de réserve. Une difficulté laisse leurs tonnages dans le vague, elle consiste en ce que leur Commerce de cabotage emploie une multitude de jonques dont le port varie depuis 5 à 6 tonnes jusqu'à 600 à 700 tonnes; en outre ce mouvement se rapportant aux consommations journalières d'une population immense, donne lieu à un Commerce de cabotage relativement plus considérable qu'ailleurs, ainsi l'élément dominant du tonnage des Ports Chinois est celui qui présente le plus d'incertitude.

Les Ports du Yang-tsé-Kiang sont figurés par aperçu; leur tonnage est supposé égal à celui de Shang-Hai d'après l'estimation vague de Mr. Blakiston dans son récent voyage sur le grand Fleuve Chinois.

Le tonnage du Port de Constantinople de cette Carte, comme des précédentes, ayant paru suspect à quelques personnes, je crois devoir dire que je l'ai tiré des Annales du Commerce extérieur (année 1857. N° de Décembre) d'où j'extrais ce qui suit : « . . . . à défaut de renseignements officiels, on a recueilli auprès des » « diverses chancelleries les éléments du tableau ci-après . . . . il ne s'agit » « ici que de résultats approximatifs, plutôt au dessous qu'au dessus de la vérité. »

Pavillons	Entrées et sorties.		Pavillons.	Entrées et sorties	
	Navires	Tonneaux		Navires	Tonneaux
Autrichien	3.831	1.303.571	Report	20.302	4.631.943
Grec	6.970	1.071.120	Hollandais	571	88.606
Anglais	4.646	912.819	Prussien	204	41.288
Sarde	1.775	389.574	Ionien	444	30.091
Français	978	277.731	Meklembourg	216	20.285
Napolitain	850	235.595	Russe	109	18.249
Suède et Norwege	874	233.334	Danois	112	14.823
Anséate	266	119.804	Belge	30	5.957
Américain	112	88.400	Espagnol	6	962
			Turc	6.346	705.760
à reporter	20.302	4.631.943	Totaux.	28.340	5.557.969

A la vérité ce total comprend les voyages sur lest (inconnus) mais non la navigation à vapeur ni le petit cabotage, j'ai supposé qu'il y avait compensation.

Paris, le 14 Septembre 1863.

42

Great Ports of the Globe, 1863

◄ "Carte figurative et approximative des
grands ports du globe"
September 14, 1863. Lithographic print, hand-colored.
82.6 × 60.6 cm.

This map is the second edition of Minard's "Great Ports of the Globe," first published two years prior [34]. It is complemented with twenty-six additional harbors, and the side note is expanded to feature an additional data table. This map and its earlier sibling are striking in their minimal aesthetics. The continents are shaded very lightly and sport a broad text label. However, there are barely any other visual features to further describe the territory. Particularly notable here is the empty space in the box in the top left corner. This is not seen in any other map by Minard, which suggests that he deliberately left room here for handwritten additions and notes.

Figurative and approximate map of the major ports of the globe

The tonnages of the ports are the tonnages of the ships entering and exiting in one year. They are represented by circles proportional in area to their tonnage, which is also indicated in the center of the circle in units of one hundred thousand tonnes. A single digit under and outside the circle designates the year of the shipment before 1860 (thus 8 means 1858).

Ports with a tonnage below one hundred thousand tonnes have been omitted.

Where there was no information on tonnages either entering or exiting, they were assumed to be equal.

The information used to prepare this map, which was difficult to collect and bring to a uniform state, was drawn from French and English customs statements, from annals of foreign trade, pseudo-official publications, from the *Dictionary of Commerce and Shipping*, from unofficial communications with French and foreign engineers, and from modern traveling.

Chinese ports were included with great reserve. One difficulty is that their maritime trade involves a multitude of junks, which carry from 5 or 6 tonnes to 600 or 700 tonnes. Moreover, this movement is linked to the daily consumption of an enormous population, leading to a relatively greater trade than elsewhere. Thus, the dominant factor in the tonnage of Chinese ports is the one presenting the most uncertainty.

The tonnage of Yang-tse-Kiang ports is assumed to be equal to Shanghai's based on estimates made by Mr. Blakiston after his recent journey on the great Chinese river.

As the tonnage of the Constantinople port used in this map has seemed implausible to some, I must state that I have drawn it from the *Annals of Foreign Trade* (December 1857), from which I extracted the following: "due to a lack of official information, the numbers in the table below were collected from various chancelleries. These results are only approximate, rather below than above the truth."

44

Tonnage of Livestock Entering Paris by Rail in 1862

➤ "Carte figurative et approximative des poids des bestiaux venus à Paris sur les chemins de fer en 1862"
April 20, 1864. Lithographic print, hand-colored.
60.5 × 48.3 cm.

This is the only flow map in Minard's oeuvre that charts movements from various places toward one center. It depicts the livestock sent from the departments to Paris via the railroads. Each color indicates an animal species. The base map is reduced to a meager coastline in the west and a dashed country border in the east. Compared with earlier flow maps, this one appears rather well organized.

Minard had by now gained experience with the method, which may have prompted him to ascertain what data sets best lent themselves to this type of visualization. He added an inset map for historical comparison. Green departments had already been supplying livestock to Paris in 1828. By 1862, twelve more departments (pink) were able to deliver livestock, thanks to the new railroad connections.

Figurative and approximative map of the weight of livestock sent to Paris via railroad in 1862

The weight of livestock is represented by the widths of the colored zones at a rate of one millimeter for every thousand tonnes, and also by the numbers written across the zones in units of one thousand tonnes or one million kilograms of livestock, all species combined. Species are also distinguished by the colors below:

    Steers and cows [tan]
    Calves [red]
    Hogs [grey]
    Sheep [blue]

Steers and cows were calculated at 300 kilograms per head, calves at 70 kilograms, hogs at 100 kilograms, and sheep at 20 kilograms.

Influence of the railroad on the supply of livestock to Paris

The principal influence of the railroads on the supply of livestock to Paris is on the scope of the market. To understand this influence, I chose two periods:

first, 1862; second, 1828, prior to the railroads, when Biot recorded in the *British Review* the arrival in Paris of 93,000 steers and cows. Having found no information on the provenance of other livestock prior to the railroads, my research was limited to steers and cows, which made up more than half of red meat.

I thus compare the extent of the imported beef market in Paris in 1828 and 1862, which are distinguished by two hues in the smaller map below.

Twelve new departments added to the supply of livestock to the capital in 1862, sending approximately 37,000 steers and cows, included in the 243,000 the railroads brought to Paris that year.

As beef consumption by each of the 750,000 inhabitants of Paris in 1828, with 93,000 steers at 300 kilos each, was 37.1 kilos of beef, and by each of the 1,700,000 inhabitants in 1862, with 243,000 steers, was 42.8 kilos of beef, can the railroads be credited for this increase of one-seventh? It could be due to, first, an increase in the wealth of the population of Paris due in part to the railroads; second, to the consumption of the greater number of wealthy travelers brought to Paris by the railroads.

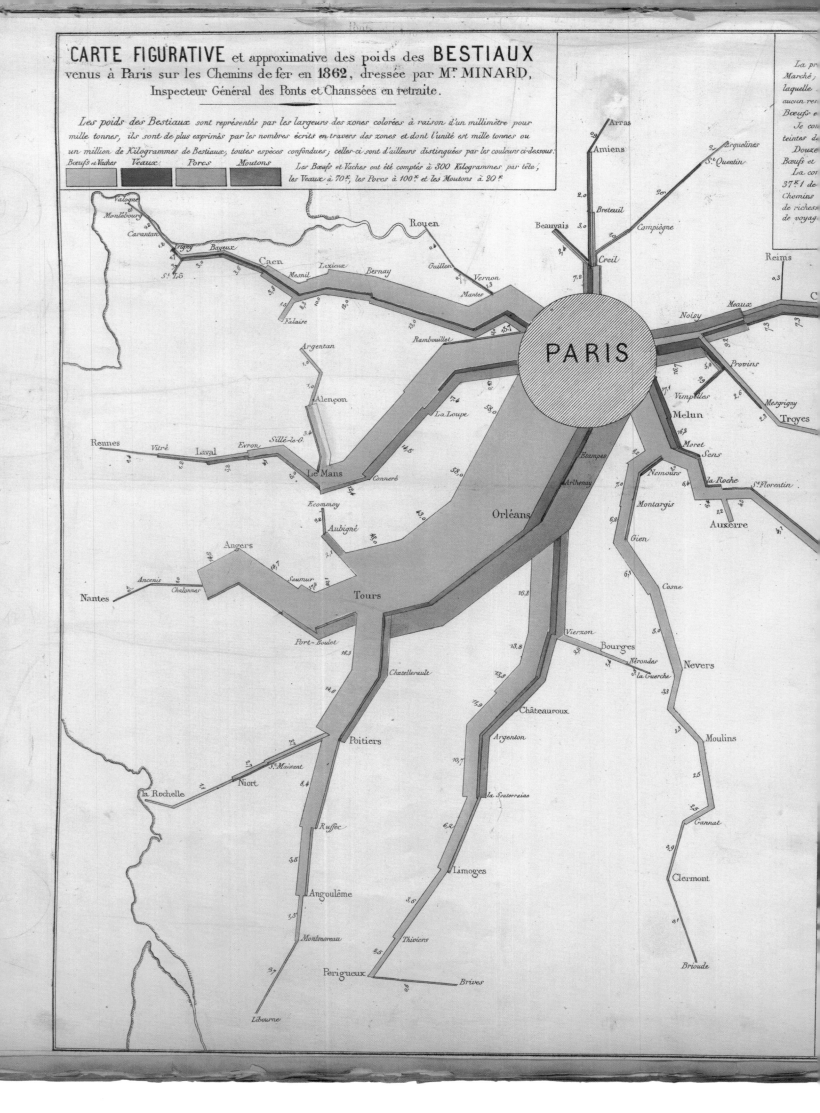

... des Chemins de fer sur l'approvisionnement de Paris en Bestiaux s'est fait sentir sur l'étendue du
... titre j'ai choisi deux époques : 1.° celle de 1862 ; 2.° celle de 1828 antérieure aux voies de fer, pour
... dans la Revue Britannique (t. 18. p. 181) l'arrivée à Paris de 93.000 Bœufs et Vaches. Ne trouvant
... les lieux de provenance d'autres Bestiaux, avant les voies de fer, j'ai dû borner mes recherches aux
... ment plus de la moitié de la viande de boucherie.

... étendue du marché des Bœufs allant à Paris en 1828 et en 1862, elles sont distinguées par deux
... ci-annexée.

... tements ont participé en 1862, à l'approvisionnement de la Capitale ; ils y ont expédié environ 37.000
... dans les 243.000 que les Chemins de fer ont amené à Paris dans la dite année.

... chacun des 750.000 habitants de Paris en 1828 et 93.000 Bœufs (à raison de 300 kilo. l'un) est de
... et pour chacun des 1.700.000 habitants en 1862 et 243.000 Bœufs de 42ᵏ8, faudrait-il attribuer aux
... tation d'un septième ? C'est peu admissible ; mais on peut dire qu'elle est due : 1.° à un accroissement
... Parisienne produit en partie par les Chemins de fer ; 2.° à la nourriture d'un plus grand nombre relatif
... nés à Paris par les Chemins de fer.

Paris, 20 Avril 1864.

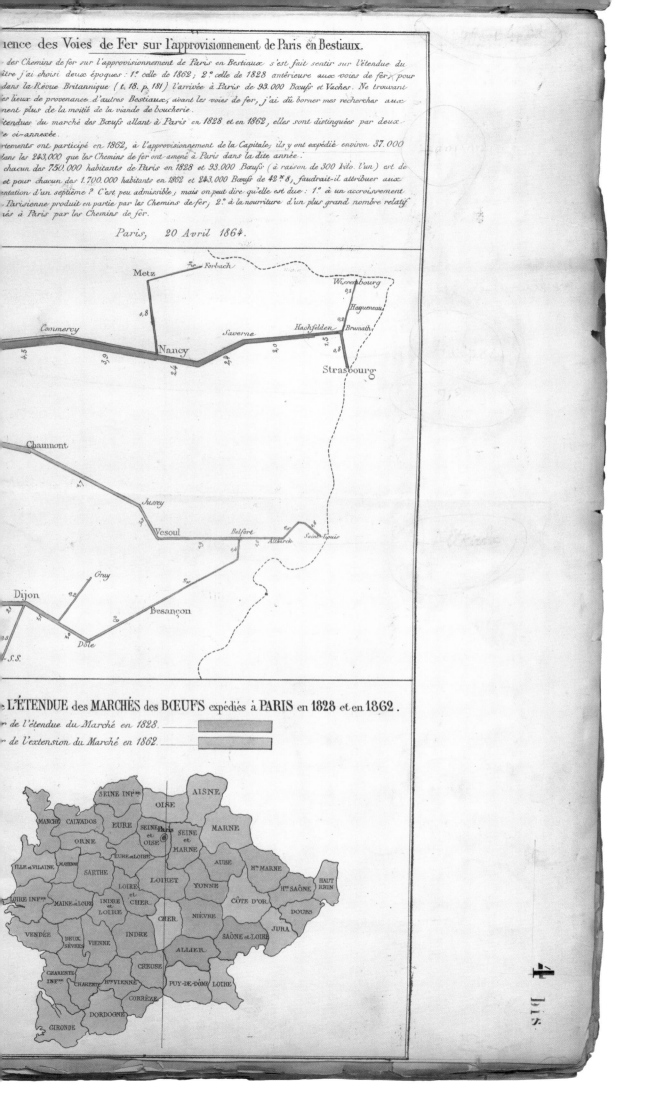

... L'ÉTENDUE des MARCHÉS des BŒUFS expédiés à PARIS en 1828 et en 1862.

... de l'étendue du Marché en 1828.
... de l'extension du Marché en 1862.

Armée *de* Charlemagne _ Campagne *de* 791 *contre les* Huns.

A _ *Armée principale marchant sur la rive droite du Danube.*

B _ *Armée sous les ordres du Comte Teudéric marchant sur la rive gauche.*

C _ *Flottille portant des troupes et les approvisionnements de la Campagne accompagnant les deux armées.*

D _ *Armée d'Italie sous les ordres de Pépin fils de Charlemagne qui, parti des rives du Pô, devait traverser les Alpes et en descendre pour attaquer les Huns en flanc.*

E _ *Remparts en pierres et terres barrant la vallée du Danube, construits par les Huns derrière des affluents du fleuve servant de fossés aux remparts dont le neuvième et dernier était derrière la Theiss et couvrait le camp principal des Huns contenant leur Trésor.*

F _ *Coupe transversale d'un rempart, d'après la description d'Adalbert guerrier de l'expédition de Charlemagne et les récits du moine de Saint - Gall.*

SIMILITUDE des DISPOSITIONS STATI... de CHARLEMAGNE et de NAPOL...

L'un dans sa Campagne en 791 contre les Huns, *l'autre...* en 1805 *contre les* Autrichiens *et les* P...

CARTE *dressée par* Mr MINARD, *Inspecteur Général des Pon...*

Cette similitude signalée par Mr Amédée Thierry (Revue... a cela de remarquable qu'une différence complète dans les armes de... n'en a point apporté dans les dispositions prises par les deux g...

Ainsi le génie militaire de Charlemagne, pour la grande guerre,... siècles celui de Napoléon.

Paris, le 15 Février, 1865...

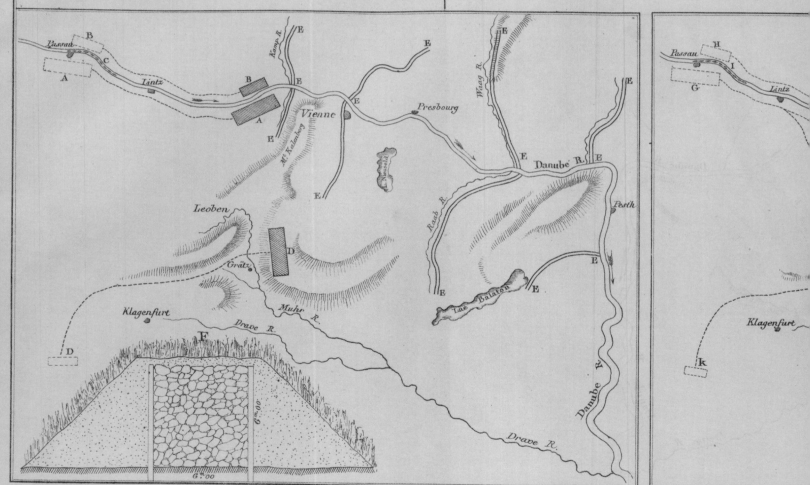

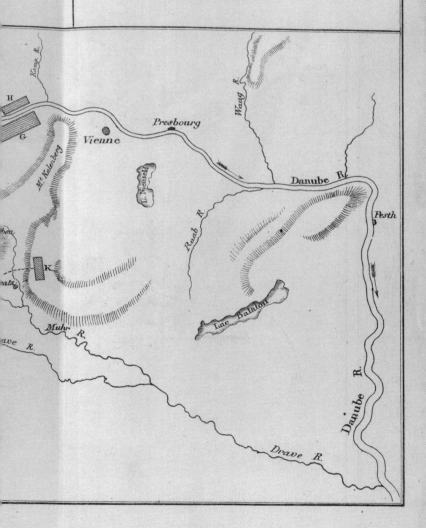

21 bis

Armée *de* Napoléon — Campagne *de* 1805,
contre les Autrichiens *et les* Russes.

G — *Armée principale marchant sur la rive droite du Danube.*

H — *Corps d'armée sous les Ordres du Maréchal Mortier marchant sur la rive gauche.*

I — *Flottille portant des troupes et des munitions de toute espèce accompagnant les deux armées.*

K — *Corps d'armée d'Italie, sous les ordres de Masséna venant des bords de l'Adige arrivant aux Alpes Juliennes.*

L — *Petit corps d'armée détaché de l'armée principale. de Lintz sur Léoben, sous les ordres de Marmont se liant avec Masséna.*

46

Similar Strategies of Charlemagne and Napoléon

◄ "Similitude des dispositions stratégiques de Charlemagne et de Napoléon Ier. L'un dans sa campagne en 791 contre les Huns, l'autre dans sa campagne en 1805 contre les Autrichiens et les Russes"
February 15, 1865. Lithographic print.
53.5 × 40.6 cm.

This uncolored work marks an interesting moment in Minard's oeuvre, as it is the first in which he applied his experience in drawing maps and plans to a historical topic. It juxtaposes two moments of military conflict on the shore of the Danube River. The left-hand map covers a campaign led by Charlemagne, who marched against the Huns in 791 AD. The right-hand map shows Napoléon's armies marching against Russian and Austrian forces in 1805 in the same region. Minard's inspirations for this map came from an article in the *Revue des deux Mondes*, which pointed to the similar strategies of each leader. The work integrates methods of military mapping and technical plans.

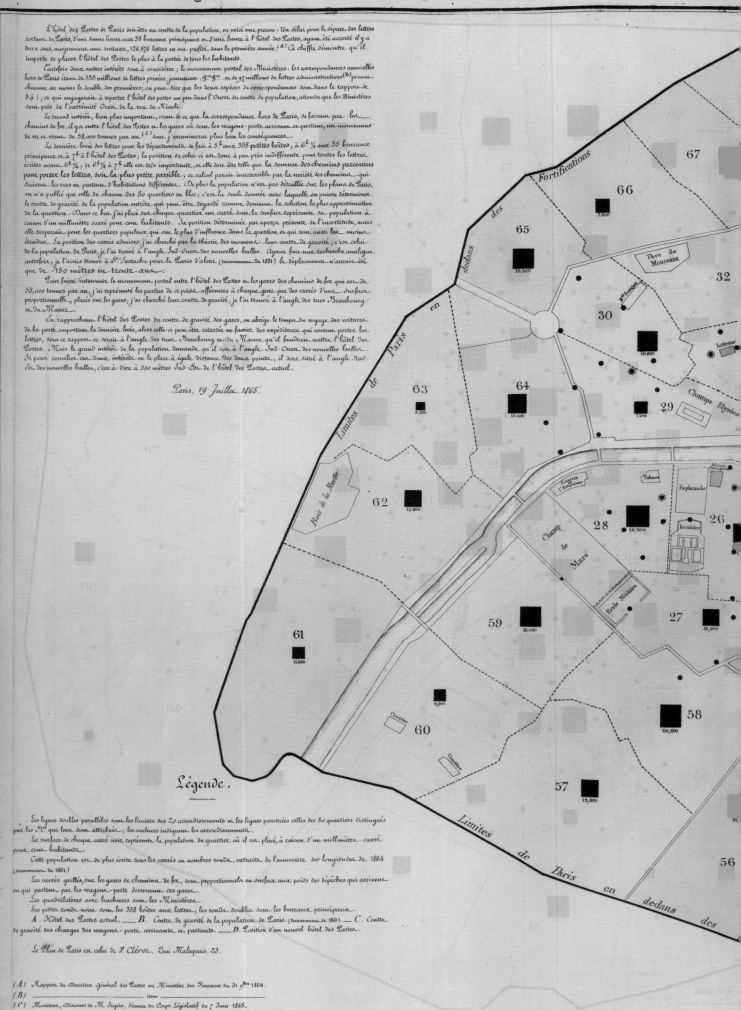

CARTE figurative relative au choix de l'emplacement d'un nouvel HÔTEL des POSTES

Paris, 19 Juillet 1865.

Légende.

Les lignes doubles parallèles sont les limites des 20 arrondissements et les lignes ponctuées celles des 80 quartiers distingués par les Nos. qui leur sont attribués ; les couleurs indiquent les arrondissements.

La surface de chaque carré noir représente la population du quartier où il est placé, à raison d'un millimètre carré pour cent habitants.

Cette population est de plus écrite sous les carrés en nombres ronds, extraite de l'annuaire des longitudes de 1864 (recensement de 1861.)

Les carrés grillés, sur les gares de chemins de fer, sont proportionnels en surface aux poids des dépêches qui arrivent ou qui partent par les wagons-poste desservant ces gares.

Les quadrilatères avec hachures sont les Ministères.

Les petits ronds noirs sont les 358 boîtes aux lettres, les ronds doubles sont les bureaux principaux.

A. Hôtel des Postes actuel. — B. Centre de gravité de la population de Paris. (recensement de 1861.) — C. Centre de gravité des charges des wagons-poste arrivants et partants. — D. Position d'un nouvel hôtel des Postes.

Le Plan de Paris est celui de P. Clérot, Quai Malaquais, 23.

(A) Rapport du Directeur Général des Postes au Ministère des Finances du 31 Xbre 1864.
(B)
(C) Moniteur, Discours de M. Segris, Séance du Corps Législatif du 7 Juin 1865.

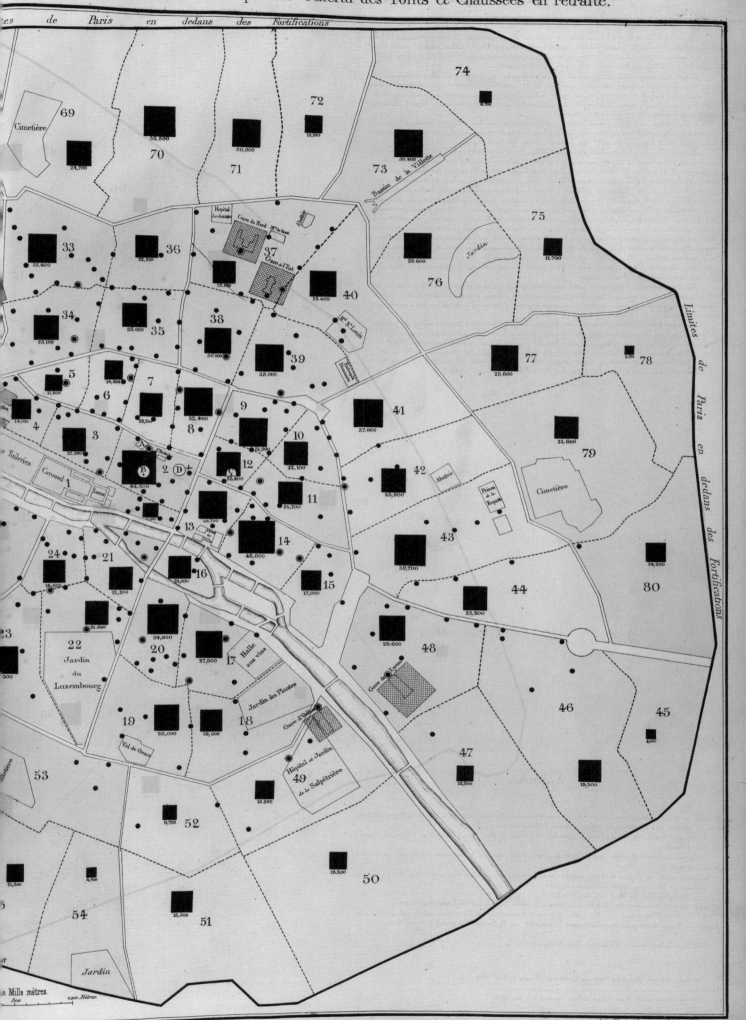

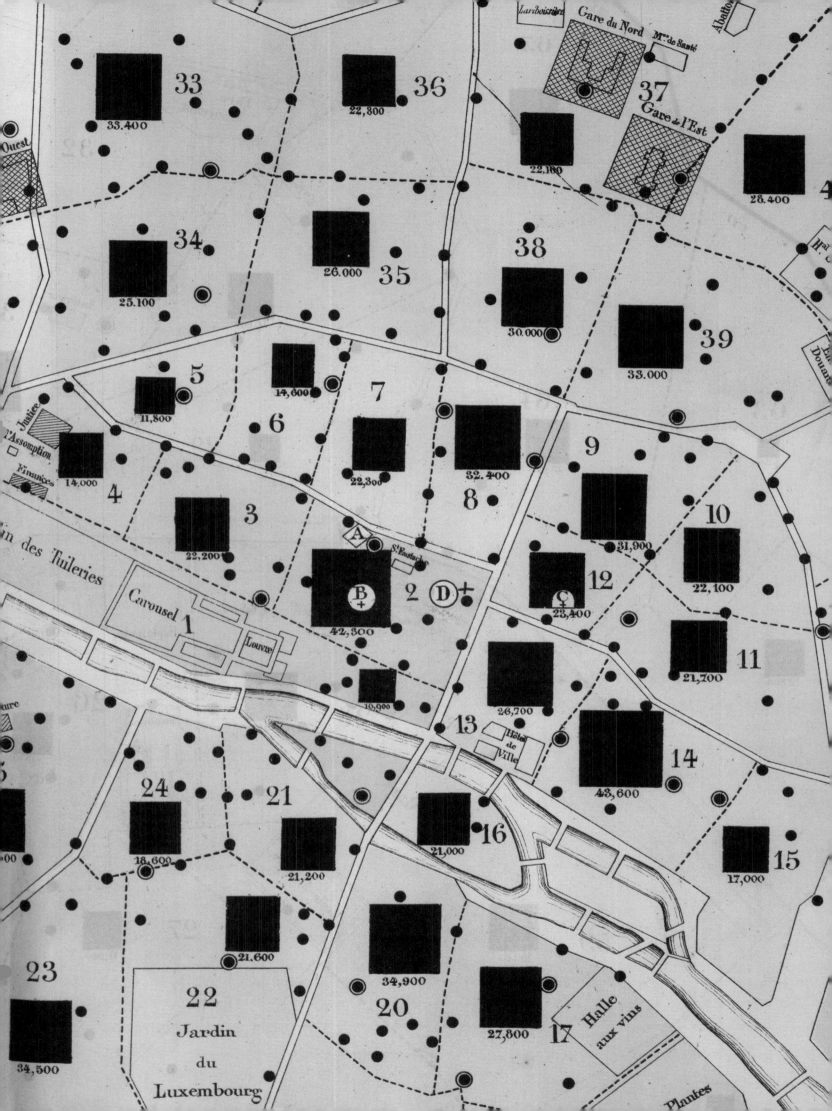

48

Location of a New Main Post Office in Paris

◄ **"Carte figurative relative au choix de l'emplacement d'un nouvel hôtel des postes de Paris"**
July 19, 1865. Lithographic print, hand-colored. 96.5 × 69.6 cm.

In this unusual map, Minard sought to find the ideal location for a new main post office in Paris. Black proportional squares indicate the population of each quartier. Railroad stations are represented with a checked square, scaled according to the amount of overland mail handled per year. He further included ministerial departments (hatched rectangles), standard mailboxes (black dots), and principal post offices (double circles). Minard included several geographical points (such as the current main post office, "A," and the center of all population, "B") that he considered in order to calculate "D"—the position he claimed to be the ideal location for a new main post office. Unfortunately, we do not have an indication as to whether this research study was considered by the municipal administration.

MINARD TRANSLATED

Figurative map to determine the location of a new main post office in Paris

Paris's main post office must be located at the center of its population, and here is one reason: Two years ago, a surtax was introduced for an express departure of letters from Paris—of half an hour from the 35 principal post offices, and of one hour from the main post office. In the first year, 126,576 letters made use of this service. This figure demonstrates the importance of placing the main post office within reach of all the city's inhabitants.

However, two other factors must be considered. First, the postal activities of the ministries: the annual correspondence outside Paris being 535 million private letters, journals, etc, etc., and 97 million administrative letters, each weighing at least double the former, we can say that the two forms of correspondence are at a ratio of 3 to 1, which would suggest siting the main post office a little to the west of the center of the population, given that the ministries are near the west end of the Rue de Rivoli.

The second and much more important consideration arises from the fact that correspondence outside Paris is transported by railroad. Between the main post office and the stations where the mail coaches arrive and depart, 58,000 tonnes of mail come and go per year.

As last collection is made at 5 p.m. at the 358 mailboxes, at 6:15 p.m. at the 35 post offices, and at 7 p.m. at the main post office, the position of the last is unimportant for all letters written before 6:15; from 6:15 to 7 it is very important that the routes traveled to carry the letters be as short as possible. What's more, plans of Paris do not detail its population—that has only been published for its 80 districts as a whole—and this is the only data by which the center of gravity of the population could be determined and the best solution identified. For this purpose, I have placed in each district a square with an area representing its population at a rate of one millimeter square for every hundred inhabitants. The positioning of the squares was determined by approximation, which introduces some uncertainty; however, this uncertainty vanishes in the most populous areas, which have the greatest influence on the question and are the most dense. I then determined, using the theory of moments, their center of gravity, and thus the center of gravity of the Paris population, which I located to the area southwest of the new Les Halles [market]. I did a similar study in the past (using census data from 1831), and traced it to Saint-Eustache back then—which means that it has moved only 150 meters in the thirty years since.

To take into account the postal activity between the main post office and the train stations, which encompasses 58,000 tonnes per year, I have represented the portions of this weight pertaining to each station in squares of proportional area located over the stations. Determining their center of gravity, I found it to be at the corner of Beaubourg and du Maure.

Moving the main post office closer to the center of gravity between the stations would shorten the traveling times for the mail carriages transporting the evening mail, so that the latest collection could be delayed in favor of the senders who rush to bring their letters. In this respect, the location of the main post office should be on the corner of Beaubourg and du Maure. However, the grand interest of the population demands it be sited on the southwest corner of the new Les Halles.

To reconcile these two interests, the main post office is placed equidistant to the two points, situated northeast of the new markets, that is to say 500 meters southwest of the existing main post office.

Legend

The double parallel lines delineate the limits of the 20 arrondissements and the dotted lines those of the 80 quartiers, which are distinguished by the number designated for each; the colors indicate the arrondissement.

The area of each black square represents the population of the quartier in which it is placed at a rate of one millimeter square for every hundred inhabitants.

This population is also written under the squares…

The cross-hatched squares over the railroad stations are proportional in area to the weight of dispatches that arrive at or depart from the station by mail coach.

The hatched quadrilaterals are the ministries.

The small black circles are the 358 mailboxes; the doubled circles are the post offices.

A. Existing main post office
B. Center of gravity of the population of Paris
C. Center of gravity of the loads of mail-coaches arriving and departing
D. Location for a new main post office

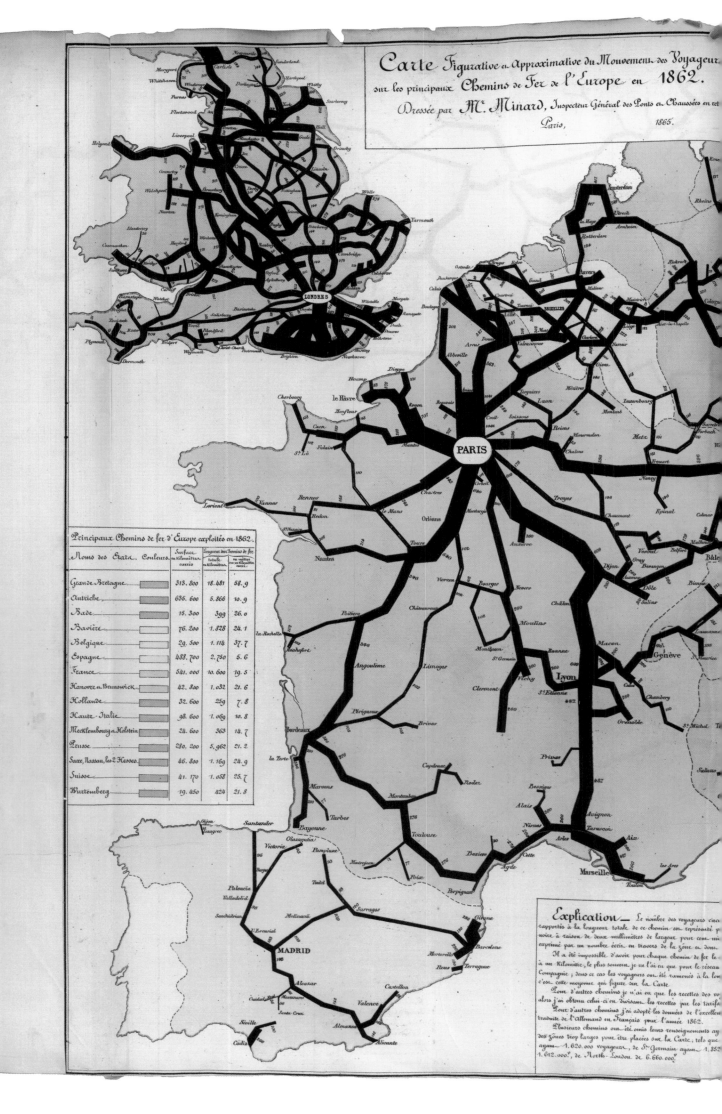

Carte Figurative et Approximative du Mouvement des Voyageurs sur les principaux Chemins de Fer de l'Europe en 1862.

Dressée par Mr. Minard, Inspecteur Général des Ponts et Chaussées en retraite.

Paris, 1865.

Principaux Chemins de fer d'Europe exploités en 1862.

Noms des États.	Couleurs.	Surface en Kilomètres carrés	Longueur des Chemins de fer totale en Kilomètres	en mètres sur un Kilomètre carré.
Grande-Bretagne		313.800	18.481	58.9
Autriche		636.600	5.866	10.9
Bade		15.300	399	26.0
Bavière		76.200	1.828	24.1
Belgique		29.500	1.114	37.7
Espagne		488.700	2.750	5.6
France		541.000	10.600	19.5
Hanovre et Brunswick		42.800	1.032	21.6
Hollande		32.600	259	7.8
Haute-Italie		98.600	1.069	10.8
Mecklembourg et Holstein		24.600	363	14.7
Prusse		280.200	5.962	21.2
Saxe, Nassau, les 2 Hesses		46.800	1.169	24.9
Suisse		41.170	1.058	25.7
Wurtemberg		19.450	424	21.8

Explication — Le nombre des voyageurs circulant rapporté à la longueur totale de ce chemin est représenté par noire à raison de deux millimètres de largeur pour cent mille, exprimé par un nombre écrit en travers de la zone en...

Il a été impossible d'avoir pour chaque chemin de fer le no... à un kilomètre, le plus souvent je ne l'ai eu que pour le réseau... Compagnie ; dans ce cas les voyageurs ont été ramenés à la long... c'est cette moyenne qui figure sur la Carte.

Pour d'autres chemins je n'ai eu que les recettes des vo... alors j'ai obtenu celui-ci en divisant les recettes par les tarifs...

Pour d'autres chemins j'ai adopté les données de l'excellent... traduite de l'allemand en français pour l'année 1862.

Plusieurs chemins ont été omis leurs renseignements a... des zones trop larges pour être placées sur la Carte, tels que... ayant 1.620.000 voyageurs, de St. Germain ayant 1.852... 1.612.000, de North-London de 6.660.000.

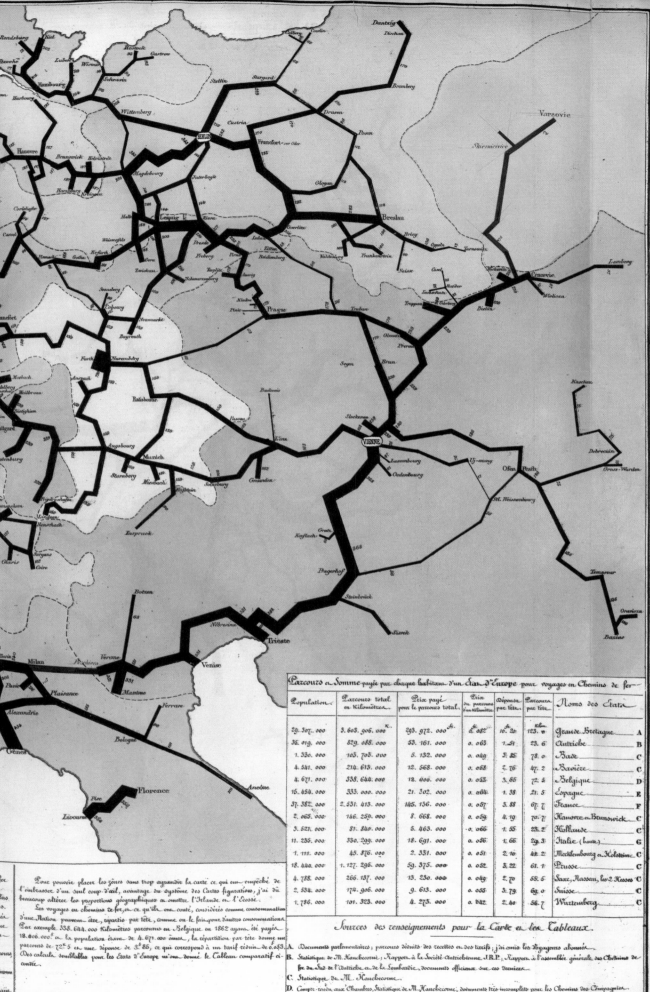

Parcours et Somme payée par chaque habitant d'un État d'Europe pour voyages en Chemins de fer

Population	Parcours total en Kilomètres	Prix payé pour le parcours total	Prix du parcours d'un Kilomètre	Dépense par tête	Parcours par tête	Noms des États	
		fr.	fr.	fr.	Kilom.		
29.307.000	3.603.906.000	293.972.000	0.082	10.20	123.0	Grande-Bretagne	A
35.019.000	829.088.000	53.161.000	0.063	1.51	23.6	Autriche	B
1.330.000	105.703.000	5.132.000	0.048	3.85	78.0	Bade	C
4.541.000	214.613.000	12.568.000	0.058	2.76	47.2	Bavière	C
4.671.000	338.644.000	18.600.000	0.055	3.85	72.5	Belgique	D
15.454.000	333.000.000	21.302.000	0.064	1.38	21.5	Espagne	E
37.382.000	2.531.413.000	145.136.000	0.057	3.88	67.7	France	F
2.065.000	146.259.000	8.668.000	0.059	4.19	70.7	Hanovre et Brunswick	C
3.521.000	81.840.000	5.463.000	-0.066	1.55	23.2	Hollande	C
11.235.000	330.299.000	18.691.000	0.056	1.66	29.3	Italie (haute)	G
1.111.000	45.876.000	2.331.000	0.051	2.10	41.2	Mecklembourg et Holstein	C
18.440.000	1.127.295.000	59.375.000	0.052	3.22	61.1	Prusse	C
4.788.000	266.137.000	13.230.000	0.049	2.70	55.5	Saxe, Nassau, les 2 Hesses	C
2.534.000	174.906.000	9.613.000	0.055	3.79	69.0	Suisse	C
1.786.000	101.323.000	4.275.000	0.042	2.40	56.7	Wurtemberg	C

Pour pouvoir placer les zones sans trop agrandir la carte ce qui eut empêché de l'embrasser d'un seul coup d'œil, avantage du système des Cartes figuratives, j'ai dû beaucoup altérer les proportions géographiques et omettre l'Irlande et l'Écosse.

Les voyages en chemins de fer, en ce qu'ils ont coûté, considérés comme consommation d'une Nation peuvent être, répartis par tête, comme on le fait pour d'autres consommations. Par exemple 338.644.000 Kilomètres parcourus en Belgique en 1862 ayant été payés 18.600.000 fr. et la population étant de 4.671.000 âmes, la répartition par tête donne un parcours de 72.5 et une dépense de 3f.85, ce qui correspond à un tarif réduit de 0.053. Des calculs semblables pour les États d'Europe m'ont donné le Tableau comparatif ci-contre.

Sources des renseignements pour la Carte et les Tableaux.

A. Documents parlementaires; parcours déduits des recettes et des tarifs; j'ai omis les voyageurs abonnés.

B. Statistique de M. Hauchecorne; Rapport à la Société Autrichienne J.R.P.; Rapport à l'assemblée générale des Chemins de fer du Sud de l'Autriche et de la Lombardie, documents officiels sur ces derniers.

C. Statistique de M. Hauchecorne.

D. Compte-rendu aux Chambres, Statistique de M. Hauchecorne; documents très incomplets pour les Chemins des Compagnies.

E. Rapport au Ministre des Travaux publics d'Espagne; ne donnant que les recettes des voyageurs, j'en ai déduit les parcours par les tarifs.

F. Rapports aux assemblées générales des Compagnies d'Orléans, du Nord, de l'Ouest, de l'Est, du Midi et de la Méditerranée, dont les résultats seuls sont compris dans ma Carte et les Tableaux, manquant de documents sur les autres Compagnies.

G. Documents officiels pour les Chemins de l'État.

49

European Railroad Travel in 1862

◀ "Carte figurative et approximative du mouvement des voyageurs
sur les principaux chemins de fer de l'Europe en 1862"
October 2, 1865. Lithographic print, hand-colored. 116.2 × 77.8 cm.

With this work Minard again took up the topic of railroad traffic, which had absorbed him since his earliest visualizations twenty years earlier. The map investigates passenger traffic on major European routes in 1862. The explanation discloses Minard's data sources and reveals how he calculated some missing figures. His aim was to allow the flows to be "embraced at a single glance," prompting him to make several major adaptions, such as dispensing with Scotland and Ireland and omitting some railroad lines whose traffic volume was excessive (such as the North London line). The map introduced a novel aesthetic in that flows are shown in black, while the countries are distinguished by a range of vivid colors.

MINARD TRANSLATED

Figurative and approximative map of the circulation of passengers on the major railroads of Europe in 1862

Explanation: The number of passengers traveling on a railroad in relation to the total length of the route is represented by the width of the black zone at a rate of two millimeters for every one hundred thousand passengers. This number is also written next to the zone in units of one thousand travelers.

It was impossible to determine the number of passengers to a kilometer for each railroad. More often I only had this number for an entire network of a country or company. In these cases, the passengers' travel was scaled to the full length of the network and it is an average that appears on the map...

For other routes I could only obtain the receipts of travelers but not their itineraries/traveled routes, therefore I calculated it by dividing the receipts by the fares.

For other routes I have adopted data from the excellent statistic of Mr. Hauchecorne for the year 1862, which was translated from German to French.

Several railroads were omitted as their information was unavailable. Others had zones too large to be placed on the map, such as the routes from Versailles, with 1,620,000 passengers, from St. Germain, with 1,852,000, from Vincennes, with 1,612,000, and from North London, with 6,600,000.

In order to place the zones without overly enlarging the map, which would have prevented it from being understood at a glance—the main advantage of the figurative map system—I altered the geographical proportions and omitted Ireland and Scotland.

Railroad travel and its costs, considered in terms of national consumption, can be divided per person. For example, for 338,644,000 kilometers traveled in Belgium in 1862 at 18,000,000 francs by a population of 4,671,000, the distance traveled per person is 72.5 kilometers at 3.85 francs. Similar calculations for the European states gave me the values in the table opposite.

Sources consulted for the map and table:
A. Parliamentary documents; routes determined by revenues and rates; pass holders were omitted.
B. Statistics of Mr. Hauchecorne; reports and official documents of the General Assembly of Railroads of Southern Austria and of Lombardy
C. Statistics of Mr. Hauchecorne.
D. Parliamentary minutes, statistics of Mr. Hauchecorne, incomplete records of the railroad companies.
E. Reports of the Spanish Ministry of Public Works; provided only travelers' receipts, I determined the routes by the tariffs.
F. Reports of the general assemblies of the Orleans Railroad Company, the Northern Railroad Company, the Western Railroad Company, the Eastern Railroad Company, the Midi Railroad Company, and the Mediterranean Railroad Company.
G. Unofficial documents of the State Railroad Administration.

50

French Wine Exported in 1864

➤ **"Carte figurative et approximative des quantités de vins français exportés par mer en 1864"**
No date. Lithographic color print. 95.7 × 74.2 cm.

This map is one of just a few works that do not bear a date. However, it must have been created sometime soon after 1864—the year of the data displayed on the map. The map investigates the worldwide overseas export of French wine. Minard wanted to study how the 1860 Anglo-French Treaty of Commerce—designed to reduce trade barriers—had affected the French wine exports.

In the right-hand box, Minard included a time series of the French wine exports (1830–1864), the total wine imports in England (1847–1864), and the French wine imports in England (1857–1864). He admitted, though, that he could not find a significant rise in the British consumption of French wine. He attributed this to the British preference for Spanish and Portuguese wines.

MINARD TRANSLATED

Figurative and approximative map of the quantities of French wine exported by sea in 1864

The widths of the red zones represent the quantity of wine exported at a rate of one millimeter for every ten thousand hectoliters. These quantities are also recorded in the black numbers across the zones in units of one thousand hectoliters.

Not included in the map are 440,000 hectoliters that were exported over land: 304,000 to Switzerland, 95,000 to Belgium, 28,000 to Italy, 11,000 to Germany, etc.

For lack of detail, all exports to a country are combined in a single delivery to one of the principal cities of that country.

Note on the graphic table: As it seemed interesting to me to represent the movement of wines in France and England a few years before and after the free trade treaty of 1860, I created the table below, in which the abscissae give the years and the ordinates the quantities in hectoliters of wine imported or exported that year, based on French and English customs documents and on *Statistical Abstract* numbers 9 and 12.

It is difficult to distinguish the influence of free trade on French wine exports. If importation of French wines into England increases slightly, we see an equal increase in the importation of other wines. When we consult the table, it is clear that the trade in French wines, which is strong worldwide, does not have an impact on the English market proportional to its wealth and to its large population, which prefers Spanish and Portuguese wines.

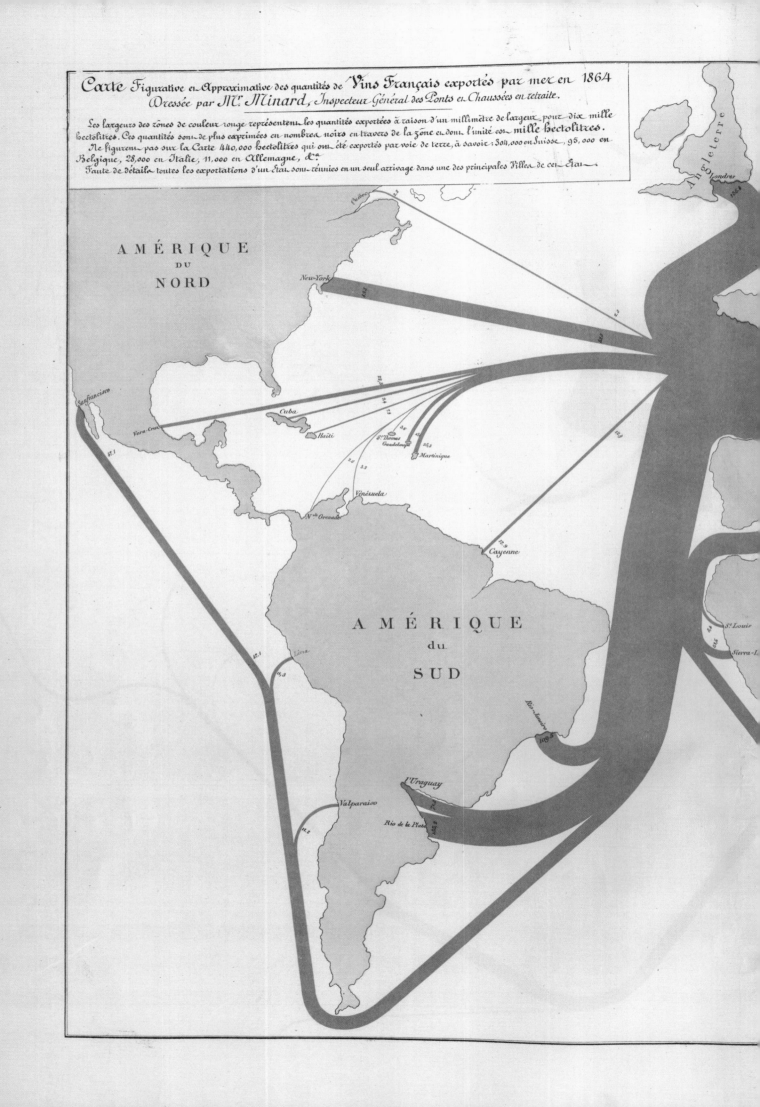

Carte Figurative et Approximative des quantités de *Vins Français exportés par mer en 1864*
Dressée par M. *Minard*, Inspecteur Général des Ponts et Chaussées en retraite.

Les largeurs des zônes de couleur rouge représentent les quantités exportées à raison d'un millimètre de largeur pour dix mille hectolitres. Ces quantités sont de plus exprimées en nombres noirs en travers de la zône et dont l'unité est mille hectolitres.

Ne figurent pas sur la Carte 440,000 hectolitres qui ont été exportés par voie de terre, à savoir : 304,000 en Suisse, 95,000 en Belgique, 28,000 en Italie, 11,000 en Allemagne, &c.

Faute de détails toutes les exportations d'un État sont réunies en un seul arrivage dans une des principales Villes de cet État.

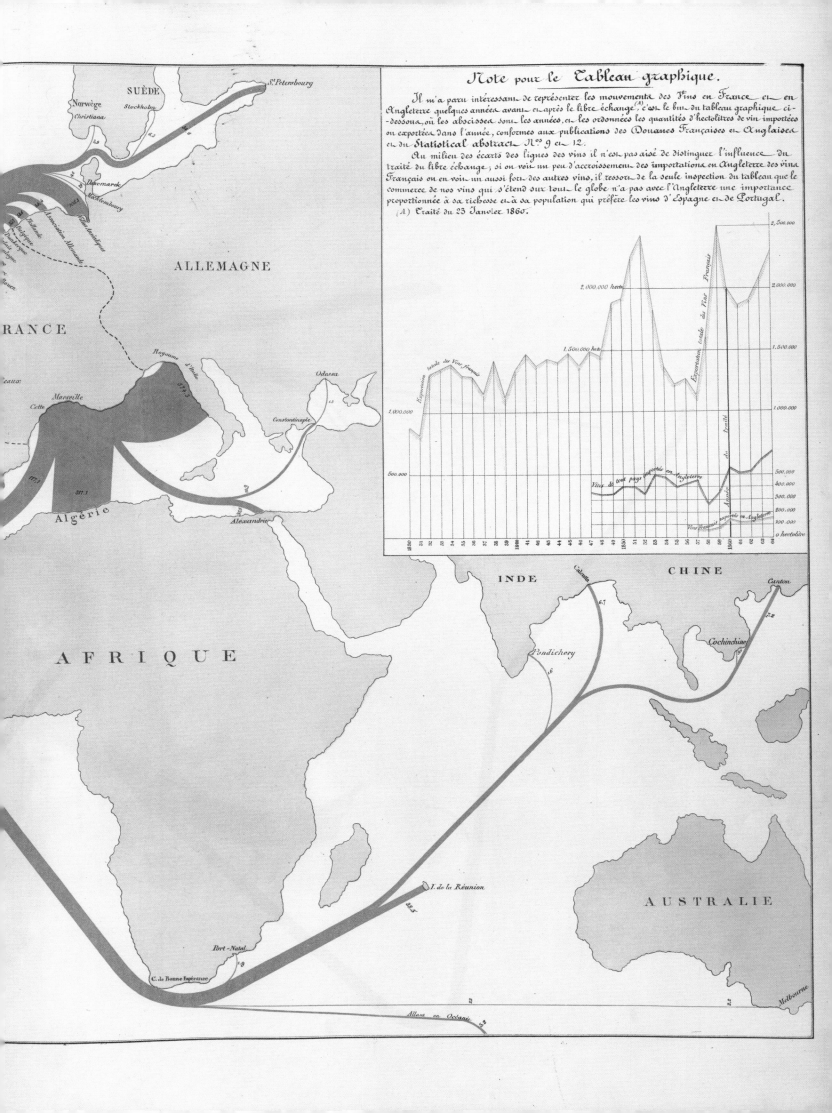

Note pour le Tableau graphique.

Il m'a paru intéressant de représenter les mouvements des Vins en France et en Angleterre quelques années avant et après le libre échange(A), c'est le but du tableau graphique ci-dessous, où les abscisses sont les années, et les ordonnées les quantités d'hectolitres de vin importées ou exportées dans l'année, conformes aux publications des Douanes Françaises et Anglaises et du **Statistical abstract** Nos 9 et 12.

Au milieu des écarts des lignes des vins il n'est pas aisé de distinguer l'influence du traité du libre échange; si on voit un peu d'accroissement des importations en Angleterre des vins Français on en voit un aussi fort des autres vins, il ressort de la seule inspection du tableau que le commerce de nos vins qui s'étend sur tout le globe n'a pas avec l'Angleterre une importance proportionnée à sa richesse et à sa population qui préfère les vins d'Espagne et de Portugal.

(A) Traité du 23 Janvier 1860.

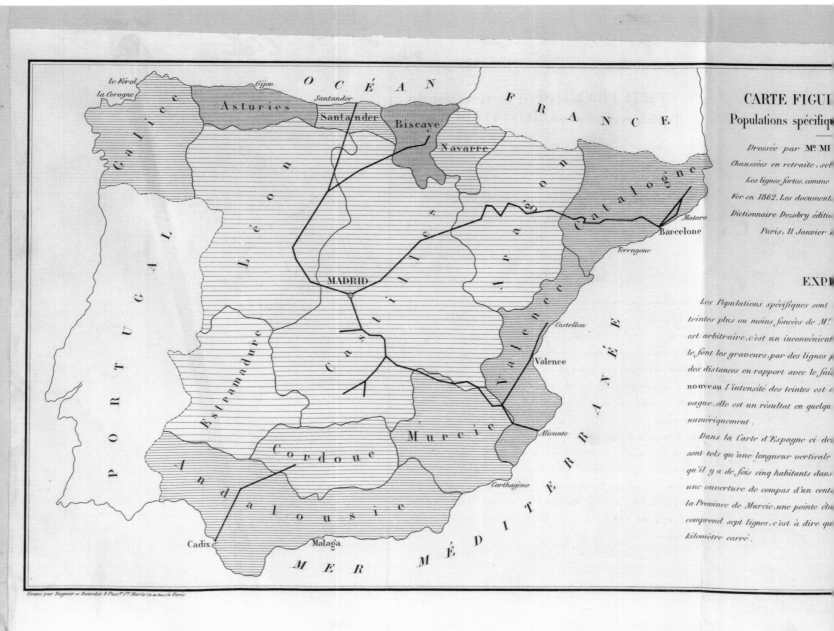

Within the map:

le Ferol
la Corogne
Gijon
Santander
O C É A N
F R A N C E
Galice
Asturies
Santander
Biscaye
Navarre
Catalogne
Mataro
Barcelone
Tervagone
Léon
PORTUGAL
Castille
Estramadure
MADRID
Valence
Castellon
Valence
Andalousie
Cordoue
Murcie
Alicante
Carthagène
Cadix
Malaga
MER MÉDITERRANÉE

Gravé par Regnier et Dourdet 8 Passe Ste Marie (à du bac) à Paris.

Right panel:

CARTE FIGU
Populations spécifiq

Dressée par M². MI

Chaussées en retraite, se

Les lignes fortes, comme

Fer en 1862. Les document.

Dictionnaire Dexobry éditio

Paris, 11 Janvier

EXPI

Les Populations spécifiques sont

teintes plus ou moins foncées de M!

est arbitraire, c'est un inconvénient

le font les graveurs, par des lignes

des distances en rapport avec le fai

nouveau l'intensité des teintes est e

vague, elle est un résultat en quelqu

numériquement .

Dans la Carte d'Espagne ci de

sont tels qu'une longueur verticale

qu'il y a de fois cinq habitants dans

une ouverture de compas d'un cent

la Province de Murcie, une pointe éta

comprend sept lignes, c'est à dire qu

kilomètre carré .

51

Populations of Spanish Provinces

▲ **"Carte figurative et approximative des populations spécifiques des provinces d'Espagne"**
January 11, 1866. Lithographic print. 53.6 × 33.3 cm. Published in: *Appendice à la Carte des voyageurs sur les chemins de fer d'Europe en 1862 suivi de considérations sur les chemins de fer* (Paris, 1867)

This map is unusual in its focus on graphical methods for choropleth maps. The explication refers to the system of shading areas according to statistical values, first used in 1827 by Charles Dupin, and asserts that the range of shades commonly used is arbitrary and flawed. He suggested a system of graduated hachures be used instead. The map shows population density in the provinces of Spain. The number of horizontal lines in the shading —within a height of one centimeter on the original map—has to be multiplied by five to deliver the population density per square kilometer. In constructing the shades mathematically, Minard hoped to elicit a more intuitive and precise perception of the values.

approximative des
VINCES D'ESPAGNE

ur général des Ponts et
le représentation graphique
Madrid, sont les Chemins de
opographiques sont tirés du
Atlas de Maltebrun.

le système ingénieux des
n. Mais ce plus ou moins
rmant les teintes, comme
stantes et je leur donne
résenter. Par ce procédé
hiquement. Elle n'est plus
ue qu'on peut apprécier

lles des lignes horizontales
e contient autant de lignes
arré. Exemple: En plaçant
culairement aux lignes de
u d'un intervalle, l'ouverture
atient 7×5=35 habitants par

Lith. Gratia

53
English Coal Exported in 1864

➤ "Carte figurative et approximative de la houille
anglaise exportée en 1864"
September 17, 1866. Lithographic print, hand-colored.
101.4 × 66.4 cm. Published in: *La houille et l'exportation
de la houille anglaise* (Paris, 1866)

This map updates two earlier maps about English coal exports [14] and [41]. Given the cartographic challenges apparent in map [41], it is notable that Minard would stick to the same scaling of flows—apparently, to make the maps in the series directly comparable. However, the English coal exports had risen further, which exacerbated the problem of placing the flows on the map.

An additional diagram provides the context of the total English coal production and consumption. It shows a time line running from 1850 through 1864, and a stacked graph charting consumption types. These are (from the bottom): export, district of London, production of cast iron, production of iron, private homes, gas lighting, steam navigation and railroads, other uses. The top graph shows the total English coal production. For the first four years it is drawn as a dashed line, indicating that Minard did not have reliable data.

MINARD TRANSLATED

Figurative and approximate map of English coal exported in 1864

The tonnages exported from the major international ports were extracted from the 1864 *Mineral Statistics* by Mr. Robert Hunt (pages 101–15)

Observation: The widths of the colored zones represent the approximate quantities of coal exported at a rate of one millimeter per twenty thousand tonnes. These quantities are also written across the zones in units of a thousand tonnes.

The grand total for each region or shipping route is greater than the sum of the tonnages detailed, since only principal exports were listed by Mr. Hunt for more than 600 points of export.

In a similar map I drew for 1860, total English coal exports were 7,100,000 tonnes, rising to 8,100,000 by 1864.

Approximate coal consumption in Great Britain from 1850 to 1864

The abscissae give the years and the ordinates the quantity of coal consumed.

The colors indicate the type of consumption. The quantities of coal consumed are represented by the length of the ordinates of each color at a rate of two millimeters per million tonnes.

Information used to prepare the table opposite:

Consumption	Sources
Exports	*Mineral Statistics*, 1865, page 214, and Parliamentary Information
London	*ibid.* page 213
Cast iron	*ibid.* page 215, and for the years prior to 1855, calculated at a rate of 3 tonnes of coal for every tonne of cast iron.
Iron production	*Mineral Statistics*, page 215, and for the years prior to 1855 calculated at a rate of 3 tonnes of coal per tonne of cast iron converted to iron.
Domestic	Including small factories. In 1848 it was estimated at 19 million tonnes, (A) which could be reduced to 18 million tonnes if considering only domestic consumption, but could be raised to 20 million considering the population in 1864.
Gas lighting	Consumption estimated at around 1/9 to 1/8 of the total production.
Railroad	Assuming total consumption of 10,000 [tonnes] per kilometer traveled, according to government data.
Steamship	Calculated at a rate of 5,000 [tonnes] of coal per horsepower and per hour, the number of horses cited in *Steam Vessels* from 1864, and assuming the steamers run half the year. For years prior to 1864, I calculated consumption proportional to the annual tonnages consumed by steamers according to the statistical abstract and to the Board of Trade.

See the excellent article on coal by Mr. Lamé Fleury published in *Dictionary of Commerce*, page 111.

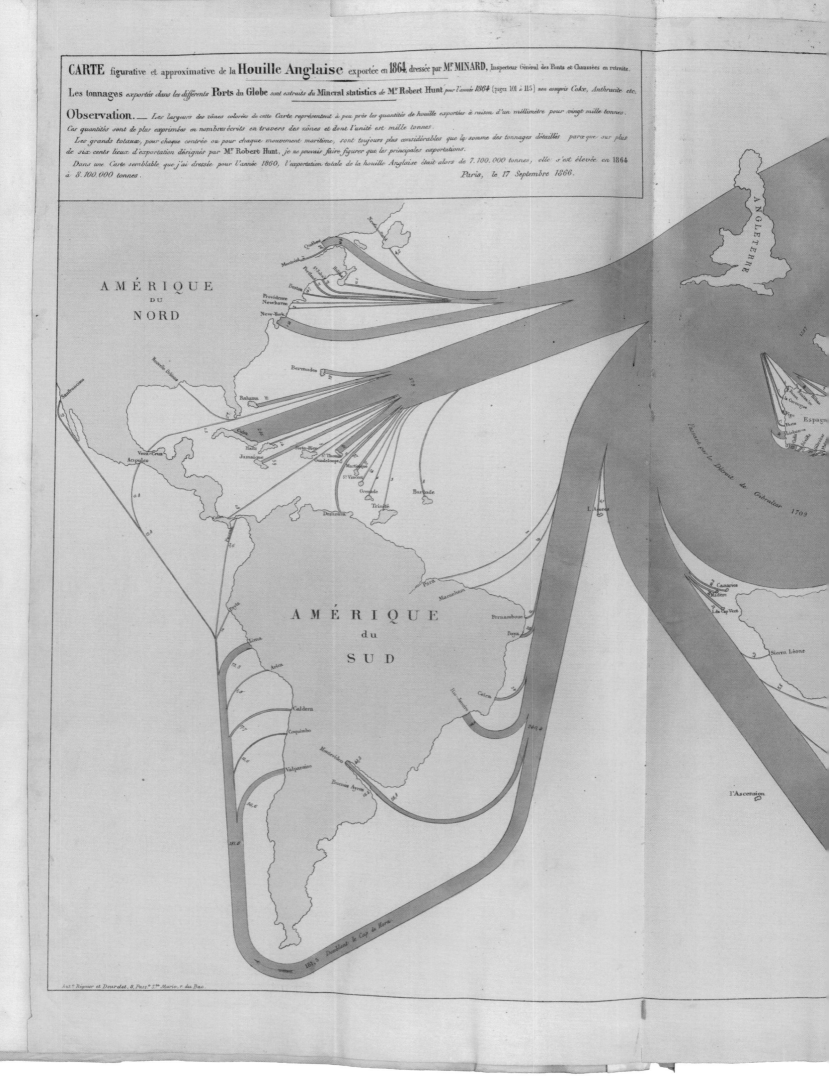

CARTE figurative et approximative de la **Houille Anglaise** exportée en **1864**, dressée par M.ʳ MINARD, Inspecteur Général des Ponts et Chaussées en retraite.

Les tonnages exportés dans les différents **Ports** du Globe sont extraits du Mineral statistics de M.ʳ Robert Hunt pour l'année 1864 (pages 101 à 115) non compris Coke, Anthracite etc.

Observation. — Les largeurs des zônes colorées de cette Carte représentent à peu près les quantités de houille exportées à raison d'un millimètre pour vingt mille tonnes. Ces quantités sont de plus exprimées en nombres écrits en travers des zônes et dont l'unité est mille tonnes.

Les grands totaux, pour chaque contrée ou pour chaque mouvement maritime, sont toujours plus considérables que la somme des tonnages détaillés parce que sur plus de six cents lieux d'exportation désignés par M.ʳ Robert Hunt, je ne pouvais faire figurer que les principales exportations.

Dans une Carte semblable que j'ai dressée pour l'année 1860, l'exportation totale de la houille Anglaise était alors de 7.100.000 tonnes, elle s'est élevée en 1864 à 8.100.000 tonnes.

Paris, le 17 Septembre 1866.

AMÉRIQUE DU NORD

AMÉRIQUE du SUD

ANGLETERRE

Espagne

l'Ascension

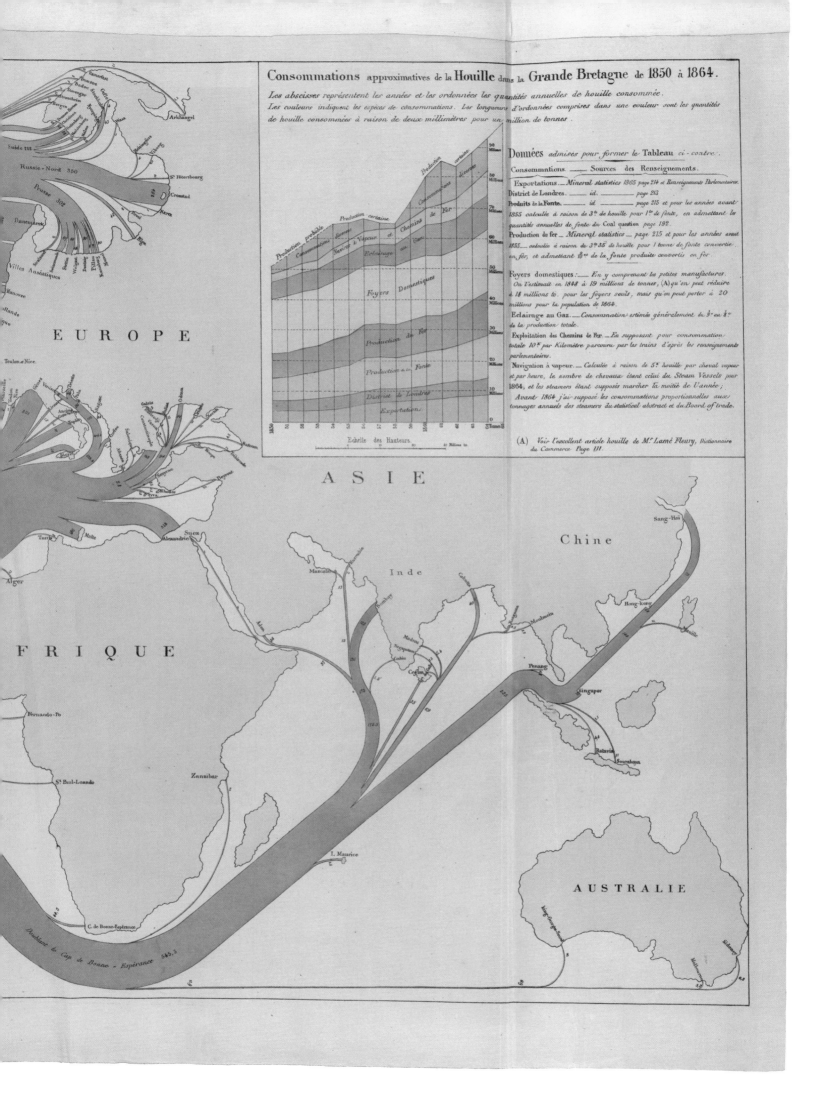

Consommations approximatives de la Houille dans la Grande Bretagne de 1850 à 1864.

Les abscisses représentent les années et les ordonnées les quantités annuelles de houille consommée.
Les couleurs indiquent les espèces de consommations. Les longueurs d'ordonnées comprises dans une couleur sont les quantités
de houille consommées à raison de deux millimètres pour un million de tonnes.

Données admises pour former le Tableau ci-contre.

Consommations. — Sources des Renseignements.

Exportations. — *Mineral statistics 1865 page 214 et Renseignements Parlementaires.*
District de Londres. — *id.* — *page 213*
Produits de la Fonte. — *id.* — *page 215 et pour les années avant*
1855 calculée à raison de 3ᵗ de houille pour 1ᵗ de fonte, en admettant les
quantités annuelles de fonte du Coal question page 192.
Production du fer — *Mineral statistics* — *page 215 et pour les années avant*
1855 — calculée à raison de 3ᵗ 35 de houille pour 1 tonne de fonte convertie
en fer, et admettant ⅚ᵗ de la fonte produite convertie en fer.

Foyers domestiques : — *En y comprenant les petites manufactures.*
On l'estimait en 1848 à 19 millions de tonnes, (A) qu'on peut réduire
à 18 millions to. pour les foyers seuls, mais qu'on peut porter à 20
millions pour la population de 1864.
Éclairage au Gaz. — *Consommation estimée généralement du ¾ au ⅘*
de la production totale.
Exploitation des Chemins de Fer. — *En supposant pour consommation*
totale 10ᵏ par Kilomètre parcouru par les trains d'après les renseignements
parlementaires.
Navigation à vapeur. — *Calculée à raison de 5ᵏ houille par cheval vapeur*
et par heure, le nombre de chevaux étant celui du Steam Vessels pour
1864, et les steamers étant supposés marcher la moitié de l'année ;
Avant 1864 j'ai supposé les consommations proportionnelles aux
tonnages annuels des steamers du statistical abstract et du Board of trade.

(A) *Voir l'excellent article houille de Mr. Lamé Fleury, Dictionnaire*
du Commerce. Page 111.

Échelle des Hauteurs.

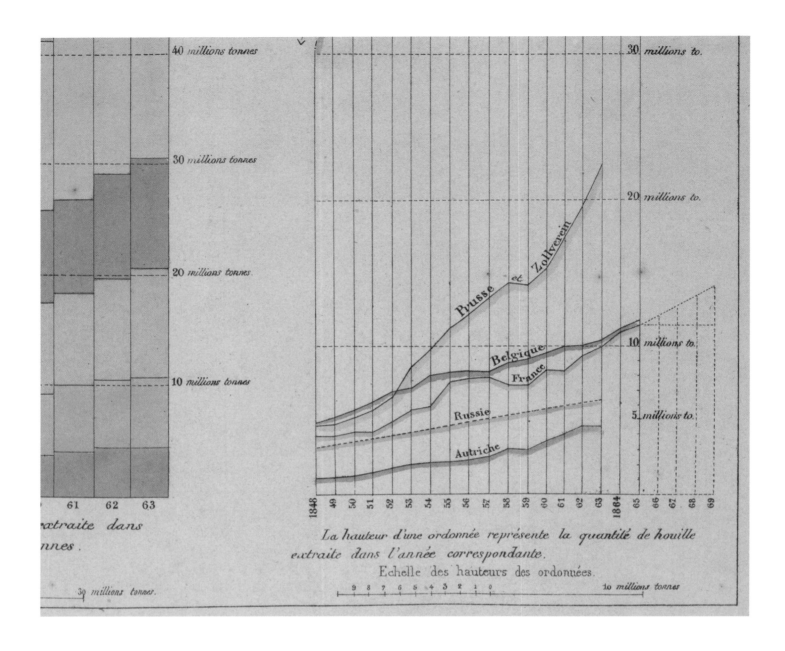

40 *millions tonnes*

30 *millions tonnes*

20 *millions tonnes.*

10 *millions tonnes*

30 *millions to.*

20 *millions to.*

Prusse et Zollverein

Belgique

France

10 *millions to.*

Russie

5 *millions to.*

Autriche

61   62   63

xtraite dans

nnes.

30 *millions tonnes.*

1848 49 50 51 52 53 54 55 56 57 58 59 60 61 62 63 1864 65 66 67 68 69

La hauteur d'une ordonnée représente la quantité de houille
extraite dans l'année correspondante.

Echelle des hauteurs des ordonnées.

9 8 7 6 5 4 3 2 1 0   10 *millions tonnes*

54

Coal Production in Europe from 1848 to 1863

➤ **"Tableaux graphiques de la production de la houille en Europe de 1848 à 1863 (y compris anthracite et lignite)"**
September 17, 1866. Lithographic print, hand-colored. 46.4 × 68.4 cm.
Published in: *La houille et l'exportation de la houille anglaise* (Paris, 1866)

Coal production was a pressing issue for all countries at the time, as consumption increased and importing countries became vulnerable to unforeseen shortages. The bar chart shows the coal production volumes in several European countries 1848–1863, emphasizing the overwhelming share of English coal. The line chart presents the same data with a different focus: countries can be compared in their development. For instance, a massive increase in Prussia (yellow) is apparent here. The Russian graph (rose) is hatched, which may indicate that Minard could not obtain reliable data. Note that Minard included a forecast for France; according to his calculations he projected the gray graph to 1869.

Tableaux Graphiques de la Production de la Houille en EUROPE de 1848 à 1863 (y compris Anthracite et lignite)

Dressés par M. MINARD, Inspecteur Général des Ponts et Chaussées en retraite — Paris, 17 Septembre 1866.

ÉTATS.

Sources des Renseignements ayant servi à dresser les tableaux.

Grande Bretagne.......... *Mineral statistics — 1865 — page 214, Coal question page 208, Dictionnaire du Commerce page 111.*
Prusse et Zollverein...... *Die Stein Kohlen — Munich 1865 pages 40, 98, 99 et 154.*
Belgique................. *Publications de la Chambre de Commerce de Mons.*
France.................. *Administration générale des Mines.*
Russie................. *Mineral statistics — 1865 — page 229.*
Autriche.............. *Die stein Kohlen pages 118 et 154.*

*L'Espagne, l'Italie, la Suisse et la Suède n'ayant produit ensemble en 1862
que 600.000 to. (Die Stein Kohlen page 154) j'ai négligé la production de ces
États dans les tableaux.*

Chaque État est distingué par une couleur.

Tableau Nº 1.

140 millions tonnes
130 millions tonnes
120 millions tonnes
110 millions tonnes
100 millions tonnes
90 millions tonnes
80 millions tonnes
70 millions tonnes
60 millions tonnes
50 millions tonnes
40 millions tonnes
30 millions tonnes
20 millions tonnes
10 millions tonnes

Grande Bretagne

Prusse et Zollverein

Belgique

France

Russie

Autriche

1848 49 50 51 52 53 54 55 56 57 58 59 60 61 62 63

*La hauteur de chaque rectangle coloré représente la quantité de houille extraite dans
l'année correspondante à raison de trois millimètres pour un million de tonnes.*

Echelle des hauteurs des rectangles

10   20   30 millions tonnes

Tableau Nº 2.

90 millions to.
80 millions to.
70 millions to.
60 millions to.
50 millions to.
40 millions to.
30 millions to.
20 millions to.
10 millions to.
5 millions to.

Angleterre

Production probable

Prusse et Zollverein

Belgique
France
Russie
Autriche

1848 49 50 51 52 53 54 55 56 57 58 59 60 61 62 63 64 65 66 67 68 69

*La hauteur d'une ordonnée représente la quantité de houille
extraite dans l'année correspondante.*

Echelle des hauteurs des ordonnées

10 millions tonnes

Imp. Régnier et Dourdet, 8 P.te S.te Marie (v du Bac)

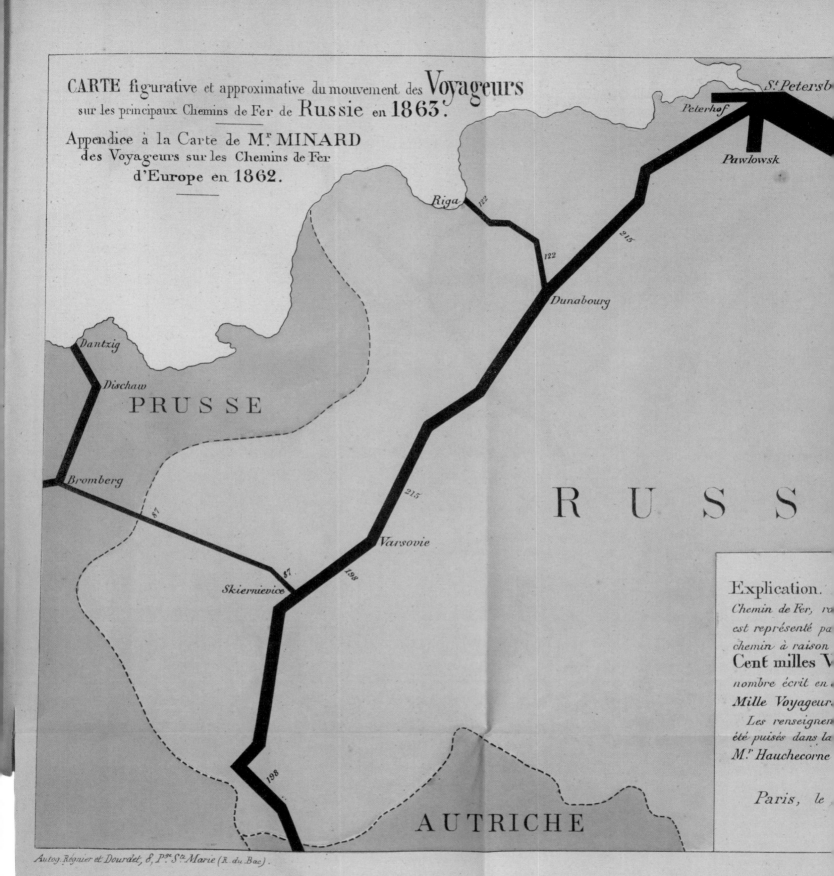

CARTE figurative et approximative du mouvement des **Voyageurs** sur les principaux Chemins de Fer de **Russie** en **1863**.

Appendice à la Carte de M.ʳ **MINARD** des Voyageurs sur les Chemins de Fer d'Europe en 1862.

PRUSSE

RUSS

AUTRICHE

St. Petersb

Peterhof

Pawlowsk

Riga

Dunabourg

Dantzig

Dischaw

Bromberg

Varsovie

Skierniewice

122

122

215

215

198

87

87

198

198

Explication.

Chemin de Fer, ra

est représenté pa

chemin à raison

Cent milles V

nombre écrit en

Mille Voyageurs

Les renseignem

été puisés dans la

M.ʳ Hauchecorne

Paris, le

Autog. Régnier et Dourdet, 8, P.ᵗᵉ S.ᵗᵉ Marie (R. du Bac).

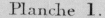

Planche 1.

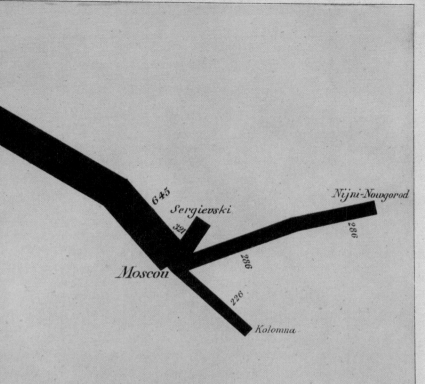

645
Sergievski
Nijni-Nowgorod
321
286
Moscou
286
226
Kolomna

E

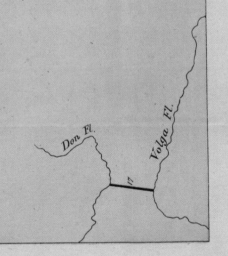

des Voyageurs circulant sur un
longueur totale de ce chemin,
r de la Zône noire indiquant le
illimètres de largeur pour
il est de plus exprimé par un
a Zône et dont l'unité est

e mouvement des Voyageurs ont
e sur les Chemins de Fer de
(Edition en Français)

1867.

Don Fl.
Volga Fl.

55

Russian Railroad Travel in 1863

◄ "Carte figurative et approximative du mouvement des voyageurs sur les principaux chemins de fer de Russie en 1863"
February 1, 1867. Lithographic print, hand-colored. 49.2 × 39.3 cm. Published in: *Appendice à la Carte des voyageurs sur les chemins de fer d'Europe en 1862 suivi de considérations sur les chemins de fer* (1867)

This map is an eastward extension of Minard's earlier work on European railway traffic [49]. He returned to this topic because data on Russia had become available in the meantime. Rather than re-draw the earlier map—it had been complicated to fit the flows into the territory of Europe—he opted for drawing an extension, keeping the coloring and scaling consistent. In the appertaining pamphlet, Minard stated that he had wanted to create a survey of European railway passenger transport for a long time and that obtaining reliable, up-to-date, and comparable data had been a laborious process. He added some observations on some national networks, on how the railroads influenced modern warfare, and on the inexplicable "fatal Friday": on Fridays, passenger numbers slumped regularly all across Europe.

MINARD TRANSLATED

Figurative and approximative map of the circulation of passengers on the major railroads of Russia in 1863

Appendix to the map by Mr. Minard representing passengers on the major railroads of Europe in 1862.

Explanation: The number of passengers traveling on a railroad, in relation to the total length of the railroad, is represented by the widths of the black zones at a rate of two millimeters for every hundred thousand passengers. This number is also written across the zones in units of a thousand passengers.

The information about the circulation of travelers was drawn from the Railroad Statistic by Mr. Hauchecorne for the year 1863 (French Edition).

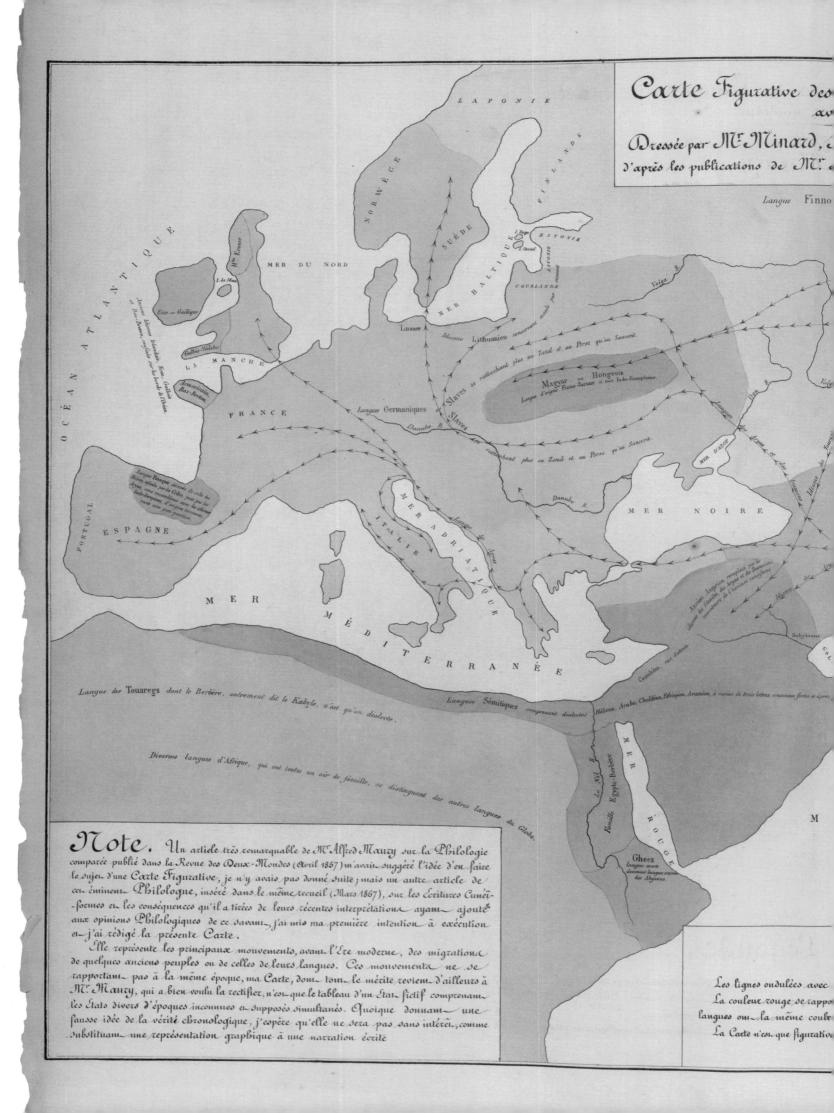

Carte Figurative des ...
av...
Dressée par Mr Minard, ...
d'après les publications de Mr ...

Langue Finno...

LAPONIE
NORVÈGE
SUÈDE
FINLANDE
ESTONIE
LIVONIE
COURLANDE
MER DU NORD
MER BALTIQUE
OCÉAN ATLANTIQUE
LA MANCHE
FRANCE
PORTUGAL
ESPAGNE
ITALIE
MER ADRIATIQUE
MER MÉDITERRANÉE
MER NOIRE
MER D'AZOF
MER ROUGE

Volga R.
Don R.
Danube R.
Danube R.

Lusace

Idiome Lithuanien conservant moule par excusant

Slaves se rattachant plus au Zend et au Perse qu'au Sanscrit.

Slaves se rattachant plus au Zend et au Perse qu'au Sanscrit.

Langues Germaniques

Slaves

Magyar ou Hongrois
Langue d'origine Finno-Tartare et non Indo-Européenne.

Langue des Touaregs dont le Berbère, autrement dit le Kabyle, n'est qu'un dialecte.

Langues Sémitiques comprenant dialectes Hébreu, Arabe, Chaldéen, Ethiopien, Araméen, à racine de trois lettres, communes fortes et aspre...

Diverses langues d'Afrique, qui ont toutes un air de famille, se distinguant des autres langues du Globe.

Famille Egypto-Berbère
Gheez
langue morte devenue langue sacrée des Abyssins.

Note. Un article très remarquable de Mr Alfred Maury sur la Philologie comparée publié dans la Revue des Deux-Mondes (Avril 1857) m'avait suggéré l'idée d'en faire le sujet d'une Carte Figurative, je n'y avais pas donné suite; mais un autre article de cet éminent Philologue, inséré dans le même recueil (Mars 1867), sur les Écritures Cunéiformes et les conséquences qu'il a tirées de leurs récentes interprétations ayant ajouté aux opinions Philologiques de ce savant, j'ai mis ma première intention à exécution et j'ai rédigé la présente Carte.

Elle représente les principaux mouvements, avant l'Ère moderne, des migrations de quelques anciens peuples ou de celles de leurs langues. Ces mouvements ne se rapportant pas à la même époque, ma Carte, dont tout le mérite revient d'ailleurs à Mr Maury, qui a bien voulu la rectifier, n'est que le tableau d'un État fictif comprenant les États divers d'époques inconnues et supposés simultanés. Quoique donnant une fausse idée de la vérité chronologique, j'espère qu'elle ne sera pas sans intérêt, comme substituant une représentation graphique à une narration écrite.

Les lignes ondulées avec ...
La couleur rouge se rapp...
langues ont la même coul...
La Carte n'est que figurativ...

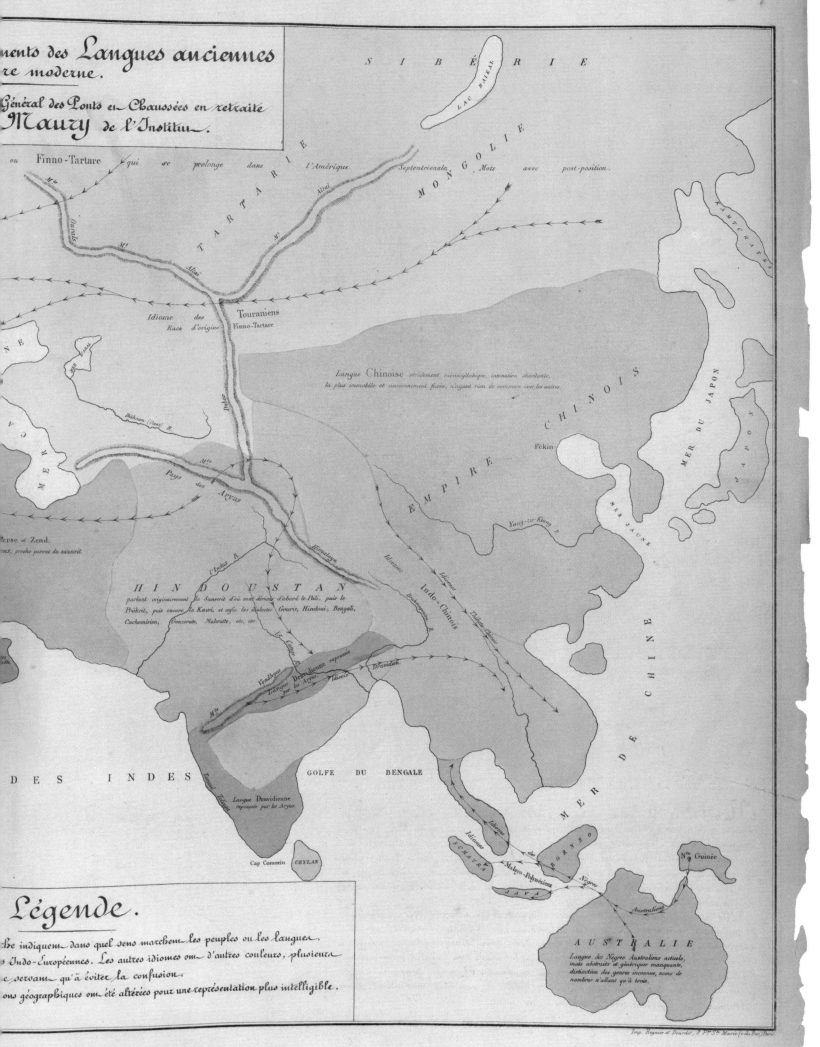

56

Dissemination of Ancient Languages

◄ "Carte figurative des mouvements des langues
anciennes avant l'ère moderne"
No date. Lithographic print, hand-colored. 97.2 × 67.6 cm.

Minard drew this map when he was eighty-six years old; even then he was still testing new topics and methods. This work is undated, but it must have been drawn in or after March 1867, as an article published that month is referenced. The map aims to show the dispersal of languages across Asia and Europe in ancient times. In Minard's era, the concept that languages evolve, and that European and Indo-Iranian languages shared a common root, was revolutionary. The map is a bold experiment in mapping events of a long duration. Minard reflects that it creates a fictional moment in time, comprising diverse unknown epochs. It is therefore more an attempt at communicating a general concept, rather than a precise mapping of events, and does not contain any single time reference.

The colors classify language areas; for instance, rose denotes the family of Indo-European languages. The migration of peoples and the diffusion of languages are streamlined into consistent movements and visualized with arrows.

MINARD TRANSLATED

Figurative map of the dissemination of ancient languages before the modern era

Note. A remarkable article by Mr. Alfred Maury on comparative philology published in the *Revue des deux mondes* inspired me to make it the subject of a map, but I did not immediately act on it. But another article by this eminent philologist, published in the same review, on cuneiform writing and the implications that he drew from its interpretation having been added to the philological opinions of this scholar, my first intention became execution and I drafted this map.

The map represents the migrations of some ancient peoples or of their languages before the modern era. As these movements did not all occur during the same period, my map, of which all the merit belongs to Mr. Maury, offers merely the picture of a fictitious state comprising the various states of unknown epochs, imagined simultaneously. Despite following a false chronology, I hope this map will not be without interest in its quest to substitute a written narrative with a graphic representation.

The undulating lines with arrows indicate the direction in which the peoples or languages moved. Red corresponds to Indo-European languages. Other languages have other colors, and several have the same color to avoid confusion. This is but a figurative map in that geographical proportions have been altered to ensure a more intelligible representation.

57
Free Trade with England

▶ **"Le libre échange avec l'Angleterre en tableaux graphiques"**
August 31, 1867. Lithographic prints, hand-colored. Each approx.
45.0 × 32.7 cm. Published in: *Le libre échange avec l'Angleterre en
tableaux graphiques.* (Paris, 1867)

In the wake of the Anglo-French Treaty of Commerce (signed in 1860), Minard published a brochure accompanied by seven plates containing a multitude of diagrams, in which he analyzed the commercial relations between France and England through the years 1854–1865. The treaty had not fully abolished prohibitions and customs, but it had substantially diminished trade barriers between both countries. Minard tried to determine whether this had advanced or choked the French national economy, noting that the trend was not always clear or easy to explain. He concluded that the accord had generally contributed to the well-being of both nations. Uncharacteristically, he did not provide his data sources (except for some isolated footnotes). It is likely he drew from public customs and trade reports.

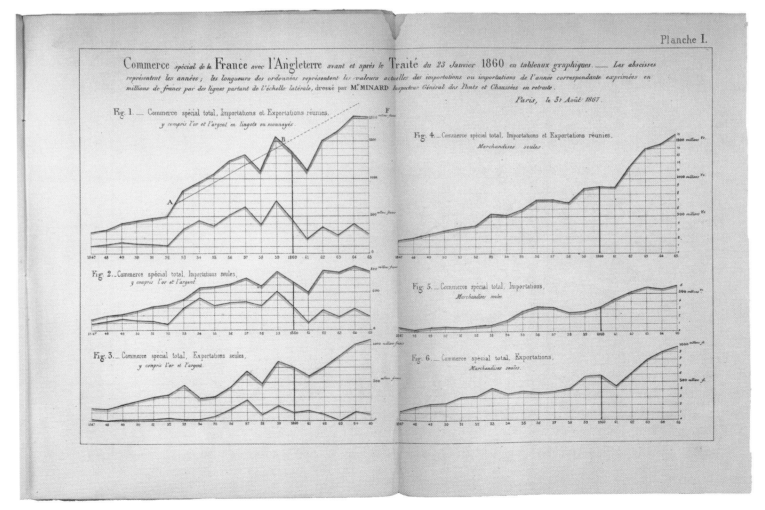

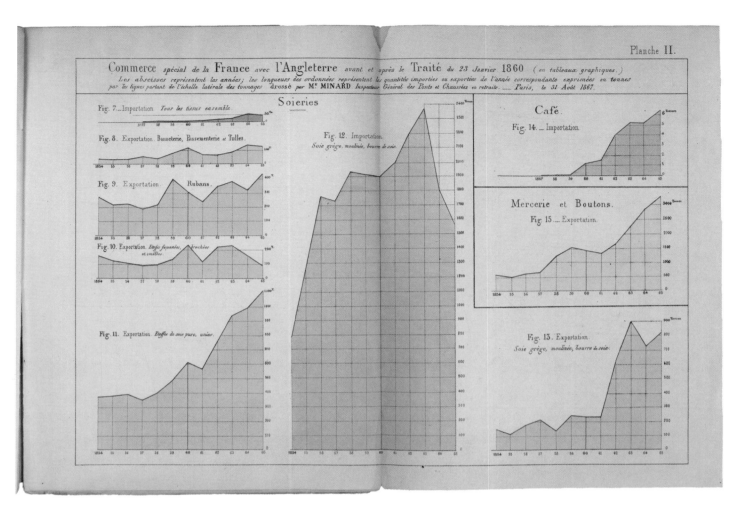

Commerce *spécial de la* France *avec* l'Angleterre *avant et après le* Traité *du 23 Janvier* 1860 *(en tableaux graphiques.)*

Les abscisses représentent les années ; les longueurs des ordonnées représentent les quantités importées ou exportées de l'année correspondante exprimées en tonnes par les lignes partant de l'échelle latérale des tonnages dressé par Mr MINARD Inspecteur Général des Ponts et Chaussées en retraite. — Paris, le 31 Août 1867.

Soieries

Fig. 7.—Importation *Tous les tissus ensemble.*

Fig. 8. Exportation *Bonneterie, Passementerie et Tulles.*

Fig. 9. Exportation. Rubans.

Fig. 10. Exportation. *Etoffes façonnées, brochées et unettées.*

Fig. 11. Exportation. *Etoffes de soie pure, unies.*

Fig. 12. Importation. *Soie grége, moulinée, bourre de soie.*

Café.
Fig. 14. — Importation.

Mercerie et Boutons.
Fig 15. — Exportation.

Fig. 13. Exportation.
Soie grége, moulinée, bourre de soie.

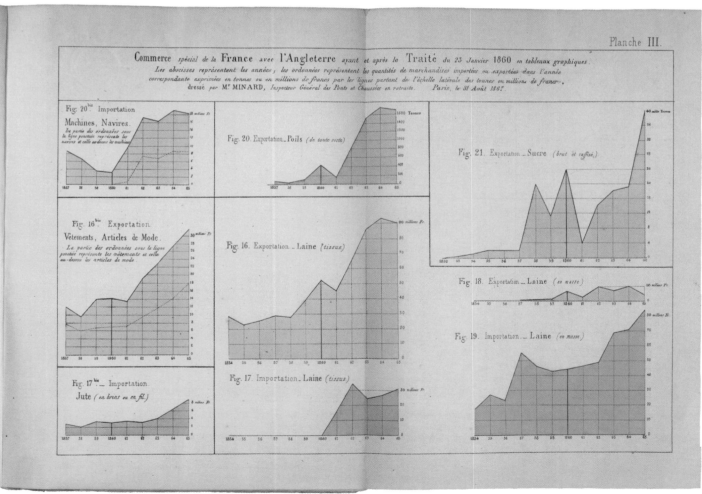

Commerce *spécial de la* France *avec* l'Angleterre *avant et après le* Traité *du 23 Janvier* 1860 *en tableaux graphiques.*

Les abscisses représentent les années ; les ordonnées représentent les quantités de marchandises importées ou exportées dans l'année correspondante exprimées en tonnes ou en millions de francs par les lignes partant de l'échelle latérale des tonnes ou millions de francs. dressé par Mr MINARD, Inspecteur Général des Ponts et Chaussées en retraite. Paris, le 31 Août 1867.

Fig. 20 bis. Importation
Machines, Navires.
La partie des ordonnées sous la ligne ponctuée représente les navires et celle au-dessus les machines

Fig. 16 bis. Exportation.
Vêtements, Articles de Mode.
La partie des ordonnées sous la ligne ponctuée représente les vêtements et celle au-dessus les articles de mode.

Fig. 17 bis. Importation.
Jute (*en brins ou en fil.*)

Fig. 20. Exportation—Poils *(de toute sorte)*

Fig. 16. Exportation — Laine *(tissus)*

Fig. 17. Importation — Laine *(tissus)*

Fig. 21. Exportation — Sucre *(brut et raffiné.)*

Fig. 18. Exportation — Laine *(en masse)*

Fig. 19. Importation — Laine *(en masse)*

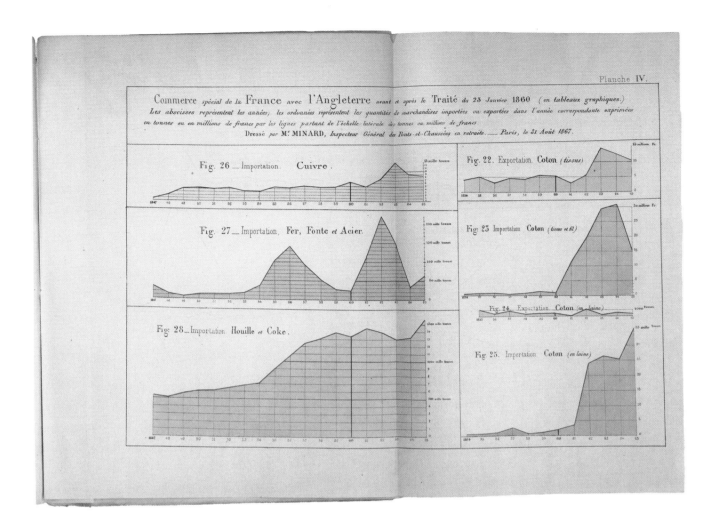

Commerce *spécial de la* France *avec* l'Angleterre *avant et après le* Traité *du 23 Janvier 1860* (*en tableaux graphiques.*)
Les abscisses représentent les années; les ordonnées représentent les quantités de marchandises importées ou exportées dans l'année correspondante exprimées en tonnes ou en millions de francs par les lignes partant de l'échelle latérale des tonnes ou millions de francs.
Dressé *par* M. MINARD, *Inspecteur Général des Ponts-et-Chaussées en retraite.* — *Paris, le 31 Août 1867.*

Fig. 26.—Importation. Cuivre.

Fig. 22. Exportation. Coton (*tissus*)

Fig. 27.—Importation. Fer, Fonte *et* Acier.

Fig. 23. Importation Coton (*tissus et fil*)

Fig. 28.—Importation Houille *et* Coke.

Fig. 24.—Exportation Coton (*en laine*)

Fig. 25. Importation Coton (*en laine*)

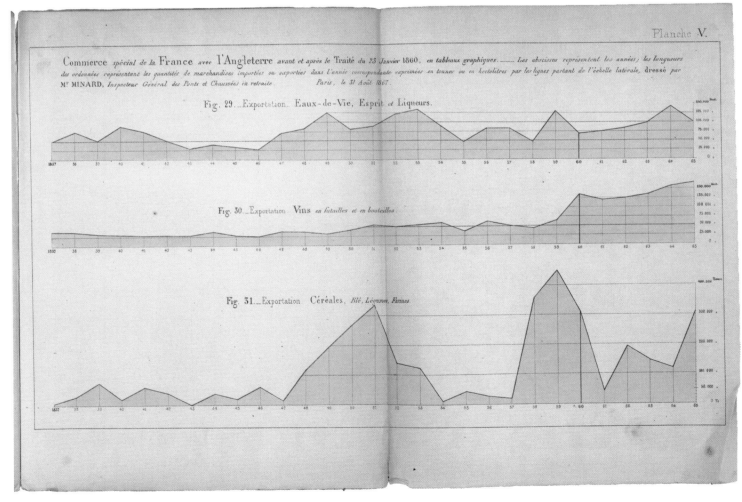

Commerce *spécial de la* France *avec* l'Angleterre *avant et après le* Traité *du 23 Janvier 1860, en tableaux graphiques.* — *Les abscisses représentent les années; les longueurs des ordonnées représentent les quantités de marchandises importées ou exportées dans l'année correspondante exprimées en tonnes ou en hectolitres par les lignes partant de l'échelle latérale, dressé par* M. MINARD, *Inspecteur Général des Ponts et Chaussées en retraite.* *Paris, le 31 Août 1867.*

Fig. 29.—Exportation. Eaux-de-Vie, Esprit *et* Liqueurs.

Fig. 30.—Exportation Vins *en futailles et en bouteilles*

Fig. 31.—Exportation Céréales, *Blé, Légumes, Farines.*

147

Tableau graphique *approximatif des quantités de* Vins *importées en* Angleterre *de 1849 à 1865,* dressé *par* M.ʳ MINARD, *Inspecteur Général des Ponts et Chaussées en retraite.* ── *Les abscisses représentent les années ; les longueurs des ordonnées représentent les quantités de vins importées dans l'année correspondante exprimées en gallons par les lignes partant de l'échelle latérale (un gallon = 4, 54 litres) ── Les renseignements ont été pris dans les publications de la Douane Anglaise ── Environ ⅓ des vins importés est réexporté, si on en juge par les consommations de l'Angleterre du Statistical abstract pour les cinq dernières années.*

Paris, le 31 Aout 1867.

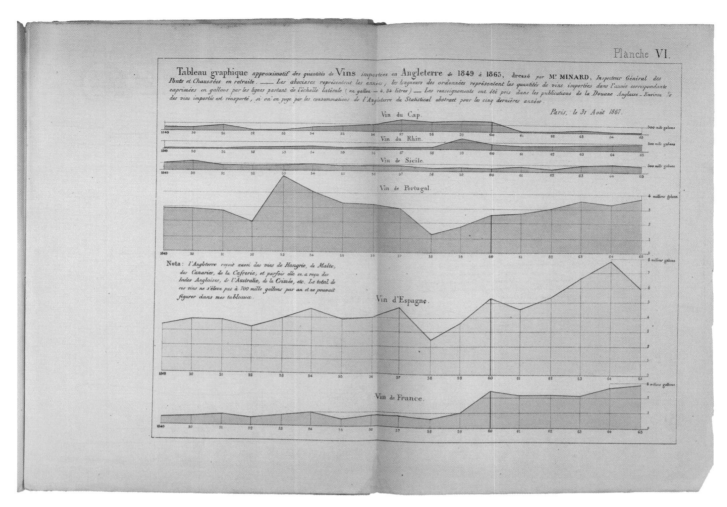

Nota : *l'Angleterre reçoit aussi des vins de Hongrie, de Malte, des Canaries, de la Cafrerie, et parfois elle en a reçu des Indes Anglaises, de l'Australie, de la Crimée, etc. Le total de ces vins ne s'élève pas à 700 mille gallons par an. et ne pouvait figurer dans mes tableaux.*

Commerce *spécial de la* France *avec* l'Angleterre *avant et après le* Traité *du 23 Janvier* 1860, (*en tableaux graphiques.*)
Les abscisses représentent les années ; les longueurs des ordonnées représentent les quantités de marchandises importées ou exportées dans l'année correspondante exprimées en tonnes par les lignes partant de l'échelle latérale.
Dressé *par* M.ʳ MINARD, *Inspecteur Général des Ponts et Chaussées en retraite.* ── *Paris, le 31 Aout 1867.*

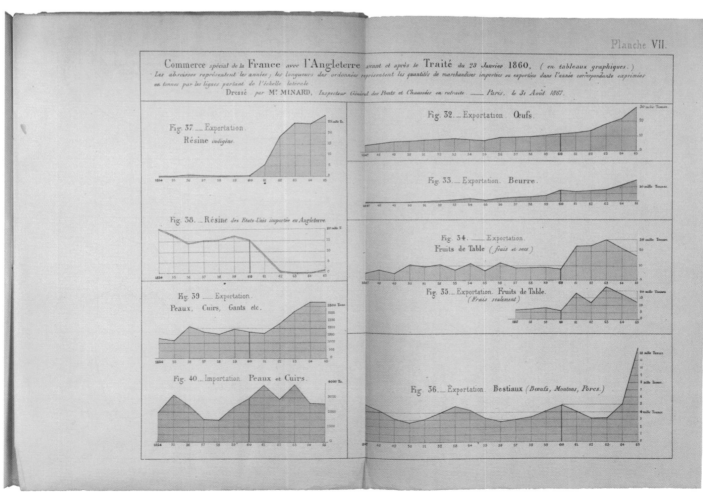

58

Cereals Imported to France in 1867

➤ **"Carte figurative des mouvements et provenances des céréales importées en France en 1867"**
May 14, 1868. Lithographic color print. 93.0 × 69.8 cm.

In this late flow map, Minard analyzed cereals imported in France. Imports from overseas are green; cereals imported on land are russet. One conspicuous feature is how he broadened the Bosphorus (which is only between 700 and 2,500 meters wide) to make room for the imports from Russia and the Ottoman Empire. Generally though, Minard seems to have developed a certain ease in working with flow maps at this point, particularly in terms of selecting suitable data. He did not have to entwine the flows very much, and their number and width can be perceived effortlessly.
To provide context, the map contains a diagram of monthly wheat prices in France, Chicago, Odessa (then Russia), Valladolid (Spain), and Budapest (then the Austro-Hungarian Empire).

MINARD TRANSLATED

Figurative and approximate map of the movements and provenance of cereal imported to France in 1867

The approximate quantities of cereal are represented by the widths of the colored zones at a rate of four millimeters for every five hundred thousand hectoliters. The numbers written below points of import are in units of one thousand hectoliters; thus [the town of] Forbach received 154 thousand hectoliters.

This map was drawn using data provided by railroad engineers and approximate information from the French Customs Administration.

Table of the average prices of wheat per month in Chicago, Odessa, Pest, and Valladolid in 1867 (broken down by hectolitres of 75 kilograms).

Observation: Prices from Chicago have been extracted from *Trade and Commerce of the City of Chicago*, page 41.

Wheat prices from Valladolid are the average of each trimester in 1867 according to Blanquille.

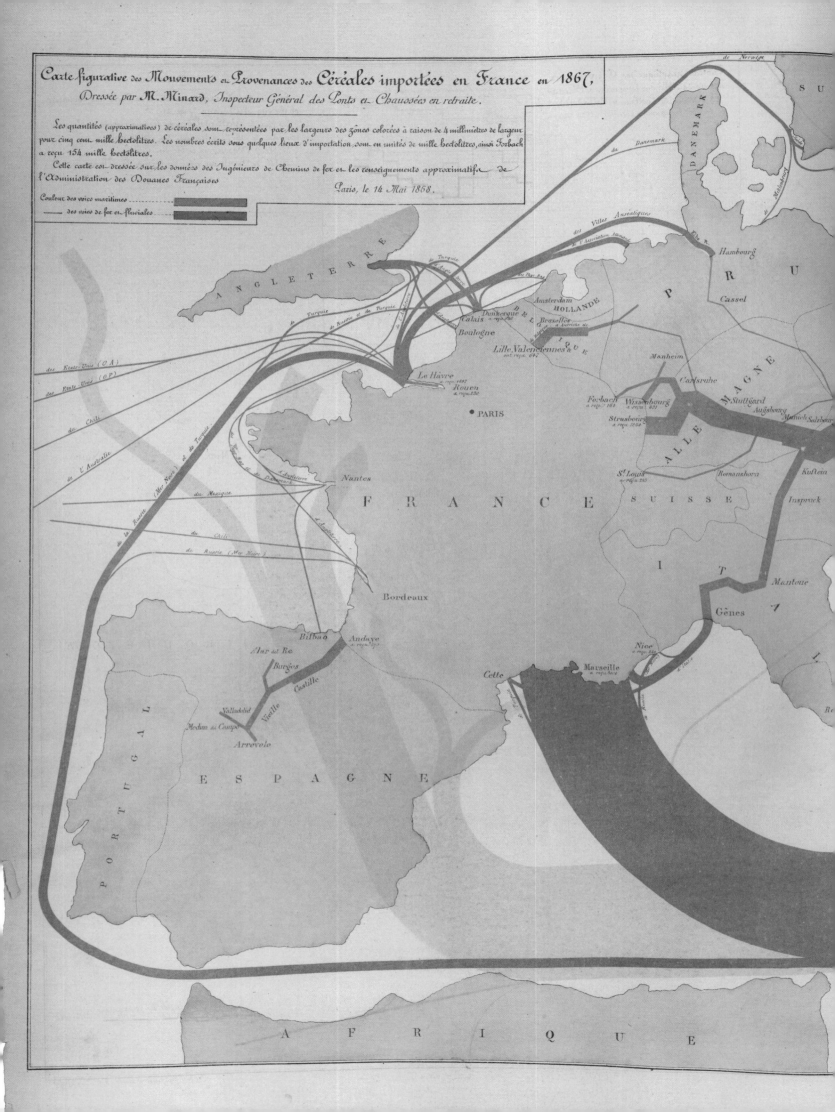

Carte figurative des Mouvements en Provenances des **Céréales importées en France en 1867,**
Dressée par M. Minard, Inspecteur Général des Ponts et Chaussées en retraite.

Les quantités (approximatives) de céréales sont représentées par les largeurs des zones colorées à raison de 4 millimètres de largeur pour cinq cent mille hectolitres. Les nombres écrits sous quelques lieux d'importation sont en unités de mille hectolitres, ainsi Forbach a reçu 154 mille hectolitres.

Cette carte est dressée sur les données des Ingénieurs de Chemins de fer et les renseignements approximatifs de l'Administration des Douanes Françaises

Paris, le 14 Mai 1868.

Couleur des voies maritimes
des voies de fer et fluviales

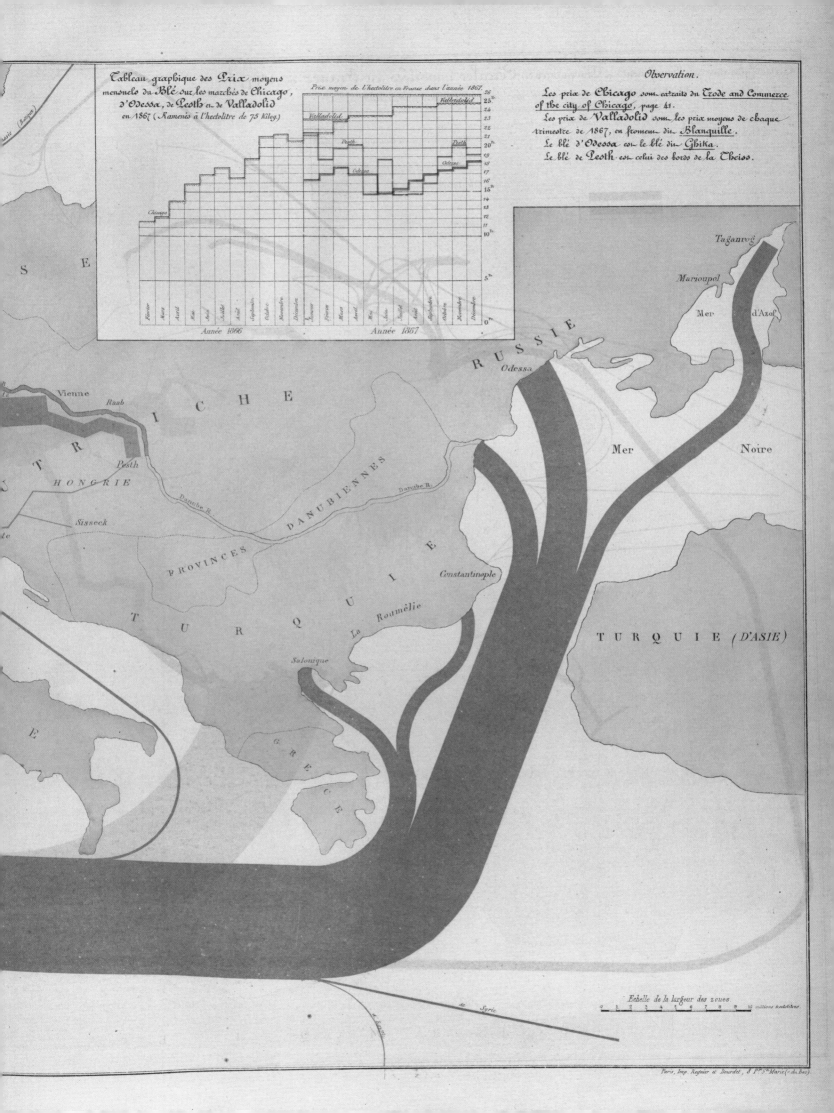

Tableau graphique des Prix moyens
mensuels du Blé sur les marchés de Chicago,
d'Odessa, de Pesth et de Valladolid
en 1867 (Ramenés à l'hectolitre de 75 Kilog.)

Prix moyen de l'hectolitre en France dans l'année 1867.

Observation.

Les prix de **Chicago** sont extraits du **Trade and Commerce**
of the city of Chicago, page 41.

Les prix de **Valladolid** sont les prix moyens de chaque
trimestre de 1867, en froment du **Blanquille**.

Le blé d'**Odessa** est le blé du **Ghika**.

Le blé de **Pesth** est celui des bords de la **Theiss**.

Année 1866   Année 1867

Echelle de la largeur des zones

Paris, Imp. Regnier et Dourdet, 8 P.ce S.te Marie (r. du Bac)

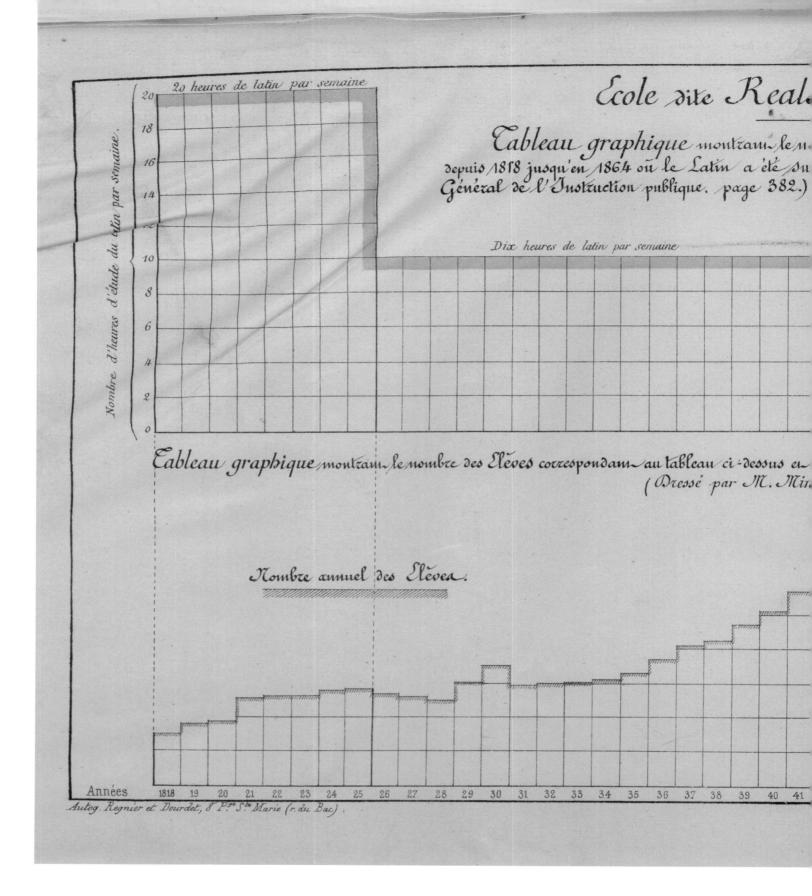

59

Hours of Latin Study in Stuttgart High Schools

▲ "École dite Realschulen de Stuttgart. Tableau graphique
montrant le nombre d'heures par semaine d'étude du latin
diminuant depuis 1818 jusqu'en 1864"
No date. Lithographic print, hand-colored. 48.5 × 28.9 cm.
Published in: *La Statistique* (Paris, 1869)

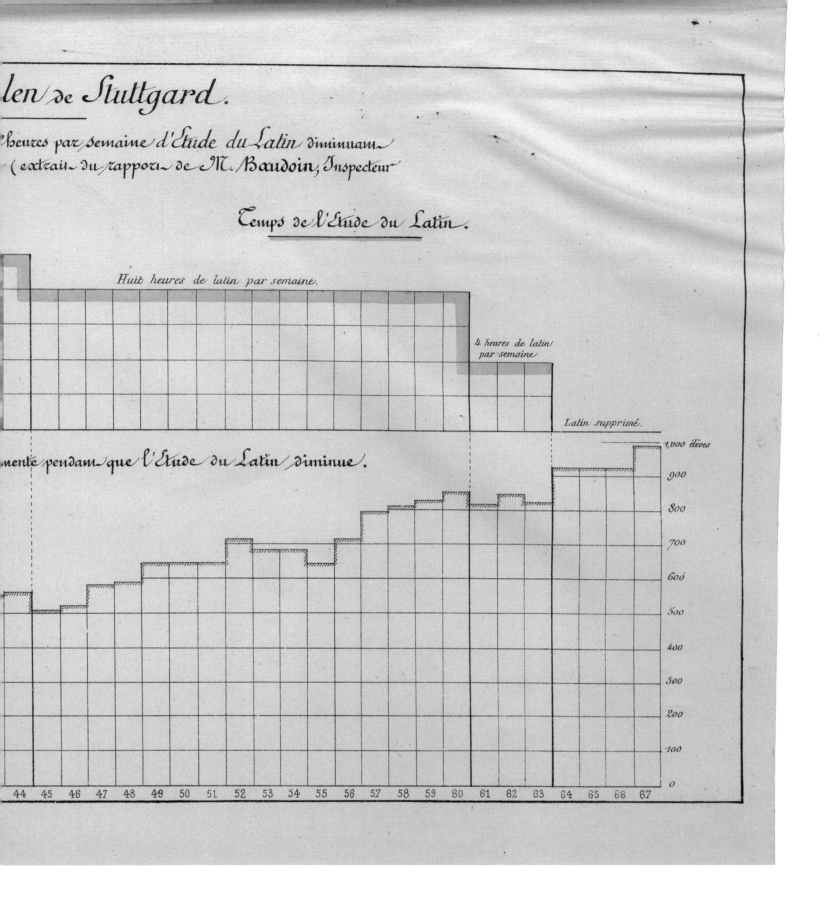

len de Stuttgard.

heures par semaine d'Etude du Latin diminuant
(extrait du rapport de M. Baudoin, Inspecteur

Temps de l'Etude du Latin.

Huit heures de latin par semaine.

4 heures de latin
par semaine

Latin supprimé.

mente pendant que l'Etude du Latin diminue.

In the paragraph "Statistics applied to education" of his brochure *La Statistique*, Minard refers to an administrative report about secondary education.[4] The publication's graphic charts had impressed him, and from one particular diagram showing the subjects taught in secondary schools in Wurttemberg (cf. page 20 in the introduction) he extracted data on the decline of Latin lessons from 1818 to 1864 (top). Minard then added a second diagram (bottom), showing the growing number of students over that same period. He expressly mentions a causal link between the two phenomena. Even though we do not know the objective of Minard's investigation here, this connection seems disputable today.

60

Hannibal's March over the Alps and Napoléon's Russian Campaign

➤ "Carte figurative des pertes successives en hommes de l'armée qu'Annibal conduisit d'Espagne en Italie en traversant les Gaules (selon Polybe)"
➤ "Carte figurative des pertes successives en hommes de l'armée française dans la campagne de Russie, 1812–1813"
November 20, 1869. Lithographic color print. 64.8 × 20.9 cm (Hannibal) and 64.8 × 26.5 cm (Napoléon).

Here is the source of Minard's prevailing fame—his flow map relating to Napoléon's Russian Campaign in 1812–1813 (bottom). It is puzzling that it is so often shown as an isolated work when it actually forms part of a comparison with a second flow map (top), which covers the 218 BC march of Carthagian commander Hannibal who, along with an army of ninety thousand men, crossed over the Alps toward Rome. The two maps show the "progressive losses in men" that both armies suffered. The flows are constructed to the same scale. It is important to note that both campaigns consisted of countless separate movements and were interrupted by battles, overnight stays, retreats and advances, and the parting and reunion of troops. To show both campaigns as a constant flow is "an effective generalization of a historic event."[5]

The Napoléon graphic manages to integrate six data variables in a condensed representation devoid of visual clutter. Its base map is strikingly reduced —except for a few rivers, barely any landscape features are delineated. The westernmost point is the city of Kowno (Kaunas, in what is today Lithuania) on the river Neman. In the east the city of Moscow is the extreme point of the flow. Note that the place names are neither consistently local nor taken from any particular language but switch from French to German to Slavic.[6] The flow enters Russia from Poland with 422,000 men; the retreating army crosses the Neman with only 10,000 men remaining. The graphic is enhanced by a temperature diagram (referring to the Réaumur scale) connected to the retreating flow. Contrary to conventional line diagrams, this one has the time running from right to left in order to follow the westward retreat.

A notable "narrative" label on the lower left-hand side of the map reads, "The Cossacks gallop over the frozen Neman."[7] This isolated text is connected

---

MINARD TRANSLATED

Figurative map of the successive losses of the French army during the Russian campaign, 1812–1813

The numbers of men present are represented by the widths of the colored zones at a rate of one millimeter for every ten thousand men, and are also written across the zones. Red designates the men entering Russia, black those exiting. The information used to draw this map was obtained from the works of Mr. Thiers, Mr. de Ségur, Mr. de Fezensac, Mr. de Chambray, and the unpublished journal of Jacob, pharmacist of the army since October 28th.

To better perceive the reduction of the army at a glance, I assumed that the corps led by Prince Jerome and Marshall Davout, which were detached at Minsk and Mogilev and rejoined near Orscha and Witebsk, had always marched with the army.

Figurative map of the successive losses of Hannibal's army during the march from Spain to Italy through Gallia (according to Polybius)

Legend: The numbers of men remaining are represented by the widths of the colored zones at a rate of one millimeter for every ten thousand men, and are also written across the zones.

As there is no consensus on where Hannibal crossed the Alps, I adopted Larosa's opinion without claiming to justify it.

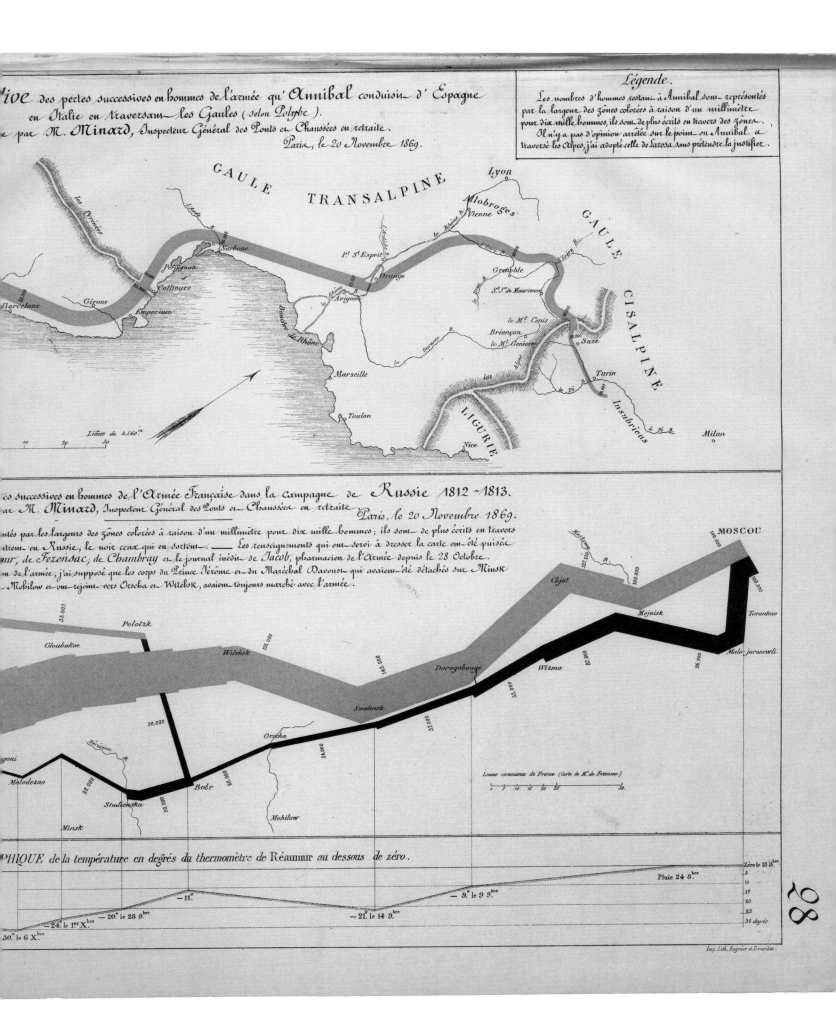

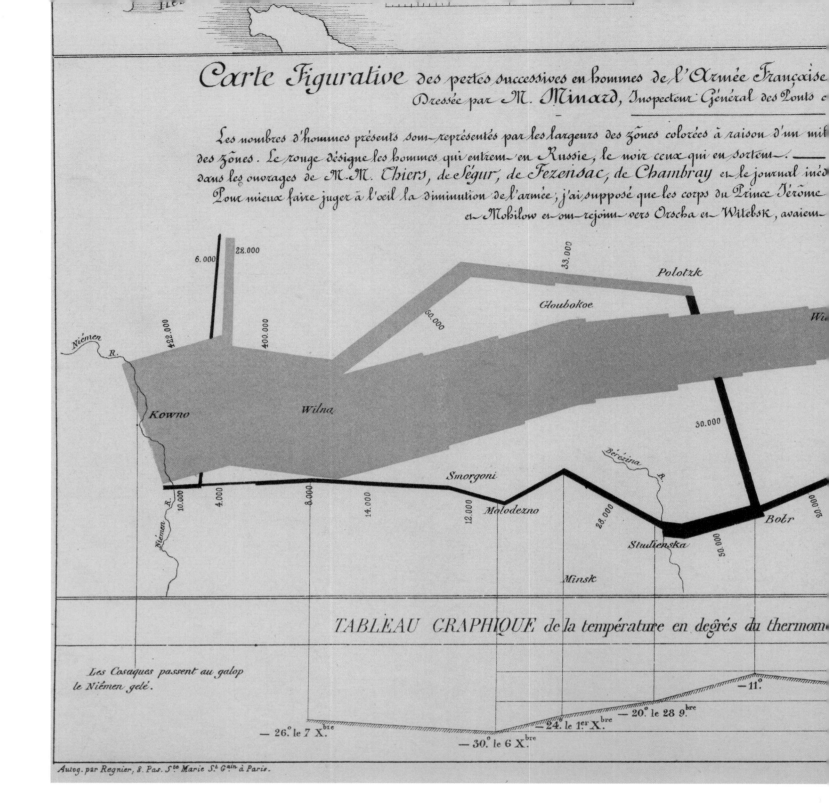

to a spot on the Neman, located in the brown flow entering Russia. However, as we speak of Cossacks and the frozen river, the label can only refer to Russian soldiers chasing the retreating French army in the winter. We may assume then, that Minard here—in an interesting impulse to complete the "narrative" contained in the map—"told" the end of the story with an anecdote from the retreat and linked it to a particular location on the river.

In the text Minard listed the books from which he had extracted his data. This must have been a rather laborious process, given that "the army" consisted of countless military units from many parts of Europe.[8]

In comparison, the Hannibal base map is more detailed. It emphasizes the coastlines of Spain, southern France, and Italy, and includes the mountain ranges of the Pyrenees and the Alps, both of which formed fatal barriers for

Hannibal's army. Note that the region is rotated eastward to make the coastline fit the horizontal format. The scale along the bottom refers to leagues, an ancient unit of length. Due to the consistent scaling in both maps—as before, this was a priority for Minard —Hannibal's losses seem rather modest. He had, however, lost some sixty-eight thousand men in this march, amounting to 72 percent of his troops.

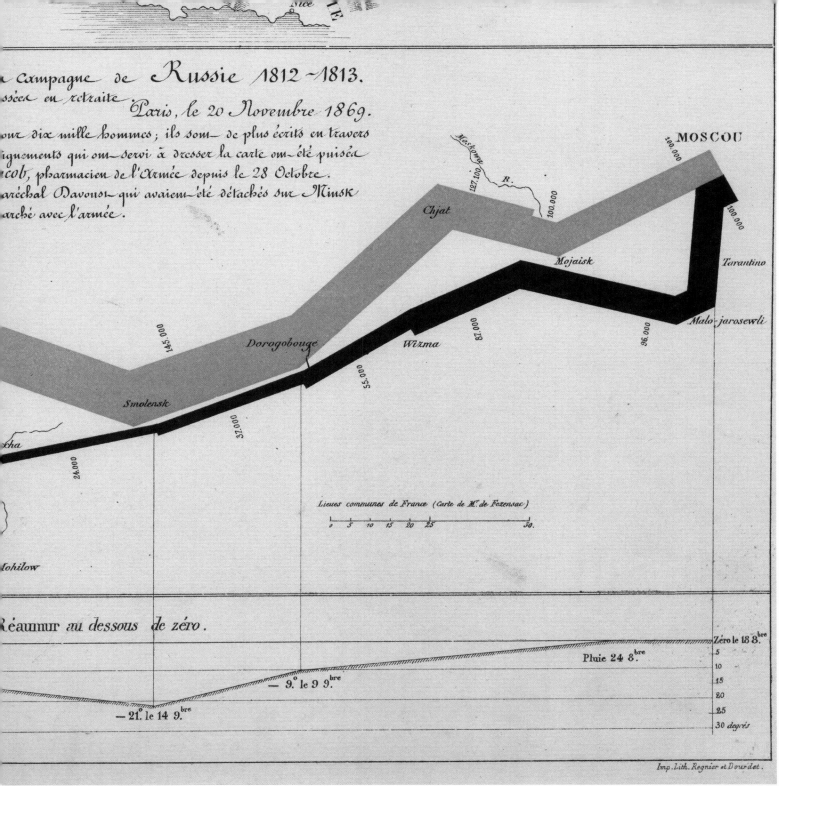

a campagne de *Russie 1812~1813.*

ssée en retraite.

Paris, le 20 Novembre 1869.

our dix mille hommes ; ils sont de plus écrits en travers

ignements qui ont servi à dresser la carte ont été puisés

COb, pharmacien de l'Armée depuis le 28 Octobre.

aréchal Davoust qui avaient été détachés sur Minsk

arché avec l'armée.

MOSCOU

Chjat

Dorogobouge

Smolensk

Wizma

Mojaisk

Tarantino

Malo-jarosewli

100.000

127.100.000

100.000

100.000

87.000

36.000

145.000

55.000

32.000

24.000

Lieues communes de France (Carte de M. de Fezensac.)

0   5   10   15   20   25   50.

Mohilow

Réaumur au dessous de zéro.

Zéro le 18 8.bre

Pluie 24 8.bre

— 9.° le 9 9.bre

— 21. le 14 9.bre

5
10
15
20
25
30 *degrés*

Imp. Lith. Regnier et Dourdet.

Minard based his representation on the ancient account in Polybius's *Histories*, as well as some advice from contemporary historians. The map arrestingly conveys a sense of the fatal moments of the campaign. When Hannibal approached the Alps, he had forty-six thousand soldiers at his command—meaning that forty-eight thousand soldiers had already been lost. For instance, the crossing of the river Ebro (today in Spain) had resulted in fourteen thousand

losses, and the Pyrenees, twenty thousand. Losses were due not only to natural obstacles such as rivers and mountains, but also to numerous unexpected battles against local tribes along the way.

This gruesome impression is deeply intensified by looking at the diminishing flow that visualizes Napoléon's army in Russia. To this day, it is an excruciating exercise to read eyewitness reports by soldiers who survived the retreat. Minard created his visualization more

than fifty years after the campaign. It is a brilliant conceptual transfer: in applying the flow method to a military campaign, Minard shifts his entire focus to a single variable: the number of people in the flow. This variable sees only one type of variation—*a sharp and steady decline*. It seems to have been this potent and poignant message that made these two maps (and particularly the Napoléon one) so successful in telling a story about the cataclysm of war.

157

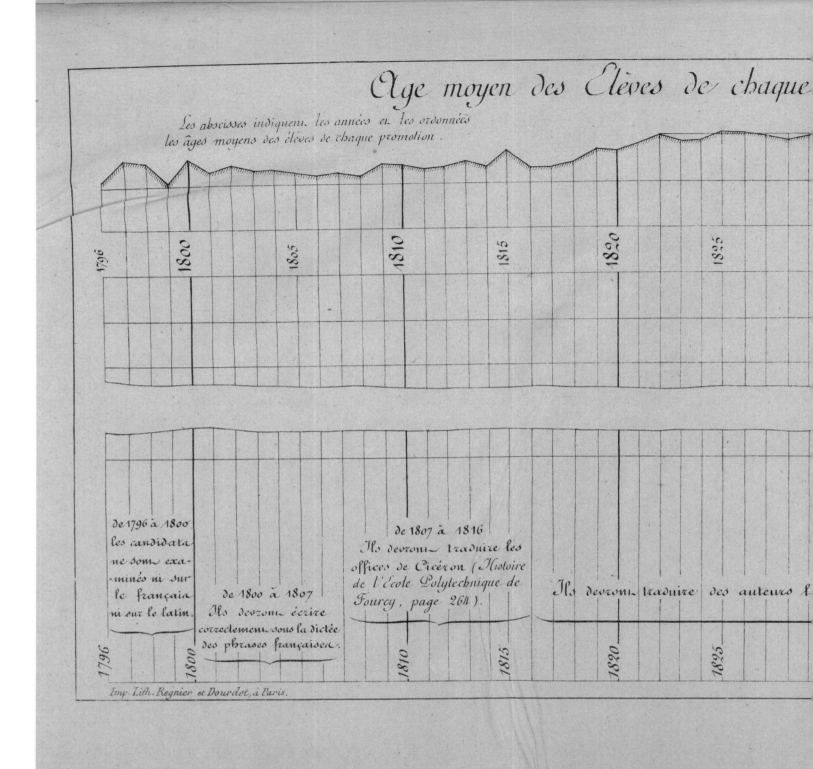

Les abscisses indiquent les années et les ordonnées les âges moyens des élèves de chaque promotion.

Age moyen des Élèves de chaque

1796   1800   1805   1810   1815   1820   1825

de 1796 à 1800 les candidats ne sont examinés ni sur le français ni sur le latin.

de 1800 à 1807 Ils devront écrire correctement sous la dictée des phrases françaises.

de 1807 à 1816 Ils devront traduire les offices de Cicéron (Histoire de l'École Polytechnique de Fourcy, page 264).

Ils devront traduire des auteurs l

1796   1800   1810   1815   1820   1825

Imp. Lith. Regnier et Dourdet, à Paris.

61

Average Age of Students at École Polytechnique

▲ "Age moyen des élèves de chaque promotion à l'École polytechnique"
May 6, 1870. Lithographic print. 64.5 × 30.8 cm.

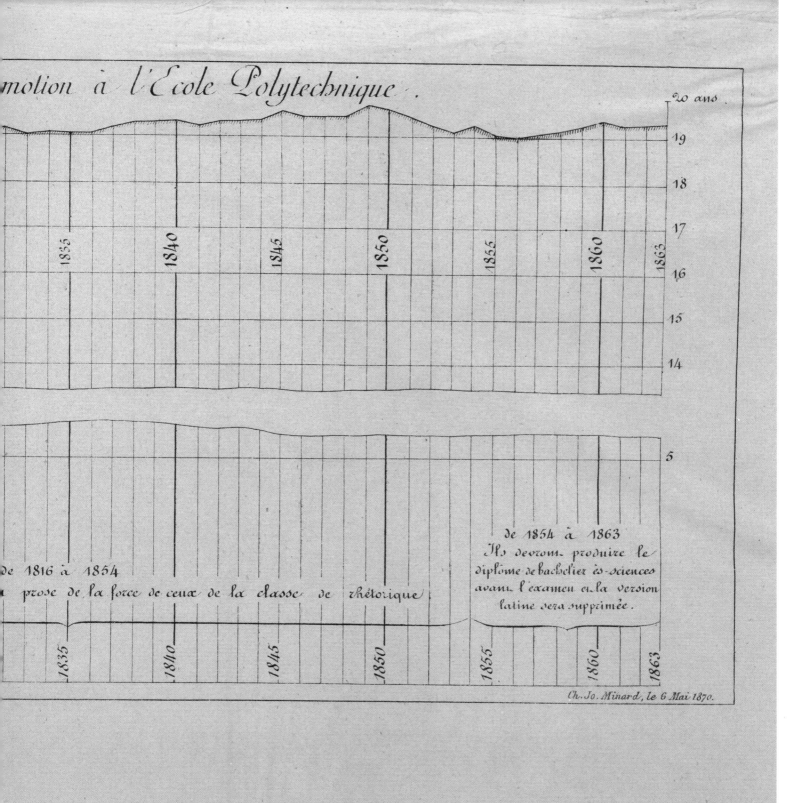

motion à l'École Polytechnique .

20 ans

19

18

17

1835   1840   1845   1850   1855   1860   1863

16

15

14

5

de 1816 à 1854
prose de la force de ceux de la classe de rhétorique

de 1854 à 1863
Ils devront produire le
diplôme de bachelier ès-sciences
avant l'examen et la version
latine sera supprimée .

1835   1840   1845   1850   1855   1860   1863

Ch. Jo. Minard, le 6 Mai 1870.

This is the last known work by Minard. The title reads: "Average student age of every admission to the École Polytechnique." The timeline shows the years 1796 through 1863. The vertical axis represents the admission age in years, with a crude breach between the ages of five and fourteen. The lower register contains text labels that explain the knowledge of Latin and French required for admission to the school. This work resonates with the layout and topic of [59]; however, we do not know why Minard investigated the importance of Latin in higher education in his last two years.

Technical Drawings

62
Paris Canal and Railroad Project

"Projet de canal et de chemins de fer pour amener à Paris, les pavés, la pierre meuliere, et l'eau de l'Yvette"
May 1, 1822. Published in: *Tableau des progrès de la dépense du pavé de Paris pendant les deux derniers siècles.* (Paris, 1825)

63
Canal du Centre, 1823

"Canal du Centre. Etanchement des filtrations de Vertempierre. Canal en maçonnerie hydraulique exécuté en 1823."
April 20, 1824. Published in: *Notice sur l'étanchement des filtrations du canal du Centre, près des carrières de Vertempierre.* (Paris, 1824)

64
Navigation, High-Speed Vessels

"Navigation — Bateaux-Rapides"
1834. Published in: MacNeill, John. "Extrait d'un mémoire anglais intitulé: De la résistance de l'eau au passage des bateaux dans les canaux (1833)," translated by Charles-Joseph Minard. (Paris, *Annales des ponts et chaussées*, 1834)

65
Railroad Lessons

"Leçons faites sur les chemins de fer"
Series of eight plates, 1834. Published in: *Leçons faites sur les chemins de fer à l'École des ponts et chaussées en 1833–1834.* (Paris, 1834)

66
Construction Course, River Navigation

"Cours de construction — Navigation des rivières"
Series of thirty-six plates, 1841. Published in: *Cours de construction des ouvrages qui établissent la navigation des rivières et des canaux, professé à l'École des ponts et chaussées de 1832 à 1841. Atlas.* (Paris, 1841)

67
Railroad from Montpellier to Cette

"Chemin de fer de Montpellier à Cette"
May 1843. Published in: *Second mémoire sur l'importance du parcours partiel sur les chemins de fer.* (Paris, 1843)

68
Construction Course, Seaports

"Cours de construction — Ports de mer"
Series of twenty-five plates, 1846. Published in: *Cours de construction des ouvrages hydrauliques des ports de mer. Atlas.* (Paris, 1846)

69
Political Economy, Graphic Tables

"Économie Politique — Tableaux Graphiques"
1850. Published in: "Notions élémentaires d'économie politique appliquées aux travaux publics," (Paris, *Annales des ponts et chaussées*, 1850)

70
The Nautical Future of Le Havre

"De l'avenir nautique du Havre"
Two plates, February 15, 1856. Published in: *De l'avenir nautique du Havre.* (Paris, 1856)

71
The Fall of Bridges in Great Floods

"De la chute des ponts dans les grandes crues"
October 24, 1856. Published in: *De la chute des ponts dans les grandes crues.* (Paris, 1856)

72
Containment of the Seine Maritime and the Clyde

"Endiguement de la Seine Maritime/Endiguement de la Clyde"
April 30, 1859. Published in: *De l'endiguement de la Seine jusqu'à Honfleur et du port du Havre.* (Paris, 1859)

73
Mouths of Navigable Rivers

"Des embouchures des rivières navigables"
Series of six plates, November 5, 1864. Published in: *Des embouchures des rivières navigables.* (Paris, 1864)

74
Great Constructions of Ancient Peoples

"Grandes constructions de quelques anciens peuples"
December 11, 1869. Published in: *Grandes constructions de quelques anciens peuples.* (Paris, 1869)

Curriculum Vitae

1781 Charles-Joseph Minard was born in Dijon on March 27. He received his secondary education in Dijon, where he formed lifelong friendships with two fellow students (Mr. Désormes, Mr. Clément).

1796–1800 At age fifteen, Minard entered the prestigious École polytechnique in Paris to pass his foundational engineering education.[1]

1800–1804 Minard went on to the influential École des ponts et chaussées to become a civil engineer for traffic-related infrastructure. The exact year of Minard's leaving the École des ponts et chaussées is unclear (1802–1804).

1802–1815 As an engineer, Minard was sent on assignments all over France: to the Canal de Charleroi between Charleroi and Brussels (1802–1804),[2] to Angers for local arrondissement services (1805), to the military haven of Rochefort (1806–1810), to Flushing and Antwerp for reconstruction works in both ports (1810–1812), to Antwerp for the construction of a war ship dock (1813–1814),[3] and to Trilport to rebuild a war-torn bridge over the river Marne. He witnessed the 1814 Siege of Antwerp, which had a lasting and traumatic impact on him.

1815–1825 Minard entered the municipal service in Paris, where he immersed himself in a study about how to ameliorate the state of the municipal pavements. He married the daughter of his friend Mr. Désormes (1822). They had two daughters; one son was lost in early infancy (1825). Minard was sent to Chalon-sur-Saône as chief engineer for the Canal du Centre.

1825–1830 Minard was assigned to the Canal de Saint-Quentin and promoted to chief engineer (1827) of the canal. He took a leave from the public corps to continue his work with the Honoré brothers, the license holders of the canal.

1830–1839 In 1830, Minard returned to public service and was promoted to inspector of the École des ponts et chaussées, which included regular teaching duties. He received the Cross of the Legion of Honor, the highest French order of merit.[4] With the foundation of the *Annales des ponts et chaussées* in 1831, Minard joined its editorial board, a position he kept until after his retirement in 1851.[5]

1839–1845 Minard was awarded Officer of the Legion of Honor[6] and promoted to inspector of the Corps des ponts et chaussées. From 1839, he oversaw the ninth inspection, which comprised six departments in the south of France. In order to reduce his traveling duties, he took over the fifteenth inspection in the center of France, closer to Paris.[7] However, due to perpetual health problems, he was unable to perform the necessary field trips in 1844–1845. In 1842, he resigned from his duties as a professor at the École des ponts et chaussées. The first significant diagrams and maps date from 1844 to 1847.

1846–1851 Minard was named inspector general and as such became a permanent member of the Conseil général des ponts et chaussées (1846). As a district inspector, he had been a temporary member of this influential council. Now, a new permanent seat was added to the council in his favor.[8] Minard was awarded Commander of the Legion of Honor (1849).

1851–1870 On his seventieth birthday (March 27, 1851), Minard officially retired due to the age limit for inspectors general. Over the following period, Minard undertook self-initiated, in-depth studies in statistical visualization. Until his death, he published about fifty-eight maps and diagram plates, along with several brochures, pamphlets, and articles.

1870 Amid the events leading up to the Siege of Paris and the Paris Commune, Minard left the city abruptly on September 11 with his wife, one daughter, and son-in-law, taking with him only light luggage and some unfinished work. Having arrived in Bordeaux, he quickly re-adopted his current studies. However, he was hit by a fever a few weeks later and died at age eighty-nine on October 24. His other daughter and son-in-law, trapped in Paris, didn't learn of the news until three months later. Minard is buried in the Montparnasse Cemetery in Paris.[9]

Notes

PREFACE

1 #dataviz apparel, "Charles Minard in Black T-Shirt," Zazzle, accessed September 4, 2017, www.zazzle.com/charles_minard_in_black_t_shirt-235775886405738885; "Minard Gifts," CafePress, accessed September 4, 2017, www.cafepress.com/+minard+gifts.

2 Edward Tufte, *The Visual Display of Quantitative Information* (Cheshire, CT: Graphics Press, 1983), 40. He printed and distributed a facsimile with the original French text as well as an English version of the map.

3 Étienne-Jules Marey, *La méthode graphique dans les sciences expérimentales et particulièrement en physiologie et en médecine* (Paris: Masson, 1878), 71–73. He described the graphic as an example for representing trajectories in space, amended by an additional variable representing a change occurring during this trajectory.

4 Marey, *La méthode graphique*, 75–78.

5 Howard Gray Funkhouser, "Historical Development of the Graphical Representation of Statistical Data," *Osiris* 3 (1937): 269–404; Arthur Howard Robinson, "The Thematic Maps of Charles-Joseph Minard," *Imago Mundi: A Review of Early Cartography* XXI (1967): 95–108; François de Dainville, "Les Bases d'une cartographie industrielle de l'Europe au XIXᵉ siècle," *La Cartographie reflet de l'Histoire* (1972; repr. Genève-Paris: Editions Slatkine, 1986), 153–175; Josef W. Konvitz, *Cartography in France 1660–1848: Science, Engineering, and Statecraft* (Chicago: University of Chicago Press, 1987); Gilles Palsky, *Des chiffres et des cartes: Naissance et développement de la cartographie quantitative française au XIXᵉ siècle*, Mémoires de la Section de géographie physique et humaine, vol. 19 (Paris: Comité des travaux historiques et scientifiques, 1996); Michael Friendly, "Visions and Re-Visions of Charles-Joseph Minard," *Journal of Educational and Behavioral Statistics* 27, no. 1 (2002): 31–52.

6 In the English-speaking realm, *flow map* is an established term for a specific type of thematic map that shows the movement of objects between areas. The term seems to have been accepted and in general use at the latest by 1939, when Willard C. Brinton devoted a chapter to flow maps in his 1939 book *Graphic Presentation*, in which he also reproduced Marey's simplified reproduction of the Napoléon map (228).

7 The term *la méthode graphique* is used widely in the statistical and scientific literature published in France throughout the nineteenth century to denote the practice of displaying measurements, statistical data, and other types of information in graphics. This is exemplified in the title of Marey's 1878 book *La méthode graphique dans les sciences expérimentales et particulièrement en physiologie et en médecine*. The use of the term points to the fact that, at the time, communicating facts and measures in diagrams was not the prevalent habit it is today but a special method that required justification.

8 Palsky, *Des chiffres et des cartes*, 118; Arthur H. Robinson, "The 1837 Maps of Henry Drury Harness," *The Geographical Journal* 121, no. 4 (December 1955): 440–50.

9 It is most probable however, that Minard and Belpaire worked independently of each other, because they conceived of the flow in a different manner. Belpaire constructed the segments of his flow as trapezoids (i.e., with varying width) from station to station, while Minard always used one consistent band width for each section. Cf. Palsky, *Des chiffres et des cartes*, 118–22. Belpaire explained his motivation and method, and provided his extensive data base in a brochure published in 1847: Belpaire, *Notice sur les cartes du mouvement des transports en Belgique* (Brussels: P. Vandermalen, 1847). Minard mentions his work in 1861, saying the two inventions had appeared in France and in Belgium at the same time. Minard, *Des tableaux graphiques*, 6.

INTRODUCTION

1 *Almanach royal et national pour l'an M DCCC XXXIX, présenté à Sa Majesté et aux princes et princesses de la famille royale* (Paris: A. Guyot et Scribe, 1839), 151. *Almanach royal et national pour l'an M DCCC XXXXIV, présenté à Sa Majesté et aux princes et princesses de la famille royale* (Paris: A. Guyot et Scribe, 1844), 165.

2 Our main source for biographical information about Minard's life and career is his obituary written by his son-in-law and fellow engineer: Victorin Chevallier, "Notice nécrologique sur M. Minard, inspecteur général des ponts et chaussées, en retraite," *Annales des ponts et chaussées* 5ᵉ série, 2ᵉ semestre (1871): 1–22; as well as a note in François Pierre Hardouin Tarbé de Saint-Hardouin, *Notices biographiques sur les ingénieurs des ponts et chaussées depuis la création du corps, en 1716, jusqu'à nos jours* (Paris: Librairie Polytechnique Baudry et Cie., 1884), 151–53.

3 Chevallier, "Notice nécrologique," (1871): 12. *Almanach royal 1839*, 151. *Almanach royal 1844*, 165.

4 Both are documented through publications: Charles-Joseph Minard, *Cours de construction des ouvrages qui établissent la navigation des rivières et des canaux, professé à l'École des ponts et chaussées de 1832 à 1841* (Paris: Carillan-Gœury et Victor Dalmont, 1841); and Charles-Joseph Minard, *Cours de construction des ouvrages hydrauliques des ports de mer* (Paris: Carillan-Gœury et Victor Dalmont, 1846). This latter one is also documented through notes taken by students: *Notes prises par les élèves au cours des ports de mer.* (Paris: École nationale des ponts et chaussées, Fol. 6512, 1841/1842).

5 Charles-Joseph Minard, *Leçons faites sur les chemins de fer à l'École des ponts et chaussées en 1833–1834* (Paris: Carillan-Gœury, 1834).

6 Konvitz, *Cartography in France*, 154.

7 We can trace this drawing tradition in engineering back to early outstanding examples such as the sketchbook of Villard d'Honnecourt (manuscript, ca. 1230), the *Bellicorum instrumentorum liber* (Venice, ca. 1420), or the rich literature about planning and projecting fortifications in the military realm.

8 Picon, "Die Ingenieure des Corps des ponts et chaussées. Von der Eroberung des nationalen Raumes zur Raumordnung," in *Ingenieure in Frankreich 1747–1990*, ed. by André Grelon (Frankfurt: Campus Verlag, 1994), 79; Konvitz, *Cartography in France*, 135ff. As an example of this regular practice, cf. a manuscript volume for teaching terrain studies and mapping by Jean-Rodolphe Perronet (the long-term director of the school), which has survived in the archive of the École nationale des ponts et chaussées: Perronet, *Cartes d'étude*. It is dated 1793, seven years before Minard would join the school.

9 Charles-Joseph Minard, *Tableau des progrès de la dépense du pavé de Paris pendant les deux derniers siècles & Projet de chemins de fer et de canal pour le transport des pavés a Paris* (Paris: no publisher, 1825).

10 This proposal is accompanied by a plan [62] that shows the region in the southwestern vicinity of Paris, distinguishing some terrain features as well as the course of the river and the location of several villages

along the route. It furthermore delineates the course of the canal and railway trails Minard suggested building. The project had been received favorably by Minard's superiors; however, its execution was prevented by a tight municipal budget in the city of Paris.

11 Minard describes his motivation to draw the diagram as follows: "Pour mieux saisir l'ensemble de toutes les circonstances de l'entretien, nous en avons dressé un registre figuré, en prenant les années pour abscisses, et pour ordonnées les divers élémens que nous avons considérés. Ce tableau chronologique renferme un intervalle de 188 années. Pendant ce laps de temps de catastrophes politiques ou financières ont porté plus d'une fois le désordre dans toutes les branches de l'administration: il n'est donc pas étonnant que la dépense de l'entretien ne suive pas des lois régulières. Mais si l'on considère une période de calme, comme celle de 1730 à 1786, où le pavé de Paris a reçu tous les soins convenables et les fonds nécessaires, où les progrès de sa surface et de sa dépense sont plus uniformes et mieux connus, on peut espérer d'y trouver des résultats exacts et utiles." Minard, *Tableau des progrès*, 3.

12 Funkhouser, *Historical Development*, 285. Minard, *Tableaux graphiques*, 4.

13 Minard, *Cours de navigation*; Minard, *Cours ports de mer*; Minard, *Leçons faites sur les chemins de fer*.

14 See, for instance, Minard, *Cours ports de mer*, atlas plates 8 and 9.

15 As a side note, we should observe that the drawings made by Minard's students in this course—a volume of which has survived in the archives of the École des ponts et chaussées—demonstrate how these drawings formed an important means of knowledge transfer. In recreating visuals in their own notes, the students not only internalized the information conveyed in the plans and diagrams, they also amplified and refined their own drawing skills. Cf. *Notes prises par les élèves* (plates at the end of the volume).

16 Bernard Grall, *Économie de forces et production d'utilités. L'émergence du calcul économique chez les ingénieurs des Ponts et chaussées (1831–1891)* (Rennes: Presses Universitaires de Rennes, 2003), 264.

17 Chevallier, "Notice nécrologique," (1871), 13f.: "Dans la plupart des grandes discussions techniques, M. Minard avait vu combien il importait pour une bonne solution de faire intervenir les saines notions de l'économie politique. En 1831, pendant son passage à l'École des ponts et chaussées, il avait proposé la création d'une chaire pour l'enseignement de cette science, et il s'était demandé alors comment celui qui serait chargé de ce cours devrait en faire l'application aux travaux publics. Depuis longtemps il avait médité et discuté ces matières, il avait lu les principaux économistes, et en 1831 il rédigea les notions qui lui semblaient indispensables aux ingénieurs."

18 Apparently not overly self-confident regarding his economic knowledge and his reasoning in this matter, he did not publish this paper until almost twenty years later: Charles-Joseph Minard, "Notions élémentaires d'économie politique appliquées aux travaux publics." *Annales des ponts et chaussées* 2ᵉ série 1ᵉʳ semestre (1850): 1–125. The paper appeared unchanged in large parts, however some chapters (particularly relating to the railroads) must have been included when revising it for publication in 1850, as they contain data and information from after 1831.

19 He emphasized the improvement of existing conditions as a goal of engineering projects in contrast to earlier times, when some public works were constructed to elevate the monarchy's or the nation's splendor, such as public monuments or triumphal arches. Minard,

"Notions élémentaires d'économie politique," 54: "Dans l'etat actuel de la societé les constructions publiques, quelles que soient leurs innovations, ont presque toujours pour but une amélioration de choses déjà existantes; c'est cette amélioration qu'on doit chercher à exprimer en économies, et ce sont des économies qui représentent l'utilité créée."

20 For instance: Georges Ribeill, "Le rôle des polytechniciens dans le développement des chemins de fer," in *La France des X. Deux siècles d'histoire*, ed. by Bruno Belhoste, Amy Dahan Dalmedico, Dominique Pestre, and Antoine Picon (Paris: Economica, 1995), 242; and François Caron, *Histoire des chemins de fer en France. Tome premier 1740–1883* (Paris: Fayard, 1997), 109: "Les possibilités techniques des chemins de fer pouvaient être contestées. À l'origine, la technologie ferroviaire pouvait ne pas paraître porteuse d'avenir. Le témoignage le plus frappant de cette incertitude initiale est celui que nous fournissent les leçons données à l'École des ponts et chaussées par l'ingénieur Minard en 1834." cf. Minard, *Notions élémentaires d'économie politique*, 39–42.

21 He laid down this conviction in two brochures in 1842 and 1843: Minard, *Importance du parcours partiel* and Minard, *Second mémoire sur l'importance du parcours partiel*. See also Palsky, *Des chiffres et des cartes*, 114.

22 Cf. also Minard's own description in Minard, *Des tableaux graphiques*, 2.

23 "Mais les nombres, d'une utilité statistiques incontestable, ne sont pas appréciés par l'œil aussi facilement que les figures qui leur sont proportionnelles; j'ai donc dressé un tableau figuratif du mouvement des voyageurs....Ce tableau parle aux yeux et fait saisir d'un seul coup d'œil l'ensemble des résultats." Charles-Joseph Minard, *Des voyageurs internationaux sur le chemin de fer entre la Belgique et la Prusse* (Paris: Fain et Thunot, 1846), 5.

24 Minard, *Des tableaux graphiques*, 2: "Ce mode de representation a un petit inconvénient sous le rapport de l'exploitation commerciale: quelquefois la marche d'une marchandise ne peut être suivie facilement de l'œil, parce que les rectangles de même couleur qui la représentent sont séparés par ceux d'une autre couleur; et si l'on veut se bien rendre compte du mouvement de cette marchandise, il faut avoir un tableau graphique pour elle seule."

25 Minard, *Des tableaux graphiques*, 3.

26 This work explicitly refers to and redesigns two flow maps by Alphonse Belpaire from 1847. See also Palsky, *Des chiffres et des cartes*, 118.

27 Again, there are clear references to questions of evaluating infrastructural investments to be found in his early maps on transportation, such as in [10]: "Le but de cette carte est de faire saisir d'un seul coup d'œil l'importance relative des voies de transport en égard aux combustibles. Une carte ainsi dressée pour l'ensemble de toutes les marchandises donnerait l'une des meilleurs bases de répartition des fonds que l'État consacre aux voies de transport. Car si cent mille francs destinés à améliorer une voie quelconque doivent donner la même baisse de prix de transport sur chacune d'elles, c'est en les appliquant à la plus fréquentée qu'on obtiendrait le plus grand bénéfice public."

28 That this is an individual focus on the part of Minard springs to mind when looking at a portfolio of visualization works collated by Minard's fellow engineer Léon Lalanne and kept at the archive of the École nationale des ponts et chaussées: Minard, Charles-Joseph. *Cartes et tableaux statistiques divers réunis par M. Lalanne* (Paris: École nationale des ponts et chaussées, 1818/1874). Although Minard is erroneously named as the sole author in the library catalog, the collection

comprises works by various contributors. In addition to several flow maps by (or inspired by) Minard, it contains also an impressive collection of elaborate diagrams—proving that among Minard's peers there was a very fruitful strand of visualization research and practice relating to diagrams.

29   For a brief outline of this development see, for instance, Michael Friendly, "The Golden Age of Statistical Graphics," *Statistical Science* 23, no. 4 (2008): 504f.

30   Minard, *La Statistique* (Paris: Cusset et Cie., 1869), 1: "La Statistique est l'enregistrement des faits similaires dans un ordre méthodique, numérique ou chronologique. La mémoire est l'enregistrement intuitif dans le cerveau d'idées ou de sensations qui nous ont plus ou moins impressionnées….En signalant de prime abord l'analogie entre la Statistique et l'un des éléments nécessaires à notre entendement, j'ai voulu la relever de l'infériorité où elle a été placée par les savants, car si la mémoire est indispensable pour acquérir nos connaissances intellectuelles, la Statistique est la base de plusieurs sciences aux-quelles nous ne serions pas arrivés sans elle."

31   William Newmarch, "The Progress of Economic Science During the Last Thirty Years:—an opening address by William Newmarch, F.R.S., as President of the Section of Economic Science and Statistics, at the Thirty-First Annual Meeting of the British Association for the Advancement of Science, at Manchester, 4th–11th September, 1861;— with a report of the closing proceedings of the section." *Journal of the Statistical Society of London* XXIV (1861): 457.

32   One example is the descriptive text of map [49], in which Minard integrated data on the circulation of railroad lines across Europe from a wide variety of different sources.

33   In addition to the descriptive texts of the maps, many of which also contain data tables, see for instance his brochures: Minard, *Des voyageurs internationaux*; Minard, *Appendice à la Carte des voyageurs sur les chemins de fer d'Europe en 1862 suivi de considérations sur les chemins de fer* (Paris: E. Thunot et Cie. 1867), or Minard, *La houille et l'exportation de la houille anglaise* (Paris: E. Thunot et Cie., 1866).

34   Regarding the interpretation of these two recurrent terms, see also Palsky, *Des chiffres et des cartes*, 127–28.

35   Minard, *Des tableaux graphiques*, 1: "La grande extension donnée de nos jours aux recherches statistiques a fait sentir le besoin d'en consigner les résultats sous des formes moins arides, plus utiles et d'une exploration plus rapide que les chiffres….En donnant à la statistique une direction figurative, j'ai suivi l'impulsion générale des esprits vers les représentations graphiques…en rendant la statistique figurative, j'ai satisfait le besoin du jour, mais n'ai-je fait que sacrifier au goût de l'epoque et n'ai-je pas contribué à augmenter l'utilité et à abréger le temps des études statistiques?"

36   Maurice Block, *Traité théorique et pratique de statistique* (Paris: Librairie Guillaumin et Cie., 2nd ed. 1886), 418: "Malgré tout ce qu'on a pu faire de vraiment remarquable, les représentations graphiques n'atteignent peut-être jamais la précision des tableaux de chiffres." Block wrote this even though, a few pages before, he acknowledged that the graphical method, once born, had quickly achieved a remarkable level of perfection (404). See also Gilles Palsky, "The debate on the standardization of statistical maps and diagrams (1857–1901): Elements for the history of graphical language." *Cybergeo: European Journal of Geography [online]* (1999): 3–4.

37   Description text on [24]: "Le but de mes Cartes Figuratives est moins d'exposer des résultats statistiques, mieux établis par des nombres, que

38   d'en faire saisir promptement les rapports à l'oeil, rapports qui arrivent spontanément à l'intelligence par les figures et qui n'y pénètrent par les nombres que par l'intermédiaire d'un calcul mental. Les Cartes figuratives sont tout-à-fait dans l'esprit du siécle où l'on cherche à économiser le temps de toutes les manières possibles."

38   This would explain why at times he would use a horizontal scale for a vertical axis—a practice that seems curious today, but does work when a diagram is printed on paper (i.e., comes without a zoom function) and is read using a ruler, as with [1] and [54].

39   Robinson, "The Thematic Maps of Charles-Joseph Minard," 100.

40   Gilles Palsky, "Cartes topographiques et cartes thématiques au XIXe siècle," in *La Cartografia Europea tra Primo Rinascimento e Fine de'll Illuminismo*, edited by Diogo Ramada Curto; Angelo Cattaneo, and André Ferrand Almeida (Florence: Leo S. Olschki Editore, 2003), 286–87.

41   Ibid.

42   Description text on [12]: "Le but de cette carte étant de faire apprécier à l'œil l'importance relative des diverses circulations, j'ai sacrifié à cette considération l'exactitude topographique. Plusieurs distances sont altérées, pour pouvoir placer les zones et pour ne pas dépasser les dimensions des plus grandes pierres de lithographie." (*Carte figurative et approximative des tonnages de marchandises, (flottage compris) qui ont circulé sur les voies navigables de France pendant l'année 1850*)

43   Two attempts to be named a member of the prestigious Académie des sciences fell through. Chevallier, "Notice nécrologique," 15.

44   Robinson, *Thematic Maps of Minard*, 100.

45   Chevallier, "Notice nécrologique," 14: "Si l'on songe aux travaux diffi-ciles executés par M. Minard dans les ports militaires et sur les canaux, aux services importants qu'il a rendus comme professeur et comme membre du conseil des ponts et chaussées, son avancement paraîtra peut-être un peu lent pour l'époque où il vivait. C'est que M. Minard ne savait pas se faire valoir."

46   [4] was published in "some one hundred copies." Likewise, [6] was distributed to some one hundred people, such as engineers, deputies, etc. (Minard, *Des tableaux graphiques*, 2). The first flow map, [5], was printed in two hundred copies and sent to members of the Conseil des ponts et chaussées, to deputies of the districts concerned, and to fellow engineers (Minard, *Des tableaux graphiques*, 3).

47   Aside from the complete oeuvre kept at the École nationale des ponts et chaussées, the Bibliothèque nationale de France holds a substantial collection and the Library of Congress a smaller selection of maps. Only single copies are known in other libraries. As for the rare book market, copies of Minard maps appear scarcely and sometimes in bad condition due to the poor quality of the paper used. At the time of writing this book, two extensive collections of maps in good condition were available through Daniel Crouch Rare Books in London. Both originated with fellow engineers and colleagues of Minard from the École des ponts et chaussées whose families had preserved the collections.

48   Chevallier, "Notice nécrologique," 17. There was a considerable fluctu-ation of officeholders in that position during the period of Minard's late career and retirement.

49   Minard, *Des tableaux graphiques*, 6. This must have happened at some point between 1855 (when Rouher became Minister of Agriculture, Commerce and Public Works) and the publication of the brochure in 1861.

50 Minard, *Des tableaux graphiques,* 6. Given Eugène Rouher's close ties with Napoléon III it might have been he who made the connection to His Majesty.

51 Chevallier, "Notice nécrologique," 17. See also Palsky, *Des chiffres et des cartes,* 135. The map depicted in the painting seems to be an early version from the series on the *Tonnages de marchandises qui ont circulé sur les chemins de fer et les voies d'eau en France* (see page 66).

52 Minard, *Des tableaux graphiques,* 6.

53 Ibid., footnote 1. This remark was apparently so important to Minard that he added it in a handwritten note on a copy of this diagram, which he bequeathed to the École nationale des ponts et chaussées as part of his big portfolio in 1870 [5].

54 Minard, *Des tableaux graphiques,* 6. See also Palsky, *Des chiffres et des cartes,* 137.

55 Palsky, *Des chiffres et des cartes,* 138: "Si ces travaux ont une influence immédiate, ils annoncent surtout une période d'engouement pour la statistique graphique, entre 1860 et 1900." In the subsequent upsurge of statistical graphics in France, it is particularly worth noting a series of *Albums de statistique graphiques*, which were published by the administration of public works between 1879 and 1906 under the direction of Émile Cheysson.

56 Tarbé de Saint-Hardouin, "Notices biographiques," 153: "La lenteur de son avancement, comparé à celui de ses contemporains, a été sans aucun doute le résultat de l'indépendance de son esprit et du choix qu'il faisait de ses occupations dans le but exclusif de satisfaire ses goûts d'étude, et sans se préoccuper des progrès de sa carrière administrative."

CATALOG OF STATISTICAL GRAPHICS

1 Minard, *Tableau des progrès,* 3, trans. by the author: "Pour mieux saisir l'ensemble de toutes circonstances de l'entretien, nous en avons dressé un registre figuré, en prennant les années our l'abscisses, et pour ordonnées les divers élémens que nous avons considérés."

2 Minard, *Importance du parcours partiel sur les chemins de fer.* (Paris: Fain et Thunot, 1842); Minard, *Second mémoire sur l'importance du parcours partiel sur les chemins de fer* (Paris: Fain et Thunot, 1843).

3 This refers to Minard's calculation methods. The number of tonnes is proportional to the square of the diameter of the circle such that the circle surface area, rather than a line, represents the tonnage.

4 Jean-Magloire Baudouin, *Rapport sur l'état actuel de l'enseignement spécial et de l'enseignement primaire en Belgique, en Allemagne et en Suisse* (Paris: Imprimerie Impériale, 1865). Mentioned in Minard, *La Statistique* (Paris: Cusset et Cie., 1869), 5.

5 Menno-Jan Kraak, *Mapping Time: Illustrated by Minard's Map of Napoléon's Russian Campaign of 1812* (Redlands, CA: Esri Press, 2014), 100.

6 Kraak, *Mapping Time,* 20.

7 "Les cosaques passent au galop le Niémen gelé."

8 Minard mentioned "the works of Mr. Thiers, Mr. de Ségur, Mr. de Fezensac, Mr. de Chambray and the unpublished journal of Jacob, pharmacist of the army from October 28th." Those works probably were: Adolphe Thiers, *histoire du Consulat et l'Empire faisant suite à l'Histoire de la Révolution française,* 20 vols. (Paris: Paulin et Lheureux, 1845–62); Philippe-Paul de Ségur, *Histoire de Napoléon et de la Grande Armée, pendant l'année 1812* 2 vols (Paris: Baudouin frères, 1824); Raymond de Montesquiou-Fezensac, *Journal de la campagne de Russie en 1812* (Tours: A. Mame, 1849) or Raymond de Montesquiou-Fezensac, *Souvenirs militaires de 1804 à 1814* (Paris, J. Dumaine, 1870); George Chambray, *Histoire de l'Expedition de Russie.* (Paris: Pillet aîné, 1823). Virginia Tufte and Dawn Finley ("MINARD'S SOURCES—From Virginia Tufte and Dawn Finley," EdwardTufte.com, August 7, 2002, www.edwardtufte.com/tufte/minard) identified "Jacob" to be Pierre-Irénée Jacob (1782–1855), with his diary published in the *Revue d'Histoire de la Pharmacie XVIII,* nos. 189–91, 1966 (www.persee.fr/collection/pharm). In the scale in the lower right of the map, Minard refers to an undetermined "Map of Mr. Fezensac." It has not yet been identified.

CURRICULUM VITAE

1 Listed as a pupil with entry date 1796 in Fourcy, Ambroise: *Histoire de l'École polytechnique,* Paris 1828, p. 499. On p. 84, Fourcy claims that the foundational course at the Polytechnique usually took two years, before pupils went on to more specialised colleges: gallica.bnf.fr/ark:/12148/bpt6k64501909/f110.double.r=corps%20des%20ingenieurs%20des%20ponts%20et%20chaussees%201804. However, Minard is listed in the general list of pupils with the date 1800 behind his name, which might indicate he spent four years at the Polytechnique, before going on to the ENPC. (ibid. p. 401)

2 Detail information: www.ronquieres.org/vionnoisetminard.html // Article published about the experiments: gallica.bnf.fr/ark:/12148/bpt6k408437x/f409.item. An 1839 map of the canal kept in the Bibliothèque nationale de France mentions Minard briefly in the legend: gallica.bnf.fr/ark:/12148/btv1b531195301/f1 (see page 12).

3 Article published about this endeavor and complications in 1856: gallica.bnf.fr/ark:/12148/bpt6k50675j/f709.item

4 Chevallier 1871, p. 9. Cf. also Almanach 1833, p. 569; Almanach 1835, p. 574

5 Chevallier 1871, p. 15

6 Chevallier 1871, p. 11

7 Almanach 1839, p. 151; Almanach 1844, p. 163.

8 Chevallier 1871, p. 13

9 Michael Friendly, personal communication with the author

Bibliography

LITERATURE BY CHARLES-JOSEPH MINARD

Observations sur un système d'écluses à petites chutes, proposé par M. P.-S. Girard, pour les canaux de navigation. Paris: Hocquet, 1821.

Notice sur l'étanchement des filtrations du canal du Centre, près des carrières de Vertempierre. Paris: A. Égron, 1824.

Tableau des progrès de la dépense du pavé de Paris pendant les deux derniers siècles & Projet de chemins de fer et de canal pour le transport des pavés a Paris. Paris: no publisher, 1825.

Expériences faites en 1802, par MM. Tourneux et Minard, sur l'écoulement de l'eau, par des orifices rectangulaires verticaux, en mince paroi, de 0,40 m de longueur, sur 2 cent. et 4 cent. de hauteur. Paris: Fain, 1831. Reprinted in *Annales des ponts et chaussées* 1ère série 1er semestre (1832): 405–7.

"Tableau comparatif de l'estimation et de la dépense de quelques canaux anglais." *Annales des ponts et chaussées* 1ère série 1er semestre (1832): 140–41.

"Expériences sur la force du cheval." *Annales des ponts et chaussées* 1ère série 2e semestre (1832): 125–43.

"De l'Action de la gelée sur les pierres." *Annales des ponts et chaussées* 1ère série 1er semestre (1833): 1–11.

"Influence de la chaleur sur l'endurcissement des mortiers hydrauliques." *Annales des ponts et chaussées* 1ère série 1er semestre (1833): 325–29.

"Notice sur une substance pouzzolanique découverte dans le département de l'Aisne." *Annales des ponts et chaussées* 1ère série 2e semestre (1833): 269–76.

Leçons faites sur les chemins de fer à l'École des ponts et chaussées en 1833-1834. Paris: Carillan-Gœury, 1834.

"Note sur le mouvement des locomotives et des waggons dans les courbes." *Annales des ponts et chaussées* 1ère série 2e semestre (1838): 126–28.

Cours de construction des ouvrages qui établissent la navigation des rivières et des canaux, professé à l'École des ponts et chaussées de 1832 à 1841. Paris: Carillan-Gœury et Victor Dalmont, 1841.

Importance du parcours partiel sur les chemins de fer. Paris: Fain et Thunot, 1842.

Second mémoire sur l'importance du parcours partiel sur les chemins de fer. Paris: Fain et Thunot, 1843.

Des pentes sur les chemins de fer de grande vitesse. Paris: Fain et Thunot, 1844.

Des conséquences du voisinage des chemins de fer et des voies navigables. Paris: Fain et Thunot, 1844.

Un épisode de la guerre ouverte entre les chemins de fer et les voies navigables. Paris: Fain et Thunot, 1845.

Cours de construction des ouvrages hydrauliques des ports de mer. Paris: Carillan-Gœury et Victor Dalmont, 1846, 2 volumes.

Des voyageurs internationaux sur le chemin de fer entre la Belgique et la Prusse. Paris: Fain et Thunot, 1846.

Canal de la Sauldre (Sologne) projet de 1849. École nationale des ponts et chaussées, Manuscript 3211, 1847.

"Notions élémentaires d'économie politique appliquées aux travaux publics." *Annales des ponts et chaussées* 2e série 1er semestre (1850): 1–125.

Note sur les mortiers exposés à la mer. Paris: E. Thunot et Cie., 1852.

"Mortiers employés à la mer. 1° Note sur les mortiers employés à la mer." *Annales des ponts et chaussées* 3e série 1er semestre (1853): 186–95.

"Mortiers employés à la mer. 3° Mortiers marins de sous-carbonates de chaux." *Annales des ponts et chaussées* 3e série 1er semestre (1853): 198–218.

"Mortiers employés à la mer. 4° Note sur des analyses de trass faites par M. Rivot, ingenieur, à l'École des mines." *Annales des ponts et chaussées* 3e série 1er semestre (1853): 218–19.

Considérations sur le durcissement des mortiers marins. Paris: E. Thunot et Cie., 1854. Reprinted in *Annales des ponts et chaussées* 3e série 1er semestre (1856): 1–5.

"Note sur l'etat de conservation de la chaux grasse, du fer et du bois dans d'anciennes fondations toujours noyées par l'eau." *Annales des ponts et chaussées* 3e série 1er semestre (1854): 214–15.

"Chaux et mortiers à la mer." *Annales des ponts et chaussées* 3e série 2e semestre (1854): 11–19.

De la chute des ponts dans les grandes crues. Paris: E. Thunot et Cie., 1856.

De l'avenir nautique du Havre. Paris: E. Thunot et Cie., 1856. Reprinted without plates in *Annales des ponts et chaussées* 3e série 1er semestre (1857): 308–20.

"Note sur une irruption d'eau pendant la fondation de la forme d'Anvers." *Annales des ponts et chaussées* 3e série 2e semestre (1857): 321–27.

D'un nouveau mode d'essai des mortiers marins dans le laboratoire. Paris: E. Thunot et Cie., 1857. Reprinted in *Annales des ponts et chaussées* 3e série 1er semestre (1858): 115–20.

Du Mortier marin de pouzzolane. Paris: E. Thunot et Cie., 1859. Reprinted in parts in *Annales des ponts et chaussées* 3e série 2e semestre (1859): 236–38.

De l'endiguement de la Seine jusqu'à Honfleur et du port du Havre. Paris: E. Thunot et Cie., 1859.

Des tableaux graphiques et des cartes figuratives. Paris: E. Thunot et Cie., 1861.

Des embouchures des rivières navigables. Paris: E. Thunot et Cie., 1864.

La houille et l'exportation de la houille anglaise. Paris: E. Thunot et Cie., 1866.

Le libre échange avec l'Angleterre en tableaux graphiques. Paris: E. Thunot et Cie., 1867.

Appendice à la Carte des voyageurs sur les chemins de fer d'Europe en 1862 suivi de considérations sur les chemins de fer. Paris: E. Thunot et Cie., 1867.

Appendice à la Carte figurative des céréales importées en France en 1867. Paris: E. Thunot et Cie., 1868.

Grandes constructions de quelques anciens peuples. Paris: Cusset et Cie., 1869.

La Statistique. Paris: Cusset et Cie., 1869.

AUXILIARY WORKS & DOCUMENTS RELATING TO MINARD'S TEACHING

"Extrait d'un mémoire anglais intitulé: De la résistance de l'eau au passage des bateaux dans les canaux (1833)," translated by Charles-Joseph Minard. In *Annales des ponts et chaussées* 1ère série 2e semestre (1834): 129–46.

"Extrait du rapport des commissaires des railways anglais du 31 mars 1848," translated and with an introductory note by Charles-Joseph Minard. In *Annales des ponts et chaussées* 2e série 2e semestre (1849): 117–28.

Minard, Charles-Joseph. *Cartes et tableaux statistiques divers réunis par M. Lalanne.* Paris: École nationale des ponts et chaussées, fol. 16080, 1818/1874. [Portfolio of maps and diagrams by Minard and several other contributors which was collected and given to the archive by Léon Lalanne]

Navier, Claude; Minard, Charles-Joseph; and Dufrénoy, Armand. *Cours et épreuves lithographiés.* Paris: École nationale des ponts et chaussées, Manuscript 3332, 1827/39.

Notes prises par les élèves au cours de ports de mer. Paris: École nationale des ponts et chaussées, fol. 6512 (lithographic print), 1841/1842.

SECONDARY LITERATURE

Almanach royal et national pour l'an M DCCC XXXIII, présenté à Sa Majesté et aux princes et princesses de la famille royale, 566–77. Paris: A. Guyot et Scribe, 1833.

Almanach royal et national pour l'an M DCCC XXXV, présenté à Sa Majesté et aux princes et princesses de la famille royale, 571–83. Paris: A. Guyot et Scribe, 1835.

Almanach royal et national pour l'an M DCCC XXXIX, présenté à Sa Majesté et aux princes et princesses de la famille royale, 147–64. Paris: A. Guyot et Scribe, 1839.

Almanach royal et national pour l'an M DCCC XXXXIV, présenté à Sa Majesté et aux princes et princesses de la famille royale, 158–177. Paris: A. Guyot et Scribe, 1844.

Baudouin, Jean-Magloire. *Rapport sur l'état actuel de l'enseignement spécial et de l'enseignement primaire en Belgique, en Allemagne et en Suisse*. Paris: Imprimerie Impériale, 1865.

Belpaire, Alphonse. *Notice sur les cartes du mouvement des transports en Belgique*. Brussels: P. Vandermalen, 1847.

Block, Maurice. *Traité théorique et pratique de statistique*. Paris: Librairie Guillaumin et Cie., 2nd ed. 1886, 403f.

Brinton, Willard Cope. *Graphic Presentation*. New York City: Brinton Associates, 1939.

Caron, François. *Histoire des Chemins de Fer en France. Tome Premier 1740–1883*. Paris: Fayard, 1997.

Chevallier, Victorin. "Notice nécrologique sur M. Minard, inspecteur général des ponts et chaussées, en retraite." *Annales des ponts et chaussées* 5ᵉ série, 2ᵉ semestre (1871): 1–22.

Coronio, Guy, ed. *250 ans de l'École des ponts en cent portraits*. Paris: Ed. des Presses des Ponts, 1997: 84–85.

de Dainville, François. "Les Bases d'une cartographie industrielle de l'Europe au XIXᵉ siècle." *La Cartographie reflet de l'histoire*. Genève-Paris: Editions Slatkine, 1986, 153–75. First published 1972.

Fourcy, Ambroise. *Histoire de l'École polytechnique*. Paris: self-published / École polytechnique, 1828.

Friendly, Michael. "Visions and Re-Visions of Charles-Joseph Minard." *Journal of Educational and Behavioral Statistics* 27, no. 1 (2002): 31–51.

Friendly, Michael. "The Golden Age of Statistical Graphics." *Statistical Science* 23, no. 4 (2008): 502–35.

Friendly, Michael and Gilles Palsky. "Visualizing Nature and Society." In *Maps. Finding our Place in the World*, edited by James R. Akerman and Robert W. Karrow. Chicago: University of Chicago Press, 2007: 207–53.

Funkhouser, Howard Gray. "Historical Development of the Graphical Representation of Statistical Data." *Osiris* 3 (1937): 269–404.

Grall, Bernard. *Économie de forces et production d'utilités. L'émergence du calcul économique chez les ingénieurs des Ponts et chaussées (1831–1891)*. Rennes: Presses Universitaires de Rennes, 2003.

Konvitz, Josef W. *Cartography in France 1660–1848: Science, Engineering, and Statecraft*. Chicago: University of Chicago Press, 1987.

Kraak, Menno-Jan. *Mapping Time: Illustrated by Minard's map of Napoléon's Russian Campaign of 1812*. Redlands, CA: Esri Press, 2014.

Malglaive, Alain. *Eugène Rouher (1814–1884), Biographie*. Broût-Vernet / Allier: Assoc. Azi la Garance, 2005.

Marey, Étienne-Jules. *La méthode graphique dans les sciences expérimentales et particulièrement en physiologie et en médecine*. Paris: Masson, 1878.

Newmarch, William. "The Progress of Economic Science during the last thirty years:—an opening address by William Newmarch, F.R.S., as President of the Section of Economic Science and Statistics, at the Thirty-First Annual Meeting of the British Association for the Advancement of Science, at Manchester, 4th–11th September, 1861;—with a report of the closing proceedings of the section." *Journal of the Statistical Society of London* XXIV (1861): 451–71.

Palsky, Gilles. *Des chiffres et des cartes. Naissance et développement de la cartographie quantitative française au XIXᵉ siècle*. Mémoires de la Section de géographie physique et humaine, vol. 19. Paris: Comité des travaux historiques et scientifiques, 1996.

Palsky, Gilles. "The debate on the standardization of statistical maps and diagrams (1857–1901): Elements for the history of graphical language." *Cybergeo: European Journal of Geography [online]*, Cartographie, Imagerie, SIG, document 85, uploaded March 16, 1999, accessed August 2, 2017. cybergeo.revues.org/148; DOI:10.4000/cybergeo.148.

Palsky, Gilles. "Cartes topographiques et cartes thématiques au XIXᵉ siècle." In *La cartografia Europea tra primo Rinascimento e fine dell'Illuminismo*, edited by Diogo Ramada Curto Angelo Cattaneo, and André Ferrand Almeida. Florence: Leo S. Olschki Editore, 2003. 275–98.

Palsky, Gilles. "François de Dainville et l'histoire de la cartographie : Orientations traditionelles et thématiques nouvelles." In *François de Dainville S.J. (1909–1971). Pionnier de l'histoire de la cartographie et de l'éducation*, edited by Catherine Bousquet-Bressolier. Paris: École des chartes, 2004: 81–99.

Perronet, Jean-Rodolphe: *Cartes d'étude pour les élèves des ponts et chaussées*. Paris: École nationale des ponts et chaussées, Manuscript 94, 1793.

Picon, Antoine. "Die Ingenieure des Corps des ponts et chaussées. Von der Eroberung des nationalen Raumes zur Raumordnung." In *Ingenieure in Frankreich 1747–1990*, edited by André Grelon. Frankfurt: Campus Verlag, 1994.

Rendgen, Sandra and Wiedemann, Julius. *Information Graphics*. Cologne: Taschen, 2012.

Ribeill, Georges. "Le rôle des polytechniciens dans le développement des chemins de fer." In *La France des X. Deux siècles d'histoire*, edited by Bruno Belhoste, Amy Dahan Dalmedico, Dominique Pestre, and Antoine Picon. Paris: Economica, 1995. 239–49.

Robinson, Arthur Howard. "The Thematic Maps of Charles-Joseph Minard." *Imago Mundi: A Review of Early Cartography* XXI (1967): 95–108.

Robinson, Arthur Howard. "The 1837 Maps of Henry Drury Harness." *The Geographical Journal* 121, no. 4 (December 1955): 440–50.

Tarbé de Saint-Hardouin, François Pierre Hardouin. *Notices biographiques sur les ingénieurs des ponts et chaussées depuis la création du corps, en 1716, jusqu'à nos jours*. Paris: Librairie Polytechnique Baudry et Cie., 1884: 151–53.

Tufte, Edward R. *The Visual Display of Quantitative Information*. Cheshire, CT: Graphics Press, 2nd ed. 2009.

Tufte, Edward R. *Visual Explanations: Images and Quantities, Evidence and Narrative*. Cheshire, CT: The Graphics Press, 2003.

List of Figures

[14] *Carte figurative de l'exportation de la houille anglaise en 1850, 1854.*

[15] *Carte figurative et approximative des tonnages de marchandises (flottage compris) qui ont circulé en 1850 et 1853 sur les voies navigables de France, 1854.*

[17] *Carte figurative et approximative des quantités de céréales qui ont circulé en 1853 sur les voies d'eau et de fer de l'Empire français, 1855.*

[21] *Carte figurative et approximative des quantités de viandes de boucherie envoyées sur pied par les départements et consommées à Paris, 1858.*

[24] *Carte figurative et approximative de l'importance des ports maritimes de l'Empire français mesurée par les tonnages effectifs des navires entrés et sortis en 1857, 1859.*

[25] *Carte figurative et approximative des tonnages des grands ports et des principales rivières d'Europe, 1859.*

[26] *Cartes figuratives et approximatives des tonnages des marchandises qui ont circulé en France en transit en 1845 et 1857, 1859.*

[28] *Carte figurative et approximative des tonnages des vins, spiritueux etc. qui ont circulé en 1857 sur les voies d'eau et de fer de l'Empire français, 1860.*

[32] 1 OF 6 *Carte figurative et approximative des quantités de coton en laine importées en Europe en 1858 et de leur circulation depuis leur origine jusqu'à leur arrivée, 1861.*

[37] 2 OF 6 *Carte figurative et approximative des quantités de coton en laine importées en Europe en 1858 et en 1861, 1862.*

[40] 3 OF 6 *Carte figurative et approximative des quantités de coton en laine importées en Europe en 1858 et en 1862, 1863.*

[45] 4 OF 6 *Carte figurative et approximative des quantités de coton en laine importées en Europe en 1858 et en 1863, 1864.*

[47] 5 OF 6 *Carte figurative et approximative des quantités de coton brut importées en Europe en 1858 et en 1864, 1865.*

[52] 6 OF 6 *Carte figurative et approximative des quantités de coton brut importées en Europe en 1858, en 1864 et en 1865, 1866.*

[33] *Carte approximative de l'étendue des marchés des houilles et cokes étrangers dans l'Empire français en 1858, 1861.*

[34] *Carte figurative et approximative des grands ports du globe, 1861.* Bibliothèque nationale de France

[38] *Carte figurative et approximative représentant pour l'année 1858 les émigrants du globe, 1862.*

[41] *Carte figurative et approximative de la houille anglaise exportée en 1860, 1863.*

[42] *Carte figurative et approximative des grands ports du globe, 1863.*

[44] *Carte figurative et approximative des poids des bestiaux venus à Paris sur les chemins de fer en 1862, 1864.*

[46] *Similitude des dispositions stratégiques de Charlemagne et de Napoléon Ier. L'un dans sa campagne en 791 contre les Huns, l'autre dans sa campagne en 1805 contre les Autrichiens et les Russes, 1865.*

[48] *Carte figurative relative au choix de l'emplacement d'un nouvel hôtel des postes de Paris, 1865.*

[49] *Carte figurative et approximative du mouvement des voyageurs sur les principaux chemins de fer de l'Europe en 1862, 1865.*

[50] *Carte figurative et approximative des quantités de vins français exportés par mer en 1864, no date.*

[51] *Carte figurative et approximative des populations spécifiques des provinces d'Espagne, 1866.*

[53] *Carte figurative et approximative de la houille anglaise exportée en 1864, 1866.*

[54] *Tableaux graphiques de la production de la houille en Europe de 1848 à 1863 (y compris anthracite et lignite), 1866.*

[55] *Carte figurative et approximative du mouvement des voyageurs sur les principaux chemins de fer de Russie en 1863, 1867.*

[56] *Carte figurative des mouvements des langues anciennes avant l'ère moderne, no date.*

[57] *Le libre échange avec l'Angleterre en tableaux graphiques (series of seven plates), 1867.*

[58] *Carte figurative des mouvements et provenances des céréales importées en France en 1867, 1868.*

[59] *École dite Realschulen de Stuttgart. Tableau graphique montrant le nombre d'heures par semaine d'étude du latin diminuant depuis 1818 jusqu'en 1864, no date.*

[60] *Carte figurative des pertes successives en hommes de l'armée qu'Annibal conduisit d'Espagne en Italie en traversant les Gaules (selon Polybe); Carte figurative des pertes successives en hommes de l'armée française dans la campagne de Russie, 1812–1813, 1869.*

[61] *Age moyen des élèves de chaque promotion à l'École polytechnique, 1870.*

All works from the École nationale des ponts et chaussées unless otherwise noted.

Index

Acknowledgments

This book was written for everyone interested in or working with data visualization and thematic cartography—a growing community of creative minds who continually strive to advance the way we glean insight from data. It is inspiring to follow your conversations on Twitter, in blogs and podcasts, and at conferences. With this book, I hope to give something back to the community, since Minard—like so many of you—continually worked to improve our methods of visualizing statistical data.

I am deeply grateful to Princeton Architectural Press for having supported this project from the beginning. Everyone involved impressed me with their professional expertise and visionary thinking. Abby Bussel, Kristen Hewitt, Nina Pick, and Barbara Darko have substantially contributed to shaping this book. Jenny Florence did an amazing job translating Minard's complicated original text into English. Ben English's design ingeniously supports the subject matter. The archivists of the École nationale des ponts et chaussées in Paris, the institution housing the most comprehensive collection of Minard's work, have been extremely supportive throughout the project. Thank you, Catherine Masteau and Johanna Descher, for paving the way for this book. Throughout the production period, Guillaume Saquet was incredibly patient in answering myriad detailed questions and providing information.

I was lucky to have had inspiration and input from many people. Gilles Palsky devoted time to sharing his immense knowledge on the subject, reviewing the essay, and helping to answer questions. Jana August is always up for a conversation on anything related to diagrams, data viz, and art history, and provided sound advice through this whole project. Julia Guther has been an unfailing source of knowledge and ideas in all matters of design, within the scope of this book and beyond. Many people have encouraged me to pursue this research, including Nigel Holmes, Philippe Rekacewicz, Michael Stoll, David Rumsey, and Raymond J. Andrews, among many others. From the field of rare book and map experts, I was lucky to have had advice from Daniel Crouch in London and Thomas Rezek in Munich.

I would like to dedicate this book to my family. You are the source of everything that I am: my late father Klaus with his insatiable appetite for intellectual stimulation, my mother Ursula with her impeccable intuition for human nature, my brother Andrej with his wit and seemingly endless energy. Most of all, I would like to thank my partner, Clemens von Lucius, for his unconditional support and love. Even our two sons have played their part: their way of embracing new experiences is magic and has left its imprint throughout these pages.

Published by Princeton Architectural Press
A MCEVOY GROUP COMPANY
202 Warren Street, Hudson, NY 12534
www.papress.com

Princeton Architectural Press is a leading publisher in architecture,
design, photography, landscape, and visual culture. We create fine
books and stationery of unsurpassed quality and production values.
With more than one thousand titles published, we find design
everywhere and in the most unlikely places.

Editor: Kristen Hewitt
Designer: Benjamin English
Translator: Jenny Florence

Special thanks to: Paula Baver, Janet Behning, Nolan Boomer,
Abby Bussel, Jan Cigliano Hartman, Susan Hershberg, Lia Hunt,
Valerie Kamen, Sara McKay, Parker Menzimer, Eliana Miller,
Nina Pick, Wes Seeley, Rob Shaeffer, Sara Stemen, Marisa Tesoro,
Paul Wagner, and Joseph Weston of Princeton Architectural Press
—Kevin C. Lippert, publisher

Library of Congress Cataloging-in-Publication Data
NAMES: Rendgen, Sandra, author.
TITLE: The Minard system : the complete statistical graphics
of Charles-Joseph Minard / by Sandra Rendgen.
DESCRIPTION: First edition. | New York : Princeton Architectural Press,
2018. | "From the Collection of the École Nationale des Ponts et
Chaussées." | Includes bibliographical references.
IDENTIFIERS: LCCN 2018003931 | ISBN 9781616896331
(hardcover : alk. paper)
SUBJECTS: LCSH: Minard, Charles Joseph, 1781–1870. | Statistics—Graphic
methods. | Minard, Charles Joseph, 1781–1870—Catalogs. | Statistics—
Charts, diagrams, etc.—France—Marne-la-Vallée—Catalogs. | École
nationale des ponts et chaussées (France)—Catalogs.
CLASSIFICATION: LCC QA276.3 .R46 2018 | DDC 001.4/226—dc23
LC record available at https://lccn.loc.gov/2018003931